'A damned good book . . . Smith provides an entertaining, thoughtful and plausible portrait of the state of contemporary public and private morality and – perhaps more importantly – sets out her grounds for optimism . . . deserves an audience from Left, Right and centre' Melanie McGrath, *Evening Standard*

'Joan Smith's latest book has all the pace of a good thriller . . . The neatly threaded eclecticism of *Moralities*, and its regular digressions into history and biography, mean that it never becomes dull' James Harkin, *Independent on Sunday*

'I disagree with this book, which is not the same as saying I dislike it. I don't. It is well written and stimulating . . . She is, in a phrase, wrong, but importantly so' Bryan Appleyard, *Literary Review*

'An intriguing and informative examination of modern morals . . . The case studies are wonderfully chosen, from international governmental hypocrisy over Saddam Hussein and General Pinochet to the World Trade Organisation and the Seattle riots . . . [Smith] guides the reader carefully through the quagmire of modern-day big business and political corruption with considerable skill' *Scotland on Sunday*

'Joan Smith's *Moralities* is . . . as gripping as any of her detective novels' Ruth Rendell, *Sunday Times*

'Joan Smith is a truly insightful and intelligent writer and critic . . . she tears into the moral maze of hypocrisy and wilful hoodwinking that are the trademarks of our mediaocracies . . . Again and again, Smith answers the questions our helpless and disempowered visionaries have been scribbling on suicide notes for decades. This is rum, definitive stuff' Paul Dale, *The List*

'Hugely readable . . . *Moralities* is both stimulating and well written. Smith is excellent at exposing the horrors that modern capitalism inflicts on the mass of people all over the world, and her book will open up debate about how best to combat them' Judith Orr, *Socialist Review*

'This lively, idiosyncratic book makes many excellent points' Karen Armstrong, *Independent*

ABOUT THE AUTHOR

Joan Smith is a columnist, novelist and critic. She is the author of the highly praised *Misogynies* and five detective novels. She has written columns for the *Independent on Sunday*, the *Guardian* and *Tribune*, and her reviews appear in the *Sunday Times* and the *Independent*. She is one of the presenters of *What the Papers Say* and a regular contributor to BBC radio. She chairs the Writers in Prison Committee of English PEN, and lives in London.

JOAN SMITH

Moralities

PENGUIN BOOKS

For my mother and in memory of my father

PENGUIN BOOKS

Published by the Penguin Group
Penguin Books Ltd, 80 Strand, London WC2R ORL, England
Penguin Putnam Inc., 375 Hudson Street, New York, New York 10014, USA
Penguin Books Australia Ltd, 250 Camberwell Road, Camberwell, Victoria 3124, Australia
Penguin Books Canada Ltd, 10 Alcorn Avenue, Toronto, Ontario, Canada M4V 3B2
Penguin Books India (P) Ltd, 11, Community Centre,
Panchsheel Park, New Delhi – 110 017, India
Penguin Books (NZ) Ltd, Cnr Rosedale and Airborne Roads, Albany, Auckland, New Zealand
Penguin Books (South Africa) (Pty) Ltd, 24 Sturdee Avenue, Rosebank 2196, South Africa

Penguin Books Ltd, Registered Offices: 80 Strand, London WC2R ORL, England

www.penguin.com

First published by Allen Lane The Penguin Press 2001
Published with updates and a new chapter in Penguin Books 2002

1

Copyright © Joan Smith, 2001, 2002
All rights reserved.

The moral right of the author has been asserted

Printed in England by Clays Ltd, St Ives plc

Contents

Either no member of the human race has real rights, or else all have the same; he who votes against the rights of another, whatever his religion, colour or sex, thereby abjures his own.

MARQUIS DE CONDORCET

Introduction

A return to puritanism?

Scandal is in the air. The tumbrils are rolling. Politicians survey the tabloids nervously, wondering when it will be their turn to have their personal lives picked apart, their ex-lovers doorstepped, their financial transactions and their private beliefs subjected to minute scrutiny. So do TV presenters, soap stars, clerics and members of the royal family. An extramarital affair here, an unwise liaison there, a moment's madness is enough to destroy a reputation or wreck a career. The final decade of the twentieth century was notable both for its obsession with celebrity and its relentless pursuit of human weakness. In the United States the most risible detail of Bill Clinton's affair with a White House intern was exposed by a politically motivated prosecutor, while the fallout from the imbroglio claimed another victim, Bob Livingston, Speaker Elect of the House of Representatives, before he had even taken up his post. In Britain a series of scandals produced a cull of public figures in a remarkably short period of time. Among them were the England football coach Glenn Hoddle and no fewer than three members of Tony Blair's Cabinet: the Welsh Secretary Ron Davies, the Paymaster-General Geoffrey Robinson and the controversial politician Peter Mandelson (twice). Other victims included the Conservative MP David Mellor, who resigned as a minister in John Major's government after his affair with an actress was exposed in a Sunday newspaper, and Lord Archer, the Tory candidate for Mayor of London, who stepped down – and eventually received a four-year prison sentence – when a decade-old scandal caught up with him. The tail-end of another episode, left over from the Conservative administration that imploded amid allegations of sleaze and corruption in the spring of 1997, had already resulted in a former minister, Jonathan Aitken, serving a short prison sentence. Even celebrities who were apparently adored by the media found it was a different matter when an ex-lover, a former business partner or a nosy stranger surfaced with a story to sell. Prince Charles was ridiculed when an intimate telephone conversation with his mistress, Camilla Parker Bowles, was illegally recorded and reported verbatim in the press. His brother's wife, the Duchess of York, was similarly mocked when a tabloid printed photographs of her in the South of France with a lover, even though they had been taken without her knowledge or permission by a paparazzo with a long lens. In the weeks before her death in 1997, the Princess of Wales complained bitterly about press intrusion into her private life, a theme taken up by her brother when he spoke at her funeral service in Westminster Abbey.

Trial by tabloid is a daily event, with everyone from pop stars to government ministers lampooned for peccadilloes that would once have been regarded as private, if regrettable, lapses of judgement. The popular press has taken over the role of scourge/confessor that used to be the exclusive domain of the Church, but without the sophisticated moral framework of Christianity, which leaves space for repentance and absolution. Fame and notoriety are uncomfortably close, as a procession of actors and footballers have learned to their cost. In such a draconian atmosphere, who would voluntarily step into the limelight, knowing that every skeleton will one day come rattling out of the cupboard? Are we creating a culture in which talented people will in future avoid public life altogether, for fear of going down in history, as Bill Clinton may well do, not as a President who left behind an unprecedented budget surplus but as a man who did unconventional things with a cigar?

Hang on a minute

Popular as this theory is across the political spectrum – it has been articulated in dozens of articles, usually by middle-aged men glancing nervously over their own shoulders – it collapses under scrutiny. How can we be more puritan when all the sociological evidence suggests that Western Europe and the United States have become much more *tolerant* in recent decades? There has never been a moment in history when people have had so much freedom to decide how to run their private lives. Marriage is no longer the sole model for adults who wish to live together and have children, homosexuality has been legalized, contraception and abortion are widely available, and the stigma of illegitimacy has vanished, to name but four key areas in which attitudes – and, crucially, the law – have relaxed. Women no longer live in terror of becoming pregnant outside marriage; homosexual couples enjoy some of the legal rights that apply to heterosexual partners; and, with a few exceptions, gay politicians no longer agonize over whether to come out. Tony Blair's Cabinets after the 1997 general election included, at different times, as many as four gay or bisexual men; in the spring of 2000 the Mayor of a Welsh town announced she had appointed her lesbian lover as her Mayoress. Ironically, much of the hostility to one or other of these developments, particularly those involving radical redefinitions of the family, has come from the same commentators who deplore the so-called new puritanism most vociferously (and who defended Clinton during the impeachment crisis of 1998/9). Scratch the surface and you will find them talking about family values, singing the praises of the old system in which the vast majority of people subscribed to identical standards throughout their lives or paid a heavy price; they are also, in at least one notable case, unabashed advocates of the double standard that assumes it is a man's inalienable *right* to cheat on his wife.

What they fail to recognize, as they launch jeremiads against what they characterize as political correctness, is the mismatch between their liberal politics, in the narrowly defined sense, and cultural and social attitudes that are deeply conservative and even verge on misogyny. Nor do they appreciate how much they have in common with genuine fundamentalists, Christian and Muslim alike, who denounce homosexuality, adultery, abortion and feminism as examples of the decadence that is supposedly ruining the West.

Recasting the riddle

So what is really going on here? Is there a way of bringing together these apparently opposed developments into a coherent analysis? This book will argue that there is, but it requires a framework in which the excesses of what used to be called the yellow press can be seen for what they really are: a distraction from a much broader picture. Ghastly as much popular journalism is on both sides of the Atlantic, it has provided a useful scapegoat, allowing powerful men and women – those who have the most to lose – to complain bitterly about intrusion into private life instead of admitting the part their own double standards have played in engineering their embarrassment. In that sense, the high-profile scandals of the final decades of the twentieth century, superficially riveting though they are, have diverted attention from a process that has been going on, largely unremarked, since the end of the Second World War. This is no less than a dramatic shift in moral discourse *away* from the sexual arrangements of individuals, and towards areas on which morality has traditionally been silent or equivocal, principally money and power. I am aware that what I am proposing may seem at first sight counter-intuitive or paradoxical, especially in the light of the Clinton–Lewinsky circus; at a time when sex appears to be a Western obsession, it is not the obvious moment to suggest that there has been a dramatic increase in tolerance on sexual matters.

Yet that is one of the central arguments of this book. The obsessions of the tabloids are a diversion, demonstrating only that sex sells newspapers, a phenomenon I link to Freud's observation of the fascination of the primal scene – that moment, real or imagined, when children realize that their parents have sex with each other. If we put these infantile impulses to one side, which is where they belong, something much more significant emerges. What we are witnessing is no less than the ejection of Church and State from private life, where they have very little business to be, and the adoption instead of a secular code whose chief concerns are justice, equality and universal human rights. (I should perhaps point out here that I have always taken it as read that belief in a supernatural deity is not necessary to lead a moral life. On the contrary, as the early chapters of this book attest, religious convictions are a very poor predictor of how well someone is likely to behave; I am inclined to agree with Nietzsche, who wrote that 'the Christian resolution to find the world ugly and bad has made the world ugly and bad'. Humanist beliefs, because they are argued logically and accepted voluntarily, have if anything greater force than the primitive threat-and-reward systems employed by religions like Christianity.) This is an exciting as well as a liberating development, freeing us from centuries of bigotry and orthodoxy imposed from above. The new morality is democratic and international, asserting that men and women have exactly the same rights throughout the world, and it assumes for the first time that the same rules of conduct apply to the people who govern as well as to the governed. In the new scale of values, an absence of transparency and misuse of power are more serious matters than consensual sexual acts between adults, and it is symptomatic of this shift that so many of the career-threatening scandals we have witnessed in recent years have little or nothing to do with sex. Indeed, an attempt by a scurrilous magazine to smear Peter Mandelson because of his homosexuality failed when other editors decided his sexual orientation was his own affair.

Blair's administration had been in office for only six months when the first scandal erupted about money, a revelation that the Labour Party had accepted a donation of £1m from Bernie Ecclestone, the Formula One racing boss, who was lobbying against the government's plans to outlaw cigarette advertising in sport; to its chagrin, when the donation became public knowledge, Labour had to hand the money back. A couple of years later there was an outcry when the Home Secretary, Jack Straw, allowed Mike Tyson, a convicted and unrepentant rapist, to enter the country to take part in a boxing tournament, on the grounds that the promoters would lose money if he was excluded. A few months after this, Straw made the same decision again, outraging women's groups and traditional Labour supporters who could not square his concern for the promoters with his tough stance against crime; Straw's critics were vindicated when Tyson went to Scotland for the second fight and boasted to journalists about how much he liked hurting people. More injudicious remarks, this time about God punishing disabled people, cost Glenn Hoddle his job as England football coach. Labour got into trouble again when the then Foreign Secretary, Robin Cook, unveiled an 'ethical dimension' to the government's foreign policy but refused to revoke existing licences to sell arms, including Hawk aircraft, to the repressive regime in Indonesia. The Conservatives fared even worse, with Lord Archer's career destroyed by the revelation that he had asked a friend to lie in a court case, while Jonathan Aitken ended up in prison because he dissembled about the identity of the benefactor who paid his hotel bill at the Ritz in Paris. In stark contrast, Princess Diana not only survived her admission on television in 1995 that she had had an affair with James Hewitt, but won public sympathy for the way he (in her extremely partisan account) let her down. Even Prince Charles weathered revelations about his adultery – a sin frowned upon by the Church of England, whose titular head he may one day become – to a point where Camilla Parker Bowles was eventually accepted as his semi-official partner, perhaps even his future second wife.

This is little short of a revolution, given that traditional morality, like the tabloids that are its degenerate heirs, is obsessed with sex and the regulation of private life. With its twin roots in religion and patriarchy, it is an elite and oppressive set of values, invented by a white, male oligarchy and working principally to the benefit of its members. To take just one example, marriage as we know it in

Britain dates back to the middle of the eighteenth century and is essentially a law to regulate the passage of property. Elevated to a moral principle, and heavily propagandized by the Church, it forced unhappy spouses to suffer lifelong misery for an ideal of Christian marriage whose real purpose was to devolve control of sex to clerics and reassure the oligarchy by reducing the risk of bogus heirs. The persecution of 'deviants' – gay men, prostitutes, unmarried mothers – was a pernicious consequence of this system. So was the licence it afforded to powerful men to flout the standards they ruthlessly imposed on everyone else; for centuries it was rightly assumed that power bestowed a degree of protection on those who achieved it, however much their ambitions and appetites diverged from the norm. Indeed, sexual greed was – sometimes still is, as we can see from the more sympathetic reactions to Clinton's travails – regarded as a character trait and even a prerogative of powerful men. What this meant, in practice, was that they were allowed to indulge their sexual tastes as they wished, with little fear of exposure, even while making public statements about their allegiance to family values. A collusive press, owned by wealthy and titled men, ensured that the British public was kept in the dark in the 1930s about Edward VIII's affair with Wallis Simpson, while few Americans, three decades later, knew about the compulsive sexual conquests of their Roman Catholic President and his younger brother Bobby. Although Clinton was not ultimately removed from office, this book will argue that one of the few clear signals sent by the impeachment process is that these assumptions can no longer be taken for granted. (And that men who marry feminists might spend a little more time considering the practical implications for their own behaviour.)

One of the most beneficial effects of the old morality, for its upholders, was the way in which it acted as a diversion from issues the ruling elite did not choose to have discussed: finance, race, empire, inequality, even the drug trafficking that British companies indulged in during the nineteenth century. These were not questions with which Church or State willingly concerned themselves, unless they were forced to confront moral issues by an unusually determined reformer like the anti-slavery campaigner William Wilberforce, an evangelical Anglican. The Vatican's recent apologies for its treatment of women and the Inquisition are shocking reminders that, far from condemning violence and exploitation, the Church not only condoned but *colluded* in the use of torture as an instrument of political will. The maintenance of ethical no-go areas continues to suit governments very well, as we can see from their reluctance to admit the scale of their involvement in the flourishing international arms trade. For all their very public commitment to human rights, the US and Britain remain number one and number two respectively in the list of global arms exporters.

But what I am suggesting in this book is not that we have already arrived in a glorious future shaped by feminists, environmentalists, human rights activists and animal liberationists. It is that we are in transition, that the old standards have come under increasingly effective challenge as the pernicious link between morality and sex is seen for what it really is: a cover for a reactionary means of social control. This development has been immeasurably assisted by new forms of communication, difficult for hostile governments to control, such as fax machines and the internet. It has also been fostered by a commitment, stronger in some democracies than in others, to freedom of information. Again and again, while I was writing this book, new light was thrown on old controversies, such as the Vatican's collusion with fascism in the twentieth century, by documents that had just been released, usually in Washington. (British governments, by contrast, have a disgraceful record of hostility towards a Freedom of Information Act, or a determination to include so many exceptions as to render it meaningless.) Ministers in democratic countries know they can no longer ignore green politics, torture in the states with which they trade or protests on the streets against globalization; the demonstrations against capitalism in the City of London in June 1999, Seattle in November of that year and Washington in April 2000 shocked world leaders, especially when they realized how much popular support the cause was attracting. By the time they assembled for a G8 summit in Genoa in 2001, a right-wing Italian government was sufficiently panicked to create a siege atmosphere in the city, and a young man was killed during clashes between demonstrators and police. While violence is clearly not the answer, change is in the air, alarming politicians on the left and right alike, even though its effects are not fully worked out. Nor is the process I am charting one of seamless advance; in a world plagued by several varieties of fundamentalism, the forces of reaction should never be underestimated. The events of 11 September reinforce this point, and the urgent need to defend the secular values that are a cornerstone of democratic societies in the twenty-first century.

Illuminating the confusion: a note on structure

This book tackles big themes, and for that reason I have adopted a somewhat unconventional structure. The first section, which I have called 'Sins of the Fathers', looks at public life, using contemporary examples to illustrate the conflict between the old and emerging moralities. In essence, what it demonstrates is the *failure* of traditional morality to operate in the public sphere, either because of its absence from the self-interested deliberations of the rich and powerful, or because of its tendency towards interpretations of events that work in their favour. This is particularly true of Chapter 2, an analysis of President's Clinton's relations with women, which is where the accusation of a 'new puritanism' has surfaced most often. Some readers may be surprised to find this subject included in this part of the book, given that one of the defences advanced on Clinton's behalf was that his relationship with Lewinsky was a private matter; central to my argument, however, is the contention that he used his *public* position, first as Attorney-General and Governor of Arkansas, later as President, to get access to and seek sexual favours from women who were in effect his employees. His private life, principally his marriage to Hillary Rodham, was never an issue, even if it prompted prurient speculation; what came under scrutiny, quite rightly, was his abuse of office and a pattern of behaviour that, I argue, amounts to sexual harassment. We are dealing here not with intrusion into someone's private life but the way in which the old morality tolerates the existence of a powerful man's *secret* life, as long as two conditions are in place: that he pays lip service to its tenets in public, and that he takes care not to get found out.

I also examine, in this section of the book, foreign involvement in the overthrow of the democratic government of Chile in 1973 and relations between Western governments, chiefly Britain and the US, and Saddam Hussein in the run-up to the 1991 Gulf War (actually the second Gulf War, that title also belonging to the earlier and much bloodier conflict between Iraq and its neighbour Iran). Both these chapters have benefited immeasurably from documents released under the American Freedom of Information Act and their availability in easily accessible form on the internet. In 1961, in the aftermath of the failed, American-backed invasion of Cuba known as the Bay of Pigs, President John F. Kennedy grumbled about the speed with which news travels in democracies. 'One of the problems of a free society, a problem not met by a dictatorship,' he complained, 'is this problem of information.' Kennedy could not have envisaged a situation in which cables to and from the American embassies in Santiago and Baghdad would be accessible to researchers anywhere in the world with a computer, a modem and a minimum of technical knowledge. What they allow us to do, along with the monumental report of the Scott Inquiry into British arms sales to Iraq, is piece together two shocking stories: in Chapter 1, how the United States, one of the biggest democracies in the world, conspired to overthrow the elected leader of another free country and condemned its citizens to seventeen years of terror and servitude; in Chapter 3, how Britain and the US tried to ingratiate themselves with one of the nastiest regimes in the world, in full awareness of its sickening human rights record, because they were terrified of its theocratic neighbour Iran and viewed oil-rich Iraq as a profitable market. Some of this material makes distressing reading, particularly the details of the charges laid against General Augusto Pinochet by a Spanish judge, Baltasar

Garzón, but it is essential to air these matters in order to expose the moral bankruptcy of the regime's few remaining supporters in Santiago, London and Washington. I also hope, in describing what happened to them, to honour some of Pinochet's victims whose ghastly fate has not in my view been sufficiently acknowledged, except by their relatives and human rights activists.

The second section of the book turns from public life, which has been afforded too little attention by upholders of morality, to an area that has received far too much. 'The Policing of Private Life' examines the double standards of the white male oligarchies, the ferocity with which their members pursued anyone who deviated from rigid Christian tenets about sex and private life, while committing the very same 'sins' themselves in private. In Chapter 4, I look at the way in which immorality came to be synonymous with sex, especially in the United States. I go on to suggest that the history of feminism, of gay rights, of marriage and illegitimacy, is in effect a catalogue of the injustices done to people who did not conform; it should become clear from this historical context, so often forgotten or ignored, that the near-hysterical opposition to abortion we have witnessed in our own time is rooted in nostalgia for the rigid control that used to be exercised over women's bodies. How that degree of control was achieved and maintained, from the middle of the eighteenth century onwards, is the subject of Chapter 5. Chapter 6 traces the grim history of gay men from the second half of the nineteenth century until the legalization of homosexuality in Britain in 1967 and its decriminalization in some American states in 1961, when individual legislatures began to lift the ban on oral and anal sex between people of the same gender. It also draws parallels between the demonization of gay men and single mothers in the final decades of the twentieth century, suggesting that both are victims not just of a lingering busybody attitude to private life, especially on the right, but of an entrenched reluctance to countenance new definitions of the family. It also suggests that this 'moral' argument is really a diversion from admitting the shortcomings of patriarchy, which is to say the alarming inflexibility of some *heterosexual* men.

The third section of the book focuses on the emerging morality, tracing its roots back to the political radicalism of the 1960s. It argues that the sexual revolution and the anti-war movement triggered off other struggles in the Western democracies – feminism, anti-racism, green politics, animal rights and most recently the protests against globalization – that the original protagonists may not have foreseen, but that nevertheless take forward their challenge to the old order. Vastly increased tolerance of the way adults express their sexuality has gone hand in hand with an increasing respect for human rights and the non-human world – a development I want to characterize as a *democratization* of morality. Nor is it surprising, in that sense, that some of the most strident denunciations of this development have come from theocratic states, whose rulers understand and fear the link between personal and political freedom. An absolutely essential step in this process was liberating people from the straitjacket of lifelong monogamy, a development Freud looked forward to half a century before it began to happen. The Church's insistence on absolute fidelity within marriage and chastity outside it remains one of the most bizarre aspects of the old morality, turning what is essentially a private arrangement between adults into a *sine qua non* of ethical life. This nonsense has now been seen for what it is, and the family has already assumed a very different shape (or shapes) as a result. The transition is neither complete nor unproblematic, given the currently unequal status of men and women, but what we can identify with confidence is a new pattern of serial relationships in which adults are no longer expected to make unrealistic commitments to each other. The vital next step in this process, I argue, is that they should recognize binding obligations to their *children*, at least until they are grown up, which does not always happen when spouses and offspring are regarded as elements in the same package. Although they have been confused in the past, parent and partner are actually different roles: the first should and does continue even if the second does not. Recognizing this separation, as many people have begun to do, should reduce the possibility of children being drawn into disputes and used as bargaining chips when their parents decide to go their separate ways.

Freeing private life from its old anxieties about extramarital sex, illegitimacy, adultery and homosexuality opens up a useful space. It allows us to think instead about real and urgent moral questions, most of them linked to our place in the wider world. In that sense, of recognizing connections and obligations beyond the narrow ones of family and race, globalization can be seen as a benign phenomenon, a redefinition of what it means to be human, which is why I have give Chapter 8 the title 'Globalize This!', the ironic slogan of protesters at the World Trade Organization Summit in Seattle in 1999. What I am suggesting here is that the so-called triumph of capitalism, which famously led Francis Fukuyama to theorize that we had come to the end of history, actually represented the nadir of the old morality. As Communism collapsed in Eastern Europe, the West made little attempt to assist the new governments that were struggling to get inefficient centralized economies back on their feet; a single-minded commitment to the free market allowed the rise of virulent forms of nationalism, the emergence of a powerful gangster mafia and the disastrous attempted coup that nearly toppled the elected government in Russia in 1991. Ironically it was Vladimir Putin, a former KGB apparatchik, who benefited from this short-sighted policy. At the same time Western governments responded to the arrival of refugees from Central and Eastern Europe, who had been lured to leave their countries by propaganda about the superiority of capitalism, by dismissing them as 'economic migrants'. The European Union, including Britain, rapidly erected more barriers against foreigners, while rich nations delayed the promised cancellation of debt and failed to meet UN targets on overseas aid. As conventional political parties struggled and for the most part failed to confront this moral bankruptcy, in which many of them were complicit, a new movement came into being from below, organizing itself by word of mouth and the internet; it startled the world when it burst into colourful action during the Battle of Seattle, forcing the summit to be abandoned and a surprisingly rapid re-evaluation of the supposed virtues of free trade.

If the twentieth century came to be characterized as the struggle between freedom and tyranny, which is to say the democratic countries of the West versus fascism and Communism, the new century is already shaping up for a different kind of confrontation: unfettered capitalism versus universal human rights. It would be easy, after the terrorist attacks on the US, to lose sight of this fact and accept instead the tendentious 'clash of civilizations' analysis – the West versus Islam – advanced by Bernard Lewis and Samuel Huntingdon. Yet it would be closer to the truth to see the events of 11 September as a manifestation of the contempt for life common to all forms of fundamentalism, and evidence of the need to understand its origins in imperialism and economic injustice. The methods of al-Quaida are no less fascist than those of the Nazis, and just as inimical to any notion of universal rights; they lend increased urgency to the project of establishing international mechanisms to bring mass murderers to justice. The principles were laid down by the Nuremberg Tribunal at the end of the Scond World War, but for too long it has been left to individuals, rather than governments, to put them into practice. Long before anyone had heard of Osama bin Laden, lawyers working in countries all over the world had been trying to obtain justice for the victims of a long list of twentieth-century tyrants and their subordinates: not just Pinochet in Chile but Hissène Habré for crimes committed in Chad; ex-President Idi Amin in Uganda; ex-President Soeharto in Indonesia; Saddam Hussein in Iraq; Pol Pot in Cambodia; Slobodan Milosevic, Radovan Karadzic and Ratko Mladic in former Yugoslavia; Colonel Mengistu in Ethiopia; ex-President Leopoldo Galtieri in Argentina; and Foday Sankoh in Sierra Leone. But the exercise also has a broader aim, which is to send a warning to contemporary leaders that even if their own citizens do not currently have the power or resources to call them to account, other states have a moral and indeed a legal obligation under international treaties to do so. The horrors inflicted on defenceless civilians in the 1990s, from the civil wars in former Yugoslavia to genocide in

Rwanda, have forced a dramatic reconsideration of the relations between states: an urgent and radical reappraisal of when it is right for governments to intervene in the affairs of another country, as NATO did in Kosovo in 1999. If world leaders had behaved as decisively in Afghanistan in 1996, when it was taken over by a bunch of flagrant human rights abusers, the lives of many Afghan civilians and thousands of American office workers might have been spared.

I would not for a moment suggest that this process does not involve considerable risks. Foreign intervention in former Yugoslavia was sometimes disastrously ill judged, such as Germany's premature announcement at the end of 1991 that it was about to recognize the breakaway states of Croatia and Slovenia, which is widely believed to have made war in Bosnia inevitable. Yet we are witnessing the emergence of a new world order in which the broken promise made after the Holocaust – never again – is finally beginning to mean something; in which the democratic nations of the world are no longer prepared to stand by while authoritarian and overtly racist regimes get away with ethnic cleansing, forced evacuations and mass murder. The Bush administration's decision to start bombing Afghanistan in October 2001 signalled an unwelcome return to unilateralism, but the opposition to that action – and the practical alternatives advocated by anti-war campaigners and human rights activists – was articulate and impressive. That is why the book's guiding spirit is cautiously optimistic, arguing that for all the unsolved problems I have drawn attention to along the way, we are already inhabiting a very different moral universe from our grandparents – even from our parents. Those of us who live in Western democracies are no longer bound by rigid rules, handed down from above, in whose formulation we have little say. What we have instead is a framework of common values that recognizes the dignity of individual human beings, along with their rights and responsibilities. Some of these are expressed in the European Convention on Human Rights, which became enforceable in English courts in October 2000. But we also understand that supporters of al-Quaida are as much a threat to these recently won liberties as

Christian fundamentalists, which is why both have to be resisted. After 11 September, *especially* after 11 September, it is all the more important to continue the task of creating a new kind of society whose values, because they are based on respect rather than coercion, can truly claim to be more moral than anything that has gone before.

Acknowledgements

The ideas in this book evolved over a long period, a process that was immeasurably assisted by discussions with friends, colleagues and people working in the field of human rights. Among my friends I would particularly like to thank Sue Ayling, Lelia Green, Paul Levy, Hanan Al-Shaykh, Digby Ricci, David May, Alev Adil, Dido Powell, Denis MacShane, Alison Gorringe, Christine Ruth, Maureen Freely, John Collins, Barbra Evans, Mark Seddon, Rosemary Goad, Caroline Coon, Nick Lezard, Lucy Hooberman, Duska Andric-Ruzicic, and Lyndall and Siamon Gordon. Moyra Ashford was invaluable when I was thinking aloud and helped with the translations from Spanish in Chapter 1. I don't expect them to agree with everything in the book and they are not to blame for any errors, which an author can usually manage to insert all on her own.

Karl Waldron and Hugh Dowson generously contributed material to the chapters on Chile and Iraq respectively, while Roger Willott's tireless campaigning on behalf of East Timor was an example of what determined individuals can achieve. Rachel Harford of the Campaign Against the Arms Trade kindly allowed me access to the organization's superb archive, which was an invaluable source of material on the international weapons trade with Iraq. Claire Walsh suggested useful sources of information for the paperback edition. I am grateful to my agent, Jane Bradish-Ellames of Curtis Brown, for understanding what I wanted to do at a very early stage, and above all to my editor, Margaret Bluman, whose enthusiasm revived me (and occasionally alarmed me) when I was exhausted by long hours in front of my laptop. Donna Poppy's copyediting was meticulous and unobtrusive, the perfect combination. Finally, I would like to add that the work of human rights organizations, particularly Amnesty International and Human Rights Watch, has been an inspiration while I was writing this book. It is a project I could have undertaken only in my lifelong conviction that this world, the only one we have, can and should be made a better place.

PART ONE

Sins of the Fathers

I

One of Us: Augusto Pinochet Ugarte

It is firm and continuing policy that Allende be overthrown by a coup ... Please review all your present and possibly new activities to include propaganda, black operations, surfacing of intelligence or disinformation, personal contacts, or anything else imagination can conjure which will permit you to continue to press forward toward our [deleted] objective in a secure manner.

— SECRET CABLE FROM THOMAS KARAMESSINES, CIA DEPUTY
DIRECTOR OF PLANS, TO HENRY HECKSHER, CIA STATION
CHIEF IN SANTIAGO, 16 OCTOBER 1970

Chile's coup de etat [sic] was close to perfect.
SITUATION REPORT BY PATRICK RYAN, US NAVAL ATTACHÉ,
VALPARAISO, 1 OCTOBER 1973

The pain of those who suffered was not alien to me in the past, nor now. I lament all the situations of belligerence and acts of violence that caused them.

— GENERAL PINOCHET, 11 SEPTEMBER 1999

The photograph resembles a film still, a black-and-white picture of men in dark uniforms glaring at the camera with the comic-opera menace of actors playing army chiefs in a celluloid banana republic. It is not difficult to imagine it as a poster advertising a new movie, *Stick It Up Your Junta!*, perhaps, in an ironic appropriation of the notorious tabloid newspaper headline from the Falklands War in 1982. If so, it looks as though the two main figures – a pugnacious fellow with folded arms, seated with his cap on his knees, and a languidly bored thug standing behind him – have chosen contrasting methods to convey the utter absurdity of their roles in this *Carry On*-type caper. There are few clues about time and place, the stiff collars and military insignia suggesting a B-movie about the Second World War except that one of them is wearing what look like cheap sunglasses. This is Gestapo chic, Hitler moustaches camped up with plastic accessories, an image designed to do what? Amuse? Terrify? Who could possibly take this Hollywood version of a tinpot dictator seriously?

But millions did, and none more seriously than the seated figure himself. Here he is again, in another carefully staged photo opportunity, this time without his sinister entourage. Either he has aged or someone has done a fantastic make-up job, turning the uniformed thug from Central Casting into a passable simulacrum of a world statesman: silver hair, benign smile, dark civilian suit. Perhaps he is a better actor than we have given him credit for, easily slipping into a deferential pose in startling contrast to his earlier gangsterish demeanour; on this occasion he stands back almost shyly as his companion, no Mafioso but the West's chief spiritual leader, raises his right hand in blessing. The juxtaposition is startling, as though the Archbishop of Canterbury had suddenly agreed to a photocall with one of the Kray twins or an American President offered to appear in public with Charles Manson. What do they make of it, the invisible masses below, peering up to get a glimpse of the figures on the balcony? What we do know is that several days later, as the Pope conducts an open-air mass for reconciliation, a group of demonstrators holding banners denouncing Pinochet will be tear-gassed by his goon squads as John Paul II looks on.

His next appearance is, incongruously, in a suburban house in the English Home Counties. It is not quite the setting for a French farce, more an am-dram production of a drawing-room comedy, with every available surface covered in pastel carpet or tightly stretched

Dralon; matching drapes frame the neo-Georgian windows, while heavy mahogany dining-chairs – reproduction, naturally – have been turned to face a square sofa, as though more guests are expected than the room can comfortably hold. This is obviously a rented house rather than a family home, although it is a fair bet that the rent would be beyond the means of your average council tenant. Our quarry, unsteady on his feet these days, to judge by the walking-stick in his right hand, is grasping a visitor by the arm, gesturing imperiously towards the sofa; he has undergone a second transfor-mation, elder statesman to frail pensioner, unable to walk without assistance but determined to put his important guest at ease. She is a politician, retired but instantly recognizable, not quite as old as her host and in better shape, if the high heels of her court shoes are anything to go by. Together they act out a defiant ritual: long-standing friends, neither in robust health, preparing to reminisce about old times over a very English cup of tea. It is not quite a farewell performance, much as he would like it to be, but an attempt to stage-manage a return to the public arena that has been forced upon him by the enemies who have been manoeuvring against him – motivated by spite, or so he and his distinguished visitor believe – during a career that has hitherto encountered very few setbacks.

Even if he is no longer able to call the shots, he still knows how to present himself to best advantage. The old machismo has been put aside for so long, it is as if it never existed; on the contrary, here he is a few months later, in a photograph taken in the garden of the same suburban house, a genial grandfather surrounded by a younger generation that has never known him in any other role. The tinpot dictator is now the living embodiment of the family values promoted by the spiritual and political leaders with whom he still mixes so easily, beaming with pride as his youngest grandchild slumbers peacefully in the crook of his left arm. Yet there are jarring notes in the photograph, from the makeshift flagpole thrust into the top left-hand corner of the picture – a prop, surely, from the old banana republic days – to the awkward posture of the little boy who perches on the old man's right knee. 'Do as you're told,' a spectral voice seems to be whispering in the child's ear, 'or grandad will get the cattle prods out. You know what he's like.'

And we do know what he's like, what dreadful crimes General Augusto Pinochet Ugarte ordered to be carried out after he overthrew the elected government in his native Chile on 11 September 1973. They have been extensively documented by the relatives of his victims – the Agrupación de Familiares de los Detenidos Desaparecidos (Group of Families of the Detained Disappeared) – by Amnesty International and by the Rettig Commission set up by President Patricio Aylwin after Chile reverted to democratic rule in 1990. Combining figures from various sources, the Chilean government concluded in 1995 that 1,102 people disappeared under the Pinochet regime and 2,095 were subject to extra-judicial executions or death under torture – a total of 3,197 victims. But this is far from painting a true picture of the terror visited on Chile by the junta. When Baltasar Garzón of the Spanish National High Court filed the *commission rogatoire* (official petition to question) that led to Pinochet's arrest in London on 17 October 1998, he produced a 48-page indictment alleging human rights violations on a much wider scale: around 5,000 people disappeared or murdered; more than 100,000 expelled or forced into exile; around half a million detained and subjected, in one form or another, to torture. We know that the junta adopted sadistic methods reminiscent of the Gestapo not just to wipe out their enemies but to discourage all forms of opposition. We know that surviving members of the legal government were kidnapped and taken to remote Dawson Island, a two-hour flight from the bitter cold of the Antarctic, where they were eventually herded into Rio Chico, a purpose-built concentration camp on the Nazi model (one of its architects, Walter Rauff, was a former Nazi gauleiter who subsequently held an important post, along with his son, in Pinochet's secret police). We know that women victims of the regime were raped and sexually humiliated; that male prisoners were forced to bugger each other and their own sons; that detainees were subjected to mock executions, dragged through barbed wire and flung out of helicopters; that both sexes were subject to degrading methods of physical, sexual and psychological torture. (Even Pinochet's offer of safe passage out of Chile to President Salvador Allende, under siege in the Moneda Palace in Santiago, was a sham. A secret recording of a conversation between the General and his co-conspirator Vice-Admiral Patricio Carvajal reveals this remark from Pinochet: 'The offer to take him out of the country is maintained ... but the plane falls, old boy, when it's in flight.')

Yet the man responsible for these horrors not only escaped justice until his arrest in London in 1998 but continued to receive the public support of the Vatican and the former British Prime Minister Baroness Thatcher, as well as senior members of the Roman Catholic hierarchy and prominent right-wing politicians in Britain. The Vatican, of course, has a long and discreditable history of supporting fascists, with whom it would much rather deal than atheistic Communists. The wartime pontiff – Eugenio Pacelli, Pope Pius XII – presided over the destruction of the Catholic Centre Party, the only remaining democratic opposition to the Nazis in Germany, long before he was elected to the highest office in 1939. One of his first actions as Pope was to send a letter to the 'Illustrious Herr Adolf Hitler', assuring him that the new pontiff was devoted to the spiritual welfare of the German people 'entrusted to your leadership'. Pius consistently refused to denounce the Nazis and also supported the fascist regime in Croatia, where half a million Serbs were murdered by a regime endorsed by the Archbishop of Zagreb, Alojzije Stepinac. Pius's refusal to condemn the Holocaust led his most recent biographer, John Cornwell, to designate him 'Hitler's Pope', and it comes as no surprise to learn that he was also an enthusiastic admirer of Spain's General Franco. At the conclusion of the Spanish Civil War, Pacelli sent a telegram to Franco, congratulating him on Spain's 'Catholic victory'. Two weeks later, in a Vatican Radio broadcast to Spanish pilgrims, he recommended 'the principles taught by the Church and proclaimed with such nobility by the Generalissimo: namely, justice for crime and benevolent generosity for those who have been misled'. Summing up the role of the Church in this wartime period, Cornwell argues that it appeared to have links with 'the very right-wing nationalism, corporatism, and Fascism that sustained anti-Semitism or complicity in anti-Semitism on racial grounds'. The Vatican reveres this staunch anti-Communist Pope to the point of preparing to canonize him. Nor was Pius alone in his willingness to accommodate the Nazis. According to documents released in July 2000, the Catholic Church helped them to launder money as the German Army retreated from Italy in October 1943; according to a message intercepted by Allied codebreakers, Cardinal Ildefonso Schuster, Archbishop of Milan, agreed to transfer 300,000 lire that was needed to pay an SS agent. James Walston, a historian at the American University of Rome, commented that Schuster's behaviour was 'part of a wider pattern of church cooperation, motivated by a strong anti-Communist ideology'. In that sense, when another fanatically anti-Communist Pope, John Paul II, beatified Archbishop Stepinac in 1998 and also lent his authority to the campaign to secure the release of General Pinochet, it was simply business as usual; harsher critics would argue that this is because fascism is Catholicism's secular twin, sharing its authoritarianism, intolerance, fear of the outsider and contempt for women.

Indeed, eleven years earlier, immediately before John Paul publicly endorsed the Pinochet regime by appearing with him on the balcony of the presidential palace in Santiago, the Pope was happy to grant him a forty-minute private audience. What they discussed is not known, but Pinochet had always styled himself a devout Catholic, a stance that was rewarded when the British government refused to alter the General's bail conditions in December 1998 to permit him to attend midnight mass. The Pope promptly dispatched a personal confessor to Pinochet's rented home in Surrey to hear his account of his sins – a task that, if embarked on in a spirit of sincere repentance, would surely require teams of confessors working round the clock for the remaining years of the General's life. They might also have wondered at the Pope's readiness to forgive Pinochet's crimes, given that one of the victims named in the indictment drawn up by Garzón was a Catalonian priest, Joan Alsina Hurtos. Another was Antonio Llidó Mengual, a priest born in Valencia, who had electric current applied to his genitals and suffered repeated beatings all over his body.

Some of the crimes listed took place in 1987, the very year in which John Paul visited Santiago, when the Chilean Commission on Human Rights reported that 134 people had been tortured, two of them fatally. This was an improvement on the previous year, when 299 people were tortured, resulting in one death; in the year following the Pope's visit, the figure rose slightly, to 139 recorded cases of torture, but only one death. The Vatican's letter to the Foreign Office, which asked the British government to block the extradition and supported Pinochet's argument that he should be immune from prosecution as a former head of state, was signed by Cardinal Angelo Sodano, Vatican Secretary of State and number two in the Roman Catholic hierarchy. Sodano's CV included a lengthy stint, from 1977 to 1988, as papal nuncio to Santiago, in the course of which it is said he came to know Pinochet well. Garzón's original indictment, revised after a House of Lords hearing in 1999, covered the latter part of this period and its immediate aftermath, the years 1983 to 1989. It recorded that a total of 1,550 people were tortured in Chile, resulting in nine deaths; nearly 7,000 people suffered what the indictment classifies as 'cruel treatment'. As papal nuncio, Sodano played an important role in organizing the Pope's visit to Santiago and briefed him on events there since the military coup. So when the Vatican intervened on the former dictator's behalf at the end of 1998, both the men at the top knew him personally and should have had first-hand knowledge of human rights violations while he was head of state. Yet the Pope's personal involvement in seeking Pinochet's release was confirmed by Lord Lamont, a prominent British Catholic who occupied the post of Chancellor of the Exchequer in one of John Major's governments, presiding over the Black Wednesday debacle in September 1992. 'I suspect that the representations have been made at the highest level, recognizing the general's great contribution to protecting freedom during the cold war,' he said. Far from seeking to play down the pontiff's role in an attempt to secure the release of a man accused of responsibility for far more murders than any of the twentieth century's most notorious serial killers, Lamont added: 'The Pope visited General Pinochet when he was President of Chile and it is not surprising that he has taken this line. The Pope would understand the reason for saving a country from a Marxist dictatorship.' The former British Prime Minister Baroness Thatcher went even further in March 1999 when she visited Pinochet in Surrey, where he was under house arrest. Thanking him for his assistance to Britain during the Falklands War, she added: 'We are also very much aware that it was you who brought democracy to Chile. You set up a constitution, suitable for democracy, you put it into effect, elections were held, and then, in accordance with the result, you stepped down.' In a debate in the House of Lords four months later, initiated by Lamont, Thatcher repeated this claim, crediting Pinochet with establishing 'a constitution for a return to democracy'; what she did not admit, on either occasion, was that he was personally responsible for overthrowing it in the first place.

The Thatcher–Lamont version of history, in which Pinochet saved Chile from an existing or impending dictatorship, is a shameless untruth. Chile was not, at the time of the coup in 1973, a Marxist despotism, nor is there any evidence that it was about to become one. On the contrary, it was the four-man junta led by Pinochet that overthrew a long-standing tradition of democratic government and ruled illegally until 1990, when the General finally (and tardily) stepped down after failing to win the backing of a majority of voters in a referendum two years earlier. The original Spanish indictment that led to Pinochet's arrest, as presented to Interpol, is categoric about what happened in Chile under the junta and the General's responsibility for it:

Without a doubt, under the personal direction of Augusto Pinochet Ugarte, a general plan was established and aimed against diverse sectors of more than 50 per cent of the Chilean national population. This plan consisted in the elimination or disappearance of all those persons identified by government officials, under orders of Augusto Pinochet, for this final purpose, including persons from all social strata, ideological, union, religious and/or other affiliations. In this manner, children, adolescents, students, housewives, religious personnel, liberal professionals, and union, cultural, intellectual, military and political leaders, etc., were arrested, tortured and executed, including [those] without any ideological or personal connection among them.

The government overthrown by the junta, a coalition led by the Marxist President Allende, had actually increased its share in elections following his initial victory in September 1970. In March 1971 more than 50 per cent of the electorate voted for pro-Allende candidates; the vote for his Popular Unity coalition rose by 14 per cent. In congressional elections held on 4 March 1973, pro-Allende candidates won 43.4 per cent of votes in the lower house, 7 per cent more than Allende's share of the vote in the 1970 presidential election. This was in spite of what was effectively an economic blockade of Chile instigated by the US, creating hyper-inflation and shortages; 'make the economy scream', reads a note in the handwriting of the CIA Director, Richard Helms, after a meeting with President Richard Nixon and Secretary of State Henry Kissinger on 15 September 1970. These measures failed to dent Allende's popularity, particularly among the poor, and the right's frustration over its failure to make electoral inroads is widely believed to have supplied partial motivation for the coup. For a continuous period from 11 September 1973 to 12 March 1990, according to Garzón's indictment, the junta headed by Pinochet was responsible for the following forms of physical torture:

various methods, from simple, violent and continuous blows to those producing fractures and loss of blood, as well as keeping prisoners suspended upside down or balanced on the soles of their feet, naked, below bright lights, or with the head covered with a hood, tied up, in narrow spaces, left in narrow cubicles where movement is impossible, hanging by the arms, suspended in the air; a process of semi-drowning in water, known as the 'submarine', with application of electricity to the testicles, tongue and vagina; and other refined methods of torture such as one known as the 'parrot's perch', which consists of suspension of the body for lengthy periods, denial of food and water, sleep deprivation, sexual humiliations, including rape, prolonged exposure to bright light or loud music, forced ingestion of excrement or urine, simultaneous blows on both ears with the palms of both hands, burns with acid or cigarettes, pulling out of nails and other methods.

Prisoners were also subjected to many different types of psychological torture, as the indictment goes on to list:

insults and humiliations, threats of torture and death to the victim and/ or their families, mock executions, threats of detention to their families, being forced to hear or witness tortures carried out on other people, making the victim believe that friends have denounced him or her, photographing or filming victims in humiliating situations; pressuring prisoners to become collaborators or forcing them to implicate others or confess guilt.

At the extradition hearing in London in September 1999, Alun Jones, QC, representing the Spanish government, said that the 35 charges against Pinochet 'constitute some of the most serious ever to come before English criminal courts'. A member of the General's defence team, Julian Knowles, responded by trying to dismiss the charges as nothing more than 'police brutality the like of which occurred in democracies all over the world'. He also denied that Pinochet had any personal responsibility for the regime of systematic torture and brutality outlined in the indictment. Yet the General's close involvement had been confirmed in testimony to the Chilean Supreme Court by one of his closest aides, General Manuel Contreras, formerly Executive Director of the widely feared Dirección de Inteligencia Nacional (DINA). Contreras received a seven-year prison sentence in Chile in 1993 for planning the assassination in Washington DC on 21 September 1976 of Orlando Letelier, Allende's Foreign Minister, and his American driver, Ronni Moffitt, in a car bomb explosion; Brigadier Pedro Espinoza, former Chief of Operations of the DINA and the man in charge of the National Stadium concentration camp in Santiago immediately after the coup, was given a six-year sentence for his involvement. (The assassination of Letelier was excluded, at the insistence of the Carter administration, from the amnesty Pinochet granted himself and his henchmen in 1978. But the General did speak up for his old pal, insisting that Contreras should be allowed to serve his sentence in a military hospital rather than in prison.) Set up in November 1973, the DINA kidnapped, tortured and murdered opponents of the junta in Chile; it also conspired to commit terrorist attacks in Spain, France, Italy, Portugal, the US, Mexico, Costa Rica and Argentina, an operation known as Operation Condor. Contreras's statement emphasized that Pinochet was the true head of the DINA, specifically that 'it was he from whom I received the orders and dispositions that I had to execute'. He also testified that 'The President [Pinochet] had the standing order that he be informed daily of any important news, and at the same time, as standard doctrine, that he be informed constantly of the implementation of orders given. I worked in direct subordination to the President of the Republic and Commander-in-Chief of the Army, without any intermediary.'

Ernest Barcella, the American prosecutor who investigated the Letelier and Moffitt murders, confirmed both that they were the work of the DINA and that the organization was responsible for other terrorist attacks abroad 'of which Augusto Pinochet Ugarte had full knowledge and in which he participated'. The FBI certainly knew about Operation Condor, summarizing its aims in a cable written on 28 September 1976 as an attempt 'to eliminate Marxist terrorist activities in [South America]'. The author of the cable, the FBI's Attaché in Buenos Aires, Robert Scherrer, said that Chile was the centre of Operation Condor and provided information about 'special teams' that travelled abroad 'to carry out sanctions up to assassination against terrorists or supporters of terrorist organizations'. (Letelier, who was not a terrorist but nevertheless a primary target of Operation Condor, once remarked: 'Quite frankly, in the time I knew General Pinochet, I had many doubts about his intellectual capacity. However, there remains little doubt in my mind as to his talents as a traitor.') When Pinochet attended Franco's funeral in

Spain in November 1975 – the only foreign leader who could bring himself to do so – he held a private meeting with Stefano Delle Chiae, the Italian terrorist implicated in the attempted assassination of the Christian Democrat politician and former Chilean Vice-President, Bernardo Leighton, and his wife, Ana Fresno, in Rome one month earlier. Twenty years later, on 23 June 1995, a court in Rome sentenced Contreras and Colonel Raúl Eduardo Iturriaga Neumann to twenty years' imprisonment for their part in organizing this attack under the auspices of Operation Condor. Perhaps not realizing its significance, the *Sunday Telegraph* reported that Pinochet's e-mail address, during his detention in Surrey, included the word 'Condor'. The paper may also have been unaware that the word has a long pedigree in fascist circles, dating back to its use as the title of the German forces – the Condor Legion – under the command of General Hugo Sperrie, that assisted Franco in the Spanish Civil War. It was the Legion's Chief of Staff, Colonel Wolfram von Richthofen, who taught the Spanish fascists how to use an air assault to destroy civilian morale, a technique notoriously employed at Guernica.

Kidnapping and torture remained in use throughout Pinochet's rule in Chile. As late as 1987, the year of the Pope's visit, this is what happened to some of the individuals who were picked up and held without trial by his henchmen:

- José Eleodoro Cuevas-Pineda and María Victoria Lagos Higueras were kidnapped in a Santiago street on 17 May. They were beaten, and given electric shocks on the face, shoulders and hands.
- Ingrid Paola Echeverría Henríquez was detained at home in Santiago. She was beaten and given electric shocks to her hands, buttocks and sensitive parts of her body. She was denied food and water for two of the four days for which she was held.
- Jorge Martinez-Martinez was detained in Santiago on 26 August. He was tortured with electric shocks and forced to eat his own faeces.
- Carlos Vargas Hernández was detained on 31 October and beaten on the face, in the stomach and in other sensitive areas of his body. Part of his moustache was ripped out.

- Benancio Renán Veloso Hernández was detained in Coronel on 11 November. He was subjected to the 'parrot's perch' and given electric shocks to his temples and sensitive areas of his body.
- Francisco Acevedo Toro, a doctor working for the Chilean Commission on Human Rights in Valparaiso, was arrested on 30 November. He was beaten, had a cross marked on his forehead with a cutting object, and was subjected to a mock execution while tied to a tree with barbed wire.

These tortures and deliberate humiliations were bad enough for the people involved. But the savagery of the regime in its early years, when the junta's determination to liquidate its opponents knew no bounds, is almost unbearable to contemplate, even in print. In 1974, for example, a man named 'Papi', who had 'visible open syphilitic sores on his body', was employed to rape female captives; they were also exposed to a dog 'trained in sexual practices with human beings'. Two years later, according to Garzón's indictment, a whole catalogue of abuse was visited on a prisoner named Pedro Hugo Arellano Carvajal, including subjecting him to electric shocks and forcing him to bugger the son of another captive. Even pregnant women were not spared: Adriana Luz Pino Vidal had electric shocks applied to her vagina, ears, hands, feet and mouth, while cigarettes were stubbed out on her stomach. Another victim, Meduardo Paredes Barrientos, had his wrists, pelvis, ribs and skull broken; he was also burned with a blowtorch or flamethrower. Marta Lidia Ugarte Roman was suspended from a pole in a pit; her finger and toe nails were pulled out, and she was burned.

To most of us, these tortures and humiliations could scarcely be more disgusting. At a time when elderly Nazis were still being brought to justice, half a century after they committed their crimes, there seemed very little cause to complain about Pinochet's arrest in Britain, other than the fact that it came so late in his thoroughly evil career. Nor were the conditions of his detention particularly onerous, compared to the cramped cells and primitive washing facilities endured by most remand prisoners in the UK, let alone his victims in Chile; all he had to put up with was the presence in his rented house of a couple of resident policemen and prolonged exposure to someone else's choice of soft furnishings. Yet Pinochet whined about his situation when he was interviewed by Dominic Lawson, editor of the *Sunday Telegraph*, in July 1999. 'Would you be happy to be confined to 80 square metres for ten months? Always seeing the same floor, seeing the same faces, the same people, always the same?' In the weeks before the extradition hearing, stories about his failing health were commonplace, including a dramatic report in the *Daily Telegraph* that a priest had been called to administer the last rites when he collapsed two days before the court case. Shamelessly playing the old soldier, Pinochet refused to be taken to hospital and insisted he wished to die surrounded by his family – but recovered before the priest was able to perform the function for which he had been summoned. While it was abundantly clear that the General felt very sorry for himself, the struggle to feel remorse for his victims was evidently beyond him. The nearest he came was a statement, strategically issued less than two weeks before the commencement of the extradition hearing – and dated on the anniversary of the coup – at a moment when some acknowledgement of the suffering endured by the people of Chile might be regarded as politic. The statement, contained in a letter and quoted at the beginning of this chapter, is couched in language that Freudians might interpret as singularly lacking in affect. But it was all his victims were going to get.

From the beginning, Pinochet's apologists characterized his detention as a spiteful act against an ailing old man, carried out by Communists and fellow-travellers – 'the organized international Left . . . bent on revenge', as Baroness Thatcher complained in the House of Lords. The circumstances of the arrest, she said darkly – 'in hospital at dead of night, when under heavy sedation following a serious back operation' – had 'left Britain's reputation for loyalty and fair dealing in tatters'. Her colleague Lord Lamont trotted out the old canard that 'terrible things were done on both sides' and described the General as 'a political prisoner in this country', a charge repeated in an editorial by the *Daily Telegraph*. 'I find as repulsive as anyone the terrible things that happened under General Pinochet', Lamont wrote in *The Times* in December 1998. But he went on to describe the situation in Chile before the coup in terms that were a clever rewriting of history, claiming that there were 'political assassinations of army officers, hyperinflation of nearly 1,000 per cent, and a shortage of basic necessities that provoked vast street demonstrations'. Law and order were breaking down, he added. 'If ever there was a revolutionary situation, that was it.' What Lamont did not say was that the turbulent conditions he described were to a large extent the creation of Allende's *enemies*, not a consequence of his government's policies. There is no doubt at all that, from the moment Allende won the largest share of votes in the election on 4 September 1970, right-wing forces within Chile were working against him. Most significant of all, however, was the covert but determined involvement of the American government to prevent Allende becoming President on 4 November 1970.

Towards this end, President Nixon and Henry Kissinger, who served as Nixon's National Security Advisor and Secretary of State, immediately began plotting both a coup and to destabilize Chile economically. At his meeting with Nixon on 15 September 1970 – the occasion on which he made his infamous note about the Chilean economy – CIA Director Richard Helms recorded in his own hand-writing: '1 in 10 chance perhaps, but save Chile!' Ten million dollars was available for the job, he noted, 'more if necessary'. The memo continues: 'full-time job – best men we have . . . game plan . . . make the economy scream . . . forty-eight hours for plan of action'. A month later Thomas Karamessines, Deputy Director of Plans at the CIA, sent a secret cable to the CIA Station Chief in Santiago, Henry Hecksher, which outlined Kissinger's orders. They could not be more direct:

It is firm and continuing policy that Allende be overthrown by a coup. It would be much preferable to have this transpire prior to 24 October [when the Chilean Congress was due to confirm Allende's election] but efforts in this regard will continue vigorously beyond this date. We are to continue to generate maximum pressure toward this end utilizing every appropriate resource. It is imperative that these actions be implemented clandestinely so that the USG [American government] and American hand be well hidden. While this imposes upon us a high degree of selectivity in making military contacts and dictates that these contacts be made in the most secure manner it definitely does not preclude contacts such as reported in Santiago 544 which was a masterful piece of work.

The CIA was anxious that a proposed military coup led by General Roberto Viaux was likely to fail, and asked Karamessines to get a message to him along these lines:

We have reviewed your plans, and based on your information and ours, we come to the conclusion that your plans for a coup at this time cannot succeed. Failing, they may reduce your capabilities for the future. Preserve your assets. We will stay in touch. The time will come when you together with all your friends can do something. You will continue to have our support.

For the moment, thanks but no thanks, in other words. Despite the melodramatic tone of this communication, it was in deadly earnest. Viaux was to be encouraged to join forces with other plotters and the CIA was sending six gas masks and six CS canisters to Santiago by special courier. Cables sent to Santiago from CIA headquarters in Langley, Virginia, on 18 October 1970 discuss the secret shipment of weapons for use in a plot to kidnap General René Schneider, the loyalist Chilean Commander-in-Chief who was regarded as a major obstacle to a coup. The CIA provided 'sterile' weapons to General Camilo Valenzuela, hoping that the kidnap would be blamed on Allende's supporters and provoke a coup. Instead, Schneider was assassinated by General Viaux, becoming the first of several high-ranking officers who were murdered for their loyalty to Chile's elected government. Schneider's successor, the politically naive General Carlos Prats, was forced to resign by hostile army officers shortly before the coup and made the fatal mistake of recommending his number two, Augusto Pinochet, to succeed him; Pinochet has been accused of ordering the assassination of Prats and his wife in Buenos Aires a few weeks later.

These are, presumably, the 'political assassinations of army officers' Lamont referred to in his *Times* article, but they were carried out by Allende's opponents, not his supporters. Similarly, a great deal of the economic chaos that followed Allende's inauguration as President was the result of deliberate American intervention, as is made clear in yet more declassified documents. An options paper on Chile, prepared for Kissinger and the National Security Council on 3 November 1970, spelled out possible US policy towards Chile; Nixon chose option C, which was to maintain an 'outwardly cool posture' but work behind the scenes to wreck the economy. Six days later Kissinger himself wrote a memo summarizing the Nixon administration's objectives in relation to the fledgling Allende government, including a direction to US agencies to 'limit his ability to implement policies contrary to US and hemisphere interest'. Kissinger outlined the President's financial strategy towards Chile in detail, demanding that action to be taken to:

a. exclude, to the extent possible, further financing assistance or guarantees for US private investment in Chile, including those related to the Investment Guarantee Program or the operations of the Export-Import Bank;

b. determine the extent to which existing guarantees and financing arrangements can be terminated or reduced;

c. bring maximum feasible influence to bear on international financial institutions to limit credit or other financing assistance to Chile. (In this connection, efforts should be made to coordinate with and gain maximum support for this policy from other friendly nations, particularly those in Latin America, with the objective of lessening unilateral US exposure); and

d. assure that no US private business interests having investments or operations in Chile are made aware of the concern with which the US Government views the Government of Chile and the restrictive nature of the policies which the US Government intends to follow.

Thus did one of the world's great democracies conspire to ruin the economy, and overthrow the government, of a small Latin American country whose voters had had the temerity to vote for a leader of their choice. (Kissinger is said to have remarked that he didn't see why the Americans should have to stand by 'and let a country go Communist due to the irresponsibility of its own people'.) What is astonishing about the Allende administration, in retrospect, is that it held on for so long and managed to retain so much of its electoral popularity. When the coup finally happened in 1973, the junta's assumption of power was chronicled in minute-by-minute detail by American officials. Patrick Ryan, a US Naval Attaché in Chile's second city, Valparaiso, confided in a situation report to Washington that it had gone almost perfectly from his government's point of view. Allende had been found dead in his office, Ryan reported, after placing a sub-machine gun under his chin and pulling the trigger. 'Messy, but efficient,' he observed laconically. 'The gun was lying near his body, a gold metal plate embedded in the stock was inscribed "To my good friend Salvador allende [sic] from Fidel Castro." Obviously Communist Cuba had sent one too many guns to Chile for their own good.' The fact that the CIA had supplied guns to the plotters, which he almost certainly knew, did not seem to trouble him.

However upbeat Ryan's analysis, American intelligence officials were already aware of the savagery with which the junta was hunting down and eliminating its opponents. On 1 October a secret memo to the State Department conceded that there had been 320 summary executions in the nineteen days after the coup, more than three times the publicly acknowledged figure. The striking thing about this long situation report is its frankness about the human rights situation in Chile, and the willingness of the American government not just to overlook widespread abuses but to pour money into Chile – even to supply the junta with arms. 'The purpose of the executions is in part to discourage by example those who seek to organize armed resistance to the Junta,' the memo observed, adding that there were signs that the police and the military were complying with an order to desist from summary executions. Even so, it admitted that 13,500 people had been arrested, with between 7,000 and 8,000 of that total held in the notorious National Stadium in Santiago. Describing the atmosphere after the coup, it detected 'a puritanical, crusading spirit – a determination to cleanse and rejuvenate Chile'. Two days before the memo was written, the Nixon administration announced its second batch of economic assistance to Chile: $24 m for feed corn. The memo also reported that 'private US and Canadian banks have already pledged $171 m in new financing of which $70 m is in highly liquid dollar acceptances'. The Nixon administration was optimistic about getting plans to sell two 'surplus' destroyers past the Senate, while the junta, not bothering to conceal its true colours, had responded with 'several new requests for controversial military equipment'. (In 1976, at a time when the scale of human rights abuses by the Pinochet regime was well known, Britain's Labour government allowed a shipment of ammunition to Chile to arm two Leander class frigates, one of which had already been supplied to the junta, while the second was about to sail. A British diplomat, when asked why the arms sale had not been stopped because of the junta's appalling human rights record, said that 'the moral obligation to provide ammunition and other supporting equipment for weapons systems bought and sold in good faith was overriding'.)

Even the American government began to feel queasy, in time, about its relations with Pinochet's torture state. Not because it regretted its role in encouraging the coup, but because the dictator's enthusiastic use of terror was seen as both an embarrassment and a potential public relations disaster. That is why, when Pinochet proposed a visit to the US in 1975 and asked for a meeting with President Gerald Ford, there was a diplomatic flurry as the Americans tried to avoid the two men being seen together. A memo sent to Ford's National Security Adviser Brent Scowcroft, on 8 August 1975, reveals that the National Security Council had asked the US Ambassador in Santiago, David Popper, to discourage the meeting by telling the Chileans that the President's schedule was full. Pinochet's visit to the US was likely to 'stimulate criticism', the memo warned, and suggested an 'informal talk with Chile's Ambassador in Washington' to avoid embarrassment.

Others were not so squeamish. Before his arrest in 1998, Pinochet visited Britain several times, usually fitting tea with Baroness Thatcher into his schedule. Her support for the dictator never wavered, even to the point of addressing a rally for Pinochet at the Conservative Party Conference in Blackpool two days before a London magistrate was due to rule on whether his extradition to Spain would be allowed to go ahead. Thatcher's speech on his behalf, in which she accused Tony Blair's government of complicity in 'international lynch law' and complained that it 'grovels to collaborate with Spain', was widely regarded as a public relations disaster, even by members of Pinochet's defence team. 'Watch Lord Lamont join hands with Lady Thatcher at the Torturers' Rally in honour of General Pinochet,' wrote Max Hastings, a Tory voter and influential editor of the London *Evening Standard*, disgusted by the spectacle.

When the magistrate, Ronald Bartle, announced his decision on 8 October 1999 that the extradition could go ahead – a judgment Pinochet's defence reluctantly appealed, effectively ensuring his continued detention in Britain for several more months – many observers felt that justice was close to being done. The moral authority of Pinochet's accusers was enhanced by an absence of vindictiveness, a commitment to humane treatment in stark contrast with the extrajudicial terror he imposed on Chile for so many years; even if he was convicted on charges of torture, he was too old under Spanish law to receive a prison sentence, and most of the victims and their relatives would have been content to have their day in court and bear witness to the horrors inflicted by the junta. But Pinochet and his legal team were determined that they would not be allowed even this small satisfaction; the case dragged on and, to no one's surprise, his advisers in Britain claimed that the old man was too sick to stand trial. He was examined in secret by a panel of doctors appointed by the Home Office and shortly afterwards the Home Secretary, Jack Straw, announced that he was 'minded' to send Pinochet home. The decision and the absence of transparency with which it was made caused outrage, as well as prompting a legal challenge from several foreign governments, which also wanted to put him on trial. Their lawyers asked for, and got, a court ruling that they should be able to see the medical report; almost immediately, its contents were leaked to the Spanish press and reported worldwide. Pinochet, it said, had irreversible brain damage that had been confirmed by a brain scan. Although other authorities, including a neuro-radiologist, pointed out that the diagnosis was far from decisive – many people of his age would show similar damage, without a corresponding decline in capacity – Straw accepted the findings and allowed the old dictator to go home.

On 3 March 2000, after a gruelling 24-hour flight to Chile, Pinochet emerged in a wheelchair that he quickly abandoned, walking unaided to greet the thousands of army officers who defied a government order not to welcome him to Santiago. Patriotic music played in the background as the supposedly sick man waved delightedly to his supporters, not even bothering to delay his remarkable recovery to save Straw's face. But the next few months were not as comfortable as he had hoped. He was indicted (and finally placed under house arrest) by a Chilean judge, on charges arising from the so-called 'Caravan of Death', a notorious episode in which a group of officers toured Chile and executed seventy-five political prisoners. Pinochet escaped prosecution only when his lawyers argued in July 2001 that he was mentally unfit to stand trial, ending almost three years of legal manouevres. Chile's former strongman retreated to his county home in Bucalemu, eighty miles south-west of Santiago, which is where we get our final glimpse of the old dictator: isolated, humiliated and officially 'demented'.

2

One of the Boys: William Jefferson Clinton

[The] *President only wanted to do what the common man has done behind his wife's back since the world began. Puritan stupidity did not only refuse him that, it withheld his right to deny it.* — GABRIEL GARCÍA MÁRQUEZ

[Clinton] *has offended not only against the traditional moral code but against the new morality of feminism, which insists that men – and especially men in authority – should not even allow the suspicion that they are abusing their power over younger underlings.* — INDEPENDENT ON SUNDAY

The secret relationship between Bill Clinton, 42nd President of the United States, and a former White House intern called Monica Lewinsky was first mentioned in an American newspaper on 21 January 1998. That morning, the authoritative *Washington Post* published a story entitled 'Clinton Accused of Urging Aide to Lie; Starr Probes Whether President Told Woman to Deny Alleged Affair to Jones's Lawyers'. The lengthy headline assumed that readers were aware of a court case alleging lewd conduct, brought against the President by a woman named Paula Jones, but its implications were explosive. The *Post* had already claimed the scalp of one American President, Richard Nixon, after two of its reporters doggedly pursued the events surrounding the break-in at the Watergate building in Washington in the 1970s. The *Post* story, bringing into the formal public domain allegations that had previously surfaced on the internet, prompted a torrent of claims and denials that led to unprecedented scrutiny of the President's sex life, exposing acts and conversations of a type not customarily recorded or spoken aloud in courtrooms. It was part of a chain of events that would lead, eleven months later, to a vote by the House of Representatives to send Clinton for trial before the Senate on charges of perjury and obstruction of justice. He would survive, but only because of his party's majority in that house and an uneasy perception outside it that he had become the target of vengeful right-wing forces. His wife, Hillary Rodham Clinton, was quick to discover and accuse a 'vast, right-wing conspiracy' against her husband, while many ordinary people, as well as influential commentators and friends of the President, wondered aloud whose private life could possibly withstand the kind of analysis to which his affair with Lewinsky was exposed. They squirmed at the prospect of their own sexual conduct being subjected to the public gaze and published in a report whose clinical language – genitals, oral sex, ejaculation – could not ward off the lubricious pleasure some readers would take in poring over the details of a middle-aged man's encounters with a much younger woman. Men who had grown up, like the President, during the sexual revolution of the 1960s discerned a backlash by supporters of conservative values – an attempt 'to reclaim the territory lost to the permissive society', as the British journalist Henry Porter characterized the *Starr Report* when it was published in 1998.

But the affair generated as much confusion as clarity. The Nobel Prize-winning novelist Gabriel García Márquez appeared to locate the President's conduct in a previous era of genteel double standards – one that the ethos of the 1960s explicitly rejected and ridiculed – when he asserted Clinton's right to lie to his wife; he had denied his affair with Lewinsky, claimed Márquez, 'with his head held high, as any self-respecting adulterer would'. It is very rare these days, and therefore all the more instructive, to see adultery and deception claimed as not merely normal male behaviour but a man's *right*; the assumptions that underpinned the old moral order have seldom been so harshly exposed. Even more confusingly, in speaking up for the President, Márquez was placing himself on the same side as a star-spangled cast of American feminists, from the novelist Erica Jong to the singer and composer Carly Simon. The latter even went so far as to sing at an emotional rally just before Clinton was impeached, appropriating the protest songs of the anti-Vietnam war movement in defence of a serial abuser of women. Although their sexual politics were hopelessly tangled, what all of these people were trying to articulate was a view that an unwise but passionate affair had been transformed into a species of pornography by a censorious prosecutor, the independent counsel Kenneth Starr, after whom the damning report was named. Their common enemy was puritanism; the blue-collar satirist Michael Moore even dressed up in seventeenth-century costume and confronted Starr, accompanied by a chorus of wailing female hysterics and TV cameras, as he left home for work. Around twenty British and American celebrities, including the actor Emma Thompson, reacted more decorously, writing a joint letter to *Le Monde* to protest at the way Clinton had been treated. And a heavyweight from an earlier generation, the playwright Arthur Miller, rallied to his cause in the *New York Times*, drawing a parallel with one of his own plays and declaring the whole affair nothing short of a witch-hunt.

But what were they defending? A man's right to break marriage vows that he, unlike so many of us, still claimed to respect? A politician's right to use his power and position to seduce or intimidate women into sleeping with him? If their arguments were superficially persuasive, especially to commentators who are habitually on their guard against a right-wing backlash, they were also misguided. What they overlooked, in their collective distaste for Starr, was the existence of a damning case against the President, informed by the very liberal values they assumed to be under attack. It was not just, as the *Independent on Sunday* argued in London, that his sexual conduct was 'unusually sordid and reckless'. Nor was it that he had committed adultery, which is a sin according to his own somewhat unforgiving religion, Southern Baptism, but hardly infrequent behaviour among his contemporaries. The most telling charge against Clinton was that his affair with Lewinsky was the latest episode in a pattern of sexual predation, carried out against women who were variously immature, vulnerable, technically his employees and sometimes unwilling. The relationships, or encounters in which they rebuffed his crude demands, were often followed by deliberate attempts to destroy the women's credibility, in case they might feel inclined to reveal his behaviour. The principal casualty of this process was not Clinton himself, who survived against the odds to complete his presidency, but a long list of women who emerged from even fleeting contact with him with their reputations damaged or destroyed. One of these was his wife, who was doubly humiliated by her husband's conduct and what would later be exposed by a sympathetic biographer as her own collusion with it; the earliest opinion polls suggested, during her own campaign in New York for a seat in the Senate, that her chance of a political career had been injured by association with her husband's lies and cover-ups. Her election to the Senate in November 2000 followed a period in which she appeared to distance herself from her husband, prompting speculation that she might one day seek a divorce.

It was an irony of the impeachment process that someone as well informed as Arthur Miller should have forgotten an essential fact about witch-hunts, which is that the overwhelming majority of their victims are women. This is no accident: thousands died in Europe and North America during a 300-year period, usually at the hands of male inquisitors who accused them, among other things, of having sex with the devil. Female sexuality was at the heart of witchcraft trials, not peripheral to them; according to the founding text on the subject, the fifteenth-century *Malleus Maleficarum*, or *Hammer of Witches*, witches were characterized as much by their sexual un-ruliness and their ability to damage men's sexual potency as their supposed habits of blighting neighbours' crops or turning milk sour. Supposedly fearless and promiscuous, they posed a threat to the established male order that had to be dealt with ruthlessly, first by torture to extract a confession and then by strangulation or burning at the stake. Of course Miller was writing metaphorically, using the image of a witch-hunt to convey his sense that the President was being made a scapegoat, but he had unwittingly identified a supremely distasteful aspect of what was going on, while being confused about the victim. It was Monica Lewinsky's reputation, even her mental health, that was called into question as soon as her affair with Clinton became public knowledge: her lips were the target of jokes about oral sex, her mouth was said to be made for fellatio, comedians sniggered about the former intern 'getting her presidential kneepads'. She was derided as 'a little nutty, a little slutty' by Clinton's supporters, while her former lover, far from defending her, used his aides to start a rumour that she was a crazed stalker. The *Starr Report* is unequivocal on this point, revealing that Clinton's first impulse, on the day the story broke in the *Washington Post*, was not just to lie about the allegations but to discredit Lewinsky. This is its account of a conversation between the President and one of his aides, Sidney Blumenthal, a former journalist with many contacts among the press corps in Washington:

The President said to Blumenthal, 'I haven't done anything wrong.' Mr Blumenthal testified that the President told him, 'Monica Lewinsky came on to me and made a sexual demand on me.' The President said that he 'rebuffed her'. The President also told Mr Blumenthal that Ms Lewinsky had 'threatened him. She said that she would tell people they'd had an affair, that she was known as the stalker among her peers, and that she hated it and if she had an affair or said she had an affair then she wouldn't be the stalker any more.'

A similar scenario, putting all the blame on Lewinsky, would soon be advanced by sympathetic commentators on both sides of the Atlantic. The BBC's distinguished former Washington correspondent Charles Wheeler, interviewed immediately after publication of the *Starr Report*, said on BBC Radio 4 that Lewinsky was a 'minx' who had set out to seduce the President. That so many men promulgated this line is testimony, in its own shabby way, to the fear that continues to be generated by female sexuality; what is worth noting for the moment is the effect of these slanders on Lewinsky, which was visible and dramatic. The dark-haired young woman, who exuded such *joie de vivre* in film footage of her talking to the President before their relationship became public, gained weight and began dressing as a parody of a respectable American matron: she appeared in suits and pearls, carrying gloves and an old-fashioned handbag, as though she was trying to tell the world she was not the sex-obsessed stalker portrayed by Clinton and his aides. If ever there was a case of a woman being publicly hounded into closing down her sexuality, this was it, as the events of 1998 ground inexorably on, and Hillary Clinton was not above capitalizing on the physical and emotional problems of her younger rival. As Lewinsky piled on the pounds, the First Lady posed regally for the cover of American *Vogue*, emphasizing the gulf between them. The President had fallen victim to Lewinsky's temporarily eclipsed charms, and his wife made sure she would pay for it.

When Clinton was not trashing Lewinsky, he was trying to play down what had happened between them, characterizing himself as the helpless victim of his physical urges. This is how he explained it in a private conversation with his pollster Dick Morris, himself soon to be disgraced for his indiscretions with a prostitute and likely to be sympathetic to the President's position. 'You know,' Clinton told Morris, 'ever since the election, I've tried to shut myself down, sexually, I mean . . . But sometimes I slipped up and with this girl I just slipped up.' He said something similar to Lewinsky, again according to the *Starr Report*, when he ended their relationship: 'Earlier in his marriage, he told her, he had had hundreds of affairs; but since turning forty, he had made a concerted effort to be faithful.' Hillary Clinton appeared to endorse this view in a magazine interview in 1999 when she suggested her husband had a weakness that she had been aware of when she married him; she had always known, said the First Lady, that Bill would be 'a hard dog to keep on the porch'. What is striking about both these formulations is that, in their different ways, they absolve Clinton from moral responsibility; indeed, his wife's revoltingly folksy phrase seems to transfer the burden of constant vigilance from his shoulders to hers.

It was a feature of much of what was said and written about the President's relationship with Lewinsky that so many people were prepared to regard him as something less than a consenting adult, never mind the most powerful (and protected) man in the world. How this squared with his capacity, entrusted to him by the American electorate, to initiate a conflict that might obliterate vast areas of the planet was never explained; it appeared that he was adult enough to have his finger on the nuclear trigger, but not to keep his hands off a vulnerable young women who worked at the White House. It followed that if he committed adultery, the fault was someone else's: his lover for failing to exercise self-control or his wife for not policing his behaviour sufficiently closely. In fact, as Gail Sheehy's biography *Hillary's Choice* revealed in 1999, this was almost literally true and had been for a very long time when Hillary went on the offensive against Lewinsky. After surviving the Flowers allegations in 1992, she took on the task of damage control where her husband's lovers were concerned, using her assistant Betsey Wright to hire a private investigator, Jack Palladino, to track down nineteen women she regarded as a potential threat to her husband's electoral prospects. The women were being chased by tabloid reporters, hot on the trail of Clinton's reputation as a serial adulterer, and Palladino's job was 'to wrest from the targeted women signed affidavits denying any sexual or romantic involvement' with the would-be President; Palladino, who had known Hillary Clinton for many years, eventually secured six affidavits. She and Wright paid him $100,000 out of federally subsidized campaign funds, disguised as legal fees, a practice that caused a scandal when it was revealed in the *Washington Post*. The significance of this story is that, when Hillary Clinton decided to act as a kind of unofficial policewoman, it was her husband's *lovers* that she chose to target.

This theory of non-responsibility on the President's part relies on an antediluvian view of gender that can be summed up in four words: Adam, Eve, her fault. It was also, however, detonated by the existence of a sinister pattern in his sexual history. What it revealed was a career as a calculating opportunist, willing to use go-betweens to procure sex and to resort to coercion when he thought he could get away with it. What brought this history to light was the determination of Paula Jones, an Arkansas woman who spent years trying to persuade public opinion and the courts that Clinton sexually harassed her in 1991. Jones said that she met Clinton, then Governor, when she was working at a function at a hotel in Little Rock, Arkansas. Shortly afterwards, a state trooper approached her and said Clinton would like to speak to her in a hotel room. She followed the man upstairs, where the Governor astonished her by whipping out his penis and asking for a blowjob. Jones, who was a state employee, refused. When she tried to bring the incident to light, she was derided on account of her gender and her class as 'trailer trash'. In an exact parallel with Lewinsky, she was mocked for her full lips and big hair; the treatment meted out to her, until the President offered her an $850,000 settlement (around half a million pounds) to drop the case in November 1998, is a model of the character assassination women could expect to undergo if they dared call him to account. Even Gennifer Flowers, one of his consensual lovers, was dismissed as an attention-seeking nightclub singer when she first claimed to have had a lengthy affair with him in the run-up to the 1992 presidential election – and she had tapes to prove it. George Stephanopoulos, Clinton's spin-doctor, matter-of-factly included 'attacking Gennifer Flowers' as part of his job description in his autobiography, dismissing it as part and parcel of 'getting my hands dirty and doing what it took to win'. He also recorded his relief at seeing her on television and concluding that her appearance – her 'red suit and dark-rooted hair' – would count against her.

Kathleen Willey could not be brushed aside so easily. The wife of a Democratic fundraiser, Willey was a volunteer worker at the White House and a woman with impeccable middle-class credentials. When her husband got into financial trouble in 1993, she approached the President for help in finding a salaried job and found herself swept into his arms – not for comfort, as another man might do, but in order that he might guide her hand on to his erect penis. Willey's respectability was beyond question, her character much more difficult to assassinate; she later said that two days before she was due to give evidence in the Jones case, she was threatened by a stranger near her home in Richmond, Virginia. (Clinton dismissed her allegation in a conversation with Lewinsky with the revealing assertion that he would never proposition a woman with such small breasts.) But the most startling allegation, the most serious of all the claims made against him, came from a woman called Juanita Broaddrick. A nursing-home supervisor in Clinton's home state of Arkansas, Broaddrick was summoned to give evidence in the Jones case and initially denied in an affidavit that she had had a sexual encounter with him. But she changed her mind during the impeachment process and appeared on television to confirm a long-standing rumour, not just that she had been sexually harassed, but that Clinton raped her in a hotel room in 1978 when he was Attorney-General of Arkansas and running for Governor. Broaddrick said on television that Clinton came to her room, invited himself in and forced her to have sex against her will, biting her lip as he did so. As he left, she said, he advised her to put some ice on the bite because it had begun to swell up. Asked why she had not reported the rape to the police at the time, Broaddrick told the *New York Times*: 'Even though I was a respected businesswoman, what was I doing in a hotel room with the Attorney-General? No, I never even considered coming forward.'

Clinton's behaviour 'sometimes ends up being abusive', according to a 'mental-health professional' interviewed by Gail Sheehy for her book on Hillary Clinton – an observation that Sheehy glossed as meaning 'he may force himself on women'. These are extraordinarily serious allegations against a serving President, made in books and on prime-time TV; they create a much darker picture of Clinton than the good-natured philanderer his friends and his wife have presented to a largely sympathetic public. But Clinton has never sued, and his response to every allegation of a sexual relationship outside his marriage, consensual or otherwise, is either a scornful denial or the 'stalker' defence with which he tried to discredit Lewinsky. This is that a famous man inevitably attracts the attention of deranged women who want to be his girlfriend, as well as the animosity of the ones he rebuffs: end of story.

'Does it count as sexual harassment if women are harassing the President for sex?' demanded Erica Jong, turning feminist theory on its head and retreating into the long-abandoned fortress of biological determinism. 'Have we forgotten that the President is the alpha male of the tribe, and the alpha male gets the youngest and most nubile females with or without foreplay?' What his supporters were suggesting was not just that any woman who made claims against Clinton was one of his rejects, motivated by revenge, but that he was more likely to tell the truth than his accusers. While it is a fact that some of the women changed their stories over time, four of them – the exception is Broaddrick, whose allegation has neither been proved nor disproved – are now broadly accepted to have had the encounters they claimed with Clinton. The President settled with Jones when she was at her weakest, waiting to appeal against a court decision dismissing the case, while Lewinsky's account of their relationship is not contested, even by people who disapprove of the circumstances in which it was provided. 'In the evaluation of experienced prosecutors and investigators, Ms Lewinsky has provided truthful information. She has not falsely inculpated the President,' was the final judgment of the *Starr Report*. Clinton, by contrast, has been exposed as a habitual and shameless liar, someone who was prepared to lie on oath to save his skin. He dissembled about his long affair with Flowers, eventually making a grudging and partial admission that he might have slept with her once; he denied ever having met Jones, never mind asking her for a blowjob; but his most outrageous, consistent and public lies were made in response to questions about Lewinsky.

The President's reaction to the very first *Washington Post* story was immediate and categorical. On national public radio, when he was asked whether he had had an affair with a young woman and encouraged her to lie to lawyers in the Paula Jones case as the newspaper alleged, he responded: 'The charges are not true. And I haven't asked anybody to lie.' That evening, on TV, he denied an 'improper relationship'. When asked precisely what he meant by this, he replied: 'Well, I think you know what it means. It means that there is not a sexual relationship, an improper sexual relationship, or any other kind of improper relationship.' The following day, in another interview, he declared categorically that 'the relationship was not sexual.' On 26 January, in the Roosevelt Room of the White House, he made what was to become his most notorious denial: 'I want to say one thing to the American people. I want you to listen to me. I'm going to say this again: I did not have sexual relations with that woman, Miss Lewinsky. I never told anybody to lie, not a single time. Never. These allegations are false.' He was eventually to commit perjury – lying on oath – on this specific issue on five separate occasions.

When a habitual liar, which most people suspected Clinton of being after the Gennifer Flowers affair, asks you to believe his version of events, why should you listen to him? Indeed, the fact that his denials were given any credence at all demonstrates what the women he harassed were up against – what any woman is up against, anywhere in the world, when she makes allegations of sexual misconduct against a powerful man. (Remember Anita Hill? In 1991 she accused a Supreme Court nominee, Clarence Thomas, of sexual harassment, and found herself publicly ridiculed and vilified. It is also worth mentioning here that the conviction rate in rape cases reported to the police in Britain *fell* in the late 1990s to a mere 7.5 per cent.) Stephanopoulos, recalling his dismay when he realized in 1992 that Clinton had lied to him about his affair with Flowers, pondered: 'How could he have been so stupid? So arrogant? Did he want to get caught?' But while it is possible that Clinton enjoyed taking risks, they were nothing like as great as Stephanopoulos assumed. Unlike his accusers, Clinton's appearance was a definite asset; with his good looks and easy charm, he did not fit most people's notion of a sex pest, certainly not a rapist. Why would he need, people asked in genuine bewilderment, to proposition women he had just met, like Jones, or grope employees at the White House, like Lewinsky and Willey? Or, for that matter, accept a hurried, incomplete blowjob from Lewinsky and then – as she later told her aunt, Debra Finerman – masturbate until he ejaculated into a sink in a bathroom off the Oval Office?

These questions bring us to the issue at the very heart of the impeachment process, which is not puritanism but power and its relation to male sexuality. A member of the baby-boom generation that followed the Second World War, the President benefited from the opportunities that became available to men as a consequence of the sexual revolution. (What he seems not to have recognized is the link between that kind of male behaviour and the second wave of feminism, a subject I shall return to in Chapter 7.) Popular with female voters, who were credited with putting him into the White House in 1992, Clinton was sufficiently au fait with feminism to be pro-choice on abortion. He even campaigned, first time round, on an unofficial two-for-one ticket, promising voters that his wife would reform health care after his election, a pledge his administration rapidly backed away from when it emerged that she was an electoral liability. More to the point, he married an avowed feminist whose unease about something – whether it was the state of her marriage, the role of political wife or both – manifested itself in dogged and ill-judged attempts to defend herself and her husband against his accusers. During his first presidential campaign in 1992, she appeared on television at the height of the furore over the Flowers allegations, supporting him as he admitted to causing 'pain' in his marriage; she made an angry observation, in another interview, that she was not a little woman, standing by her man like Tammy Wynette, and had to apologize to the furious country-and-western singer. Outsiders speculated she had made a political deal, agreeing to sideline her own ambitions in order to further his, and did not want to lose everything she had worked for because of his infidelities. She certainly did not seem to be a woman physically at ease with herself, and her intellectual confidence contrasted with a public persona that came to look more and more rigidly constructed. Yet close associates of the couple believed, until the Lewinsky revelations proved other-wise, that Clinton had put his adulteries behind him when he became

35

leader of the free world; Stephanopoulos even made the mawkish suggestion that the couple's bond had been strengthened during his presidency, that Hillary had fallen in love with her husband a second time when he fulfilled their joint dreams for his political career. Whatever the true state of their marriage, or the private agreements between them, it was their joint failure to comprehend contemporary sexual mores – in Hillary's case, to close the gap between feminist theory and her actual experience – which would threaten both their relationship and the entire Clinton administration.

The President was as publicly uxorious as his predecessor, John F. Kennedy, frequently holding hands with his wife in an open demonstration of affection. If anything, he was even more ostentatious about his religious convictions, often carrying an oversized Bible under one arm and talking freely about its influence on policy. (Stephanopoulos even recalled the President rising at three a.m. to read the Book of Joshua before meeting the Israeli Prime Minister, Yitzhak Rabin, and the Chairman of the PLO, Yasser Arafat, in 1993.) In one sense, all this means is that Clinton *voluntarily* adopted moral precepts that regulated all aspects of his life, including sex, and then broke them repeatedly. But the charge against him is not just the obvious one of double standards; it is that his clandestine behaviour was *abusive*, an exercise whose purpose was not so much sexual fulfilment as a wanton exercise of power. That Kennedy used and abused women throughout his truncated political career did not become evident until years after his death, but the revelations – including evidence that young women were coerced into agreeing to sex with the President – have never completely tarnished his reputation as a visionary thinker. (Some people, blindly loyal to the Camelot myth, refuse to believe them to this day.) It was Clinton's misfortune, by contrast, to have one of his many extramarital relationships subjected to forensic scrutiny before a Grand Jury and in the *Starr Report* while he was still in office. Comprehensively detonating Hollywood notions of a May–September love affair, the report contained elements of French farce as the principals lurked behind doors and grappled with the President's trousers. But it was also, in the final analysis, a relentless catalogue of blowjobs, exposing dark elements of his sexuality and an attitude to women that was classically misogynist.

The stage for the drama was set on 15 November 1995, when the President happened to find himself briefly alone with Lewinsky in Stephanopoulos's office while she was still an unpaid intern at the White House. When she told him she had a crush on him, he immediately took advantage of the situation by inviting her into a study off the Oval Office and kissing her. Later that evening, when fewer people were around, Clinton approached her in the Chief of Staff's office and suggested she meet him in Stephanopoulos's room again a few minutes later. She did, but they were almost immediately interrupted; whatever Lewinsky had expected, the encounter was brief and businesslike, with Clinton giving half his attention to a telephone conversation with a Congressman or Senator. She recalled: 'I believe he took a phone call . . . and so we moved from the hallway into the back office . . . [H]e put his hand down my pants and stimulated me manually in the genital area.' Still talking on the phone, Clinton dextrously reached into his trousers and took out his penis for her to give him a blowjob. With the intern still on her knees, he eventually finished his conversation and ordered her to stop before he ejaculated. 'And then I think he made a joke,' remembered Lewinsky, 'that he hadn't had that in a long time.'

Blaming the frigidity of his wife is a classic married-man tactic at the outset of an affair with another woman, but Lewinsky may have been too young and inexperienced to recognize it. Two nights later the scene was repeated, in almost every detail, at the same time in the evening. On this occasion, Clinton told Lewinsky to use the excuse that she needed to come to his office to deliver a takeaway pizza. He had just begun feeling her breasts when they were once again interrupted by a phone call. As he chatted to a Congressman, he once again 'unzipped his pants and exposed himself' for Lewinsky to give him a blowjob. Nothing else happened until six weeks later, on New Year's Eve, when Lewinsky bumped into the President as he came out of the Oval Office. In a gesture that testifies to her assessment of her insignificance to him, she reminded him of her name, which she thought he had forgotten. He told her he had lost her phone number and led her to the study, where he once again took out his penis and indicated she should perform fellatio. This time they were not interrupted, although he stopped her before he ejaculated, saying he did not yet know her well enough.

A week later Lewinsky visited Clinton in his private office and 'we were intimate in the bathroom'. Two weeks later they had phone sex for the first time. Another week passed and Clinton invited her into the Oval Office, where she asked a question that once again betrayed her anxiety about the President's attitude to her: 'Is this just about sex . . . or do you have some interest in trying to get to know me as a person?' The President's reply, that he 'cherishe[d]' their time together, sounded odd even to Lewinsky, 'when I felt like he didn't really even know me yet'. After offering this minimal reassurance, Clinton led her into a hallway next to the study, 'unzipped his pants and sort of exposed himself'. Once again, she gave him a blowjob. Ten days later, on the occasion of their sixth sexual encounter, they had their first conversation of any length. The President unbuttoned her dress, unhooked her bra and felt her breasts, and she performed fellatio. Fifteen days later, on 19 February, he told her he no longer felt right about their relationship and they should see each other only as friends. This injunction operated for just over a month, until 31 March, when Clinton called her at her desk and suggested she should come to the Oval Office on the pretence of delivering papers to him. On this occasion Lewinsky, who was desperately anxious to see him again, persuaded herself that his actions, far from being selfish, were designed to please her. '[H]e focused on me pretty exclusively,' she said proudly, recalling that he kissed her breasts and touched her genitals. The President was for once a model of restraint, keeping his penis inside his trousers and – in what she seems to have interpreted, bizarrely, as an affectionate gesture – inserting a cigar into her vagina, which he then placed in his mouth. The following month, April 1996, she was transferred to the Pentagon.

She had no further sexual contact with Clinton that year, as she attempted to have herself moved back to the White House. When they started to meet again for sex in February 1997, the rendezvous were arranged through Betty Currie, the President's secretary, who authorized Lewinsky's entry to the White House and escorted her to the West Wing. On 28 February the President invited Lewinsky to hear him tape his weekly radio address. Afterwards, Currie, Clinton and Lewinsky went into the back office, where the secretary left them alone. He gave Lewinsky a couple of presents, then they fondled each other and the presidential penis was once again released from his trousers. On this occasion, when he pushed her away, she said she wanted to make him come, and he allowed her to continue until he ejaculated. She was wearing a navy-blue Gap dress and, next time she took it from her wardrobe, she noticed stains on the hip and chest. (The dress was later seized as evidence and DNA-tested, revealing that the stains were the President's semen.) A month later Lewinsky and the President had sex for the last time. '[T]his was another one of those occasions when I was babbling about something and he just kissed me, kind of to shut me up, I think,' she testified. 'I wanted him to touch my genitals with his genitals,' she said, but he was unwilling to allow penetration to take place. Instead, as usual, Lewinsky gave him a blowjob. Afterwards, Clinton expressed anxiety that a foreign embassy might be tapping his phones, and suggested cover stories they could use. A couple of months later, fearing Lewinsky had confided in friends and relatives about their encounters, Clinton ended the relationship for good.

A striking aspect of this workmanlike sequence of events, from the President's point of view at least, is that it has much in common with Jones's testimony. Clinton does not waste time but takes out his penis almost as soon as he is alone with Lewinsky; his interest in both women is limited to establishing (a) her availability and (b) her willingness, or otherwise, to perform the act he requires. Another is his reluctance to ejaculate, frequently remarked on by Lewinsky, who seems to have interpreted it as a failure on her part to gain her lover's trust. Clinton's preference for blowjobs has been widely discussed, the most frequently canvassed opinion suggesting it was determined by his forensic decision – like his wife, the President trained as a lawyer – that fellatio did not count as sex. Certainly this is what Clinton claimed when he was challenged over his denial at the Jones deposition that he had ever had sex with Lewinsky; oral sex, he tried to argue, was not covered by the term 'sexual relations'. This assertion is less than compelling, and not just because sexual preferences are rarely directed solely by conscious decisions.

In the first place, if oral sex doesn't count, why is it called oral *sex*? Secondly, if heterosexual intercourse is the defining test of whether sexual activity has taken place, it gives rise to the quaint proposition that all gay men and lesbians are celibate. Gore Vidal, commenting on this aspect of the case, reached like Erica Jong for biology, arguing that men are programmed to have sex with as many different partners as possible, not to form lasting relationships: 'Hence an addiction to the impersonal blowjob.' This does at least have the virtue of reminding us that what Clinton sought from his sexual partners reveals something about his psyche, rather than his legal training. But the significance of fellatio for a man like Clinton is not so much its impersonality, a proposition psychologists might well want to debate, as the relative positions of male and female in the act. Lewinsky is in a subordinate position, literally and metaphorically; she is servicing Clinton, nothing more, and the cheap gifts he offers her are the currency any boss might use to keep an employee willing to do his bidding. Lewinsky naively remarked in her testimony on Clinton's determination to keep her quiet, even using his hand to gag her on one occasion, a gesture she attributed to his fear of discovery. But it also suggests he was anxious not to waste time on unnecessary conversation, an end that was also achieved by his more usual and entirely effective expedient of putting his penis in her mouth. He did not even give her the satisfaction of completing the act, in the usual sense, until quite late into their 'relationship'. Instead, he appears to have moved the *locus* of pleasure elsewhere, from orgasm to the process itself, enjoying himself by *not* coming. The whole sequence is suggestive not just of a lust for power over others but of iron self-control, the polar opposite of the joyous surrender that customarily characterizes the moment of orgasm.

It is not uncommon for men to fear ejaculation, with its inevitable transition from the erect phallus to the limp penis. 'The effect which coitus has of discharging tensions and causing flaccidity may be the prototype of what the man fears,' Freud wrote in *The Taboo of Virginity* in 1917, 'and the realization of the influence which the woman gains over him through sexual intercourse, the consideration she thereby forces from him, may justify the extension of this fear.' For Clinton, brought up in a fractured, predominantly female household, it would not be surprising if these anxieties, which are intimately related to a larger misogyny, were unusually acute. But few men embark on a career that provides as *one of its perks* so many opportunities to confront these anxieties and disarm them, temporarily at least, by demonstrating mastery over the self and the feared object. The irony here is that, placed in this context, Clinton's claim that he could not control his sexual urges looks like the polar opposite of the truth; his avoidance of coitus, his single-minded pursuit of oral sex without orgasm during the act, circumvents all the terrors identified by Freud, from experiencing involuntary limpness to forming an emotional bond. In the circumstances, it is deliciously ironic that his worst fears are justified when he finally permits himself to come – and leaves incriminating stains on Lewinsky's dress for the FBI to find and test.

It is unsurprising that, as millions of readers goggled over the revelations in the *Starr Report*, questions of morality – other than the unilluminating fact that Clinton had committed adultery – were pushed aside. What happened, in effect, was that people identified with one or other of the protagonists, Bill, Hillary or Monica, with middle-aged men particularly likely to support the beleaguered President. Handsome, easy-going, married to what was widely assumed to be a frigid feminist, he fitted perfectly into the traditional role of helpless male, struggling and sometimes failing to inhibit his physical cravings, a lapse that was all too understandable when Lewinsky was flaunting her obvious charms. If this seems like a caricature, it is nevertheless the case for the defence, sufficiently compelling in the end for Clinton to avoid disgrace and dismissal from office. It successfully obscured a much more serious issue, which was the continuing ability of powerful men, at the end of the twentieth century, to get away with systematic sexual abuse of women. That Clinton had a narrow escape is undeniable, demonstrating that the moral climate had shifted somewhat since the 1960s, when Kennedy slept with literally hundreds of women without damaging his career. But the true irony of the episode lies in Clinton's skilful manipulation of traditional morality – by which he would be judged as a minor transgressor, if a transgressor at all, according to some of his friends and allies – as a smokescreen. Far better to be convicted of cheating on his wife, at the court of public opinion, than to own up to a pattern of behaviour that might have landed a less attractive and influential man with a criminal record.

3

Not One of Us: Saddam Hussein al-Takriti

*Those who caution delay because they hate war – as we all do
– must ask themselves this question: how much longer should
the world stand by and risk these atrocities continuing?*
— JOHN MAJOR, 15 JANUARY 1991

We used to love him, but it's all over now.
WITH APOLOGIES TO THE ROLLING STONES

In July 1981 a junior minister in the British government set off on a
visit to Baghdad, where the President of Iraq, Saddam Hussein, was
celebrating the anniversary of the 1968 revolution that brought his
Ba'ath Party to power. Douglas Hurd, an old Etonian who wrote
thrillers in his spare time, was one of several Conservative ministers
who would pack their suitcases for Baghdad after Mrs Thatcher
came to power in May 1979. They included the Foreign Secretary,
Lord Carrington, in July that year; Cecil Parkinson, then a Trade
Minister, in October; his boss John Nott, Secretary of State for Trade
and Industry, a month later; and John Biffen in October 1981,
shortly after he replaced Nott as Trade Secretary. As well as these
high-level contacts, the Committee for Middle East Trade, an area
advisory group to the British Overseas Trade Board, spent five days
in Iraq in February 1980, looking at ways to expand trade between
the two countries.

It was the beginning of a new chapter in relations between the
two countries. Iraq had imposed an embargo on British goods in

July 1978 after James Callaghan's Labour government expelled eleven Iraqi diplomats in an angry response to the assassination in London of a former Iraqi Prime Minister – a murder in which the regime in Baghdad was implicated. The Conservatives, though, took a more conciliatory view, and the embargo was lifted as a result of Carrington's post-election visit. By the early 1980s Iraq was looking for a wide range of imports from the West, including weapons, and one of the companies eager to supply them – the opening moves in a long-running farce whose conclusion would be documented, fifteen years later, in Sir Richard Scott's report on the export of defence and dual-use equipment to Iraq – was British Aerospace. Whatever the ostensible reason for Hurd's trip to Baghdad in the summer of 1981 – and it is difficult to imagine the urbane thriller-writer observing Saddam's flamboyant cult of personality with anything but wry distaste – his programme was thoroughly businesslike, including talks with Iraq's Foreign Minister and a meeting with Saddam himself at an anniversary reception on 17 July. The *Guardian* had no hesitation in describing Hurd as 'a high-level salesman' and reminded its readers of the scale of the prize that dangled before him: Iraq's requirement for a comprehensive air-defence system. If British Aerospace was successful, the paper reported, it would be the biggest order of its kind the company had ever secured. Aided by this and other ministerial contacts, Britain's trade with Iraq rose from £201 m in 1979 to £322 m in 1980, to £624 m in 1981 and £874 m in 1982.

What Hurd might have appreciated, if there was time in his schedule for sightseeing, was what little remained of the city's original culture and architecture. Baghdad's history, and its importance as a trade centre, stretches back hundreds of years. Originally a village near the old Persian capital of Ctesiphon, its moment came when the Abbasid caliphate moved there from Damascus and began building a new imperial city. Its high point was the reign of Haroun al-Rashid (786–809), when sumptuous mosques, pavilions and gardens made it the most splendid and important metropolis in the East. Haroun and his friend, the great poet Abu Nuwas, appear as characters in *The Thousand and One Nights*, and the explorer and translator Richard Burton described Baghdad as 'a Paris of the ninth century'. But the City of Peace, as it was officially known in the Abbasid period, was now in the hands of a thuggish twentieth-century dictator who would soon disfigure it with hideous modern memorials to his vanity.

Saddam Hussein has mythologized his own background, in the manner of dictators the world over, and some of the details are unclear or exist in several versions. But it is known that his childhood was violent and disrupted, teaching him to manipulate other people and inculcating savage notions of how to achieve his aims. He was born in 1937 in al-Auja, a village near the remote town of Takrit, on the River Tigris about a hundred miles north of Baghdad. His father, Hussein al-Majid, died or disappeared around the time of Saddam's birth, and he was raised by his mother and a brutal stepfather, Ibrahim Hassan. Denied an education, forced to work on the family farm, Saddam left home at the age of ten and went to live in the house in Takrit of his uncle, Khairallah Tulfah, who had been thrown out of the Iraqi Army in 1941 because of his fascist sympathies. Saddam went to a local school with his cousin Adnan, one of many relatives who would one day occupy powerful positions in his regime, then moved to Baghdad, where he attended secondary school and became interested in the recently formed Ba'ath move-ment. Expelled from school, implicated in his first murder at the age of sixteen, he was soon chosen by the party to take part in an attempt on the life of the Iraqi Prime Minister, General 'Abd al-Karim Qasim. The attempt failed and Saddam fled to Cairo, wounded by a bullet that, according to his own self-glorifying account, was removed by a doctor without anaesthetic. He finally went to college in Egypt, at the late age of twenty-three, failed his exams and returned to Baghdad, without qualifications but already a fully fledged assassin, when the Ba'athists overthrew General Qasim in 1963. The new regime was overthrown in its turn six months later, leaving Saddam to concentrate on building up the Jihaz Haneen, a terror organization modelled on Hitler's SS. With the Ba'ath Party out of power for the next five years, he had time to turn its members into a force that would suppress opposition in Iraq and murder opponents abroad – as it did, in London as well as in other foreign capitals, when the Ba'athists returned in 1968. The coup did not yet place Saddam in sole charge of the country but, with the help of the absolutely loyal Jihaz Haneen, he was well on his way.

The glittering ceremonies Saddam laid on for visiting dignitaries in the early 1980s did not disguise the fact that he was in charge of a one-party state. A year before Hurd's visit, a diplomat at the US Embassy in Baghdad reported to Washington that that year's 17 July celebrations 'produced a blatant outpouring of officially inspired fervor [sic], celebrating Saddam Hussein, the man and leader'. Behind the scenes, the secret cable remarked laconically, Saddam's security services 'root out every suspected source of trouble to the regime'. Those most affected by the intimidation were 'the Sh'ia, the Kurds and the educated, professional classes who, for the most part, we assume, remain unmoved by Saddam's appeal'. This was something of an understatement: the Ba'athist coup in 1968 had been followed by televised hangings of the new regime's opponents, including Iraqi Jews and members of the Communist Party. Saddam, as Vice-Chairman of the Revolutionary Command Council, had enjoyed a ringside seat. In 1981, the year of the Hurd and Biffen trade missions, he had been President for only two years since ousting the regime's nominal head, General Ahmad Hassan al-Bakr, but his ruthlessness was already legendary. Nor was there much ambiguity about the origins or character of his Ba'ath Party – the word means 'renaissance' in Arabic – which began as a nationalist movement in the Syrian capital, Damascus, in 1944. The objectives of the party were defined by one of its founders, a Christian teacher named Michel Aflaq, as 'freedom, unity and socialism', but the type of socialism he had in mind is usually prefaced by the adjective 'national'. Loathing Britain and France, the colonial powers that had cynically decided Syria's fate between the two world wars, Aflaq and his Muslim co-founder, Salah al-Bitar, sympathized with Germany and Italy; the political movement they founded, and its methods when it eventually achieved power, were imports from

European fascism, which the young Saddam had been brought up to revere.

To complicate matters, the two Arab states that were governed by versions of Ba'athism in the latter half of the twentieth century, Syria and Iraq, were old enemies, and there was constant tension between them, increasing Saddam's natural insecurity and belligerence. According to the historian Peter Mansfield, this was an inevitable consequence of the way the party operated; implacably hostile to democracy, the Ba'athists did not have a popular following and relied instead on 'extreme dictatorial or fascist-type methods' to keep themselves in power. In 1973, in a confidential assessment of the situation in Iraq, prepared by the US Embassy in Baghdad for the State Department, it was estimated that less than 1 per cent of the population belonged to the Ba'ath Party; after five years in power it continued to retain its 'secretive, cell-like structure and informer system'. Describing a classic one-party state, the diplomats reported that its 'principal instruments of power are the pervasive and competing intelligence and internal security organs of the Ba'ath Party, the armed forces and the ministry of the interior'. Nor was there any doubt about the real power in the land: 'The strongest figure is RCC Vice-Chairman Saddam Hussein, leader of the civilian wing. Saddam Hussein is the personification of Ba'athi Iraq; he is young (thirty-five), ambitious and ruthless. He has a limited knowledge of the outside world, speaks only Arabic, and is dogmatic in his belief that the "imperialists" led by the US are actively seeking to crush revolutionary Iraq.' This was not a promising assessment for the Americans, who were already worried by Iraq's closeness to its chief arms supplier, the Soviet Union. Yet there were compelling reasons for the Americans to court Saddam, as the British would begin to do six years later. No discussion of the West's relations with Iraq makes sense without keeping in mind the fact that the country's oil reserves are the second largest in the world, surpassed only by Saudi Arabia's; Iraq has 6 per cent – just over a sixteenth – of the world total. 'Oil revenue was $900 m in 1971 and is expected to rise to $2bn in 1975,' the US Embassy reported, reminding Washington that Saddam not only controlled a precious resource but had money to spend as a result of it. Moreover, he had recently concluded a deal that resolved the problems that had caused arguments between Iraq and the Western oil companies for years. All in all, 'the future of the Ba'ath regime, particularly in view of the encouraging economic prospects, seems bright'.

This upbeat assertion was made six years before a very different revolution took place in the capital of Iraq's next-door neighbour, Iran. The impact of this development on the stability of the region, and the attitude to it of Western powers, can hardly be emphasized enough; it is the key to understanding the troubled history of the next decade. In one of the greatest reverses ever suffered by American foreign policy, the Shah of Iran, an autocratic but modernizing pro-Western leader, was overthrown in 1979 in favour of a theocratic regime led by Ayatollah Khomeini. This 79-year-old Muslim cleric, who had spent many years in exile in Paris during the Shah's reign, horrified the American government, which saw one of its main allies in the Middle East sliding back, as it thought, into medieval – and specifically anti-American – barbarism. The seizure of the US Embassy in Tehran, denounced by Khomeini as a nest of spies, was to reverberate through American domestic politics; Jimmy Carter's bungled attempt to rescue the hostages, when American military helicopters became bogged down in the Iranian desert, and his failure to get them out in time for the 1980 presidential election – the widely anticipated 'October surprise' – is credited with bringing Ronald Reagan to power. (The naivety of many American voters towards their country's foreign policy should never be underestimated; during a trip to the States just before the presidential election, when I was interviewing the family of a US Marine who was being held hostage in the Tehran embassy, the man's father asked plaintively: 'How could they do this to my son? We gave them the best telephone system in the world.' He had never heard of SAVAK, the Shah's notorious secret police, or its role in keeping the old regime in power.)

The new regime in Iran fully reciprocated the Americans' hostility, trapping the two countries in a lengthy exchange of insults, one of whose side-effects was to be an almost wilful blindness on the part of the US and its Western allies towards the nature of Saddam's dictatorship in Iraq. 'Persian-pukes prepare to die,' taunted American F1-11 pilots, safe in their base in leafy Oxfordshire in the 1980s. 'Allah creates but we cremate.' The absence of democracy in Iran, and the intolerance of the Islamic regime, would later be graphically demonstrated when it pronounced a fatwa on the author Salman Rushdie – a PR disaster for Iran, as well as a calamity for the unfortunate novelist. This meant that there was a ready audience in the West for stories about human rights abuses in Iran, where the sight of women in their enveloping chadors became a symbol of the authoritarian character of the state. It also meant that Saddam, in his tailored Western suits, appeared as the antithesis of the elderly clerics in long black robes who were now in charge in Tehran; in an unconscious reversal, he came to seem less 'Arab' than his Iranian neighbours who, of course, are not Arabs at all. And it rapidly became clear that he was also more than willing to take on the Ayatollah, tying up Khomeini's time and resources in a way that usefully diverted him from anti-Western projects.

From the simplistic view of the West, an entirely unacceptable, fundamentalist regime in Tehran was now pitted against the secular Ba'athists in Baghdad. In less than a year, the two countries would be at war and, despite public declarations of neutrality, it was always seen as vital to the West's interests that Iran should not emerge the victor, a view shared by several Middle Eastern countries, notably Saudi Arabia and – ironically, in view of future events – tiny Kuwait. There was a religious element to this bias, among educated Westerners: Iraq's ruling class consists of Sunni Muslims, essentially Saddam's extended family from the area around Takrit, and the Sunnis have always been regarded as less extreme than the Shi'ites who make up the bulk of Iran's population. To complicate matters, most Iraqis are Shia as well, a fact that fostered Saddam's long-standing insecurity and explained his venomous hostility to Khomeini; the last thing he wanted was a Shi'ite government across one of his borders, stirring up his own people – never much enamoured of him, as declassified American documents show – against his regime. Astonishingly, this is exactly what Khomeini proceeded to do. With disastrous timing, and intentions that were hard to fathom – did the fledgling Iranian revolution really want to embroil itself in hostilities with Iraq? – he denounced Saddam and called on the Iraqi people to overthrow their 'corrupt and atheistic' government. Saddam responded by abrogating a treaty he had signed with the Shah in 1975, when he was still Vice-President. Then, in September 1980, he invaded his troublesome neighbour.

The declaration of war was a humanitarian disaster, as even the dry language of the *Scott Report* later conceded: it 'produced casualties on a massive scale, the use by Iraq of horrifying chemical weapons, and the use by Iran of children as infantry soldiers'. (This grinding conflict was known as the Gulf War, as I mentioned earlier, until Saddam's invasion and rapid expulsion from Kuwait in 1990/ 91 appropriated that title and wiped the earlier, purely local affair from the West's memory.) It was also a potential bonanza for foreign arms suppliers. In 1979 just under 7 per cent of Iraq's gross domestic product was spent on weapons. By 1984 it had risen to nearly 30 per cent, making Iraq the world's biggest importer of major weapons systems. During the war, 26 countries happily supplied arms to both sides in the conflict, while another 4 sold only to Iraq. (That two of these were Jordan and Egypt shows that the West's hostility to Iran was shared in the Middle East.) Almost half of Iraq's weapons during the war came from the Soviet Union, with France accounting for another 28 per cent. But, at the time of Hurd's visit in 1981, the Russians had imposed a short-lived arms embargo, not unconnected with Saddam's somewhat tactless purge of the Iraqi Communist Party. Saddam himself was certainly keen to do deals elsewhere; in 1980, just before he invaded Iran, he signed a £600 m deal with Italy to provide four frigates and set up a shipyard in Iraq.

The Iranian revolution had much the same effect on UK policy as it did on American. In the days of the Shah, British companies had entered into 'a large number of contracts for the sale of arms and defence-related equipment to Iran'. Although these companies were keen to complete contracts and get their money – UK exports to Iran totalled £403 m in 1981, very few of them involving military equipment – government policy was already switching, disastrously, in favour of Iraq. 'From the start of the war between Iran and Iraq in the early 1980s, the West consistently underestimated the danger Saddam Hussein posed to the stability of the region,' observed John Hughes-Wilson, a former colonel in the British Army's Intelligence Corps. That British companies did not manage to sell weapons to Iraq in the quantities they would have liked is due to considerations beyond their control: anxiety on the part of British governments about offending Iran, which had ordered two supply ships from a shipyard in Yarrow and a vessel named the *Kharg* from Swan Hunter before the conflict began, Saddam's habit of defaulting on payments and his dreadful human rights record. The latter was never regarded as a major obstacle, except in PR terms, and Britain tried to get round the problem of having to appear even-handed in its dealings with the combatants by discussing arms deals that would take place when the conflict was over.

The formal policy of the British government towards the belligerents would not be spelled out in detail until 1985 – what came to be known as the Howe guidelines – but as early as 1982 it claimed a position of neutrality. In May that year, a letter from the Ministry of Defence explained: 'We are prepared to consider requests for the supply of defence equipment from either side on a case by case basis, taking into account our neutrality obligations, our relations with the countries concerned and the need to work for a peaceful solution to the conflict.' In private, the situation was very different, as the *Scott Report* revealed. At a meeting of the Cabinet's Overseas and Defence Committee on 29 January 1981, ministers agreed that lethal arms and ammunition should not be supplied to either side but 'every opportunity should be taken to exploit Iraq's potentialities as a promising market for the sale of defence equipment'. Government policy was that the definition of 'lethal items' should be interpreted as narrowly as possible 'and the obligations of neutrality as flexibly as possible'. This is essentially a story about money and it has to be told through escalating sums, in the form of loans and credit, which demonstrate the determination of successive British governments to shore up Saddam's shaky regime in the Middle East, even when it was on the brink of bankruptcy. What the covert pro-Iraq bias meant, in the first four years of the war, was that British companies sold at least £184 m of defence-related goods to Iraq, and only a paltry £13 m to Iran – an imbalance of 14 to 1 in Saddam's favour. So much for the Thatcher government's neutrality, and if BAe had got its way, the post-war disparity would have been much higher. In July 1981, when I was working for the London *Sunday Times*, I discovered that a team of thirty Iraqi technicians was covertly in Britain to discuss a £1 bn aircraft deal. BAe's employees had been visiting Iraq regularly in the previous four months, and the deal would eventually allow the Iraqis to build 300 British Hawk fighter trainer planes under licence. The Iraqis wanted the Hawks, a ground-attack aircraft euphemistically described as a 'trainer', to replace their old Jet Provosts, also built by Britain. But it would additionally provide the groundwork for Iraq to create its own aircraft industry, making the proposal doubly controversial.

Outside the arms industry and the inner circles of Margaret Thatcher's government, other voices were less approving of Britain's new trading partner. No one realized, at the time, that the war would drag on until 1988 and kill at least a million people. Equally, no one should have been in any doubt that Iraq was in the grip of a terror comparable to that created by the Gestapo in Nazi Germany, with families living in constant fear of a knock on the door that would see their relatives dragged off, to disappear into Saddam's notorious prisons, their fate – almost certainly torture, ill health and death – pieced together only through rumours and long-ago sightings reported by released prisoners. Amnesty International issued a stream of reports about 'disappearances' in Iraq, arrests of political opponents of the regime who were never heard of again, as well as forced deportations by the authorities. Thousands of people, including Shia Muslims suspected of being of Iranian descent, were forced over the border into Iran. Another target was the Kurds, a mountainous people who constitute a quarter of Iraq's population and who have always been subject to brutal repression. A typical 'disappearance' story from Amnesty's files is that of the seven al-Hashimi brothers, arrested in Baghdad on 1 October 1980: Ahmad and Wahab, both students; Ibrahim, a post-office worker; Hussain, a chemist; Iyad, a civil engineer; 'Abd al-Ridha, who worked at Baghdad Airport; and Isma'il, a pharmacist. The brothers are believed to have been taken as 'hostages' to force the surrender of another brother, Ja'far, who had fled Iraq after opposing Saddam. The men were initially held at Abu Ghraib Prison near Baghdad, but nothing was heard of them again until 1997, when Amnesty was officially informed of the execution of the eldest, Isma'il, a full fourteen years earlier on 3 August 1983. His only offence was to fail to inform the authorities about his brother's opposition activities. An elderly Shia cleric, Sayyid Muhammad Sadeq Muhammad Ridha al-Qazwini, also disappeared in 1980, when Iraqi security agents broke into his house in Karbala', taking him away in his nightclothes. He too was last heard of in Abu Ghraib Prison, where a fellow inmate who was released in 1986 said he had seen the old man – Muhammed Sadeq al-Qazwini was born in 1900 and was in failing health at the time of his arrest – and reported he had gone blind. Iraq in this period was 'the perfect Orwellian state, complete with a Big Brother, who ruled through terror and oppression'. Sadly, with the West's attention focused on the Islamic regime in Iran – Muslim fundamentalism was shaping up nicely as the new global threat – these reports did not receive the attention they deserved. This was especially true in Britain, where contacts between London and Tehran were soured by the Rushdie affair.

Relations between Iraq and Mrs Thatcher's government began to go awry in 1983, but not because of Saddam's human rights record or the ghastly death toll in the Gulf War. The problem was the difficulty of getting money out of Iraq for trade deals that had already been signed, a situation that British ministers addressed by blithely lending money to Saddam and underwriting deals with British companies in case he defaulted. Displaying an extraordinary disregard for financial reality – or with an eye to future profits for UK companies – Mrs Thatcher announced that the Export Credits Guarantee Department was extending a £250 m loan to Iraq in 1983, with the same amount of credit available in 1984; cash contracts worth £200 m were also being converted into credit. The loan, handled by merchant bankers Morgan Grenfell, stated specifically that the money could not be used for military projects that would help Iraq in its war with Iran. But, as a briefing prepared by the Campaign Against the Arms Trade pointed out, this loan and others that followed 'could have released for the war effort funds that might otherwise have been needed for civilian projects'. In any case, after representations by the Iraqis and British defence equipment manufacturers, the government agreed that contracts for non-lethal defence equipment could be supported up to a limit of £25 m. This limit, known as the 'defence allocation', was increased to £50 m in December 1985. Yet as early as January 1984, almost two years before, ministers were aware that 'equipment exported for civilian use had been diverted to military use' by both combatants in the Gulf War. By February that year a senior official at the Ministry of Defence, Mr Sandars, was writing to the Middle East Department of the Foreign Office, expressing concern that an investigation by the House of Commons Defence Committee would force an admission that the policy of neutrality, as mentioned earlier in this chapter, had been a sham – that 'we had leaned heavily towards Iraq in the early years of the war, despite our declared policy of neutrality'. The situation became even trickier the following year, after a UN report published on 26 March confirmed that the Iraqis had used outlawed chemical weapons, mustard gas and the nerve gas, Tabun, against the Iranians.

The result, on 29 October 1995, was the publication of the Howe guidelines on arms sales to Iraq and Iran – an attempt by the government to clarify its position through a written answer by the then Foreign Secretary, Sir Geoffrey Howe, to a parliamentary question. The guidelines, which represent the government's *public* position, are an interesting contrast with the behind-the-scenes view of civil servants that ministers had unfairly favoured Iraq during the conflict. For this reason, and because they would become the focus of a fierce internal battle between ministers in Mrs Thatcher's administration in 1989 and 1990, they are worth quoting in full:

The United Kingdom has been strictly impartial in the conflict between Iran and Iraq and has refused to allow the supply of lethal defence equipment to either side. In order to reinforce our policy of doing everything possible to see this tragic conflict brought to the earliest possible end, we decided in December 1984 to apply thereafter, the following guidelines to all deliveries of defence equipment to Iran and Iraq:

(i) We should maintain our consistent refusal to supply lethal equipment to either side;

(ii) Subject to that overriding consideration, we should attempt to fulfil existing contracts and obligations;

(iii) We should not, in future, approve orders for any defence equipment which, in our view, would significantly enhance the capability of either side to prolong or exacerbate the conflict;

(iv) In line with this policy, we should continue to scrutinize rigorously all applications for export licences or the supply of defence equipment to Iran and Iraq.

With the guidelines acting as a brake on the arms trade, though not perhaps as strictly as they appeared to do, it was an enormous relief to the British government when the Gulf War combatants finally agreed a ceasefire in 1988. Iraq was widely believed to have won, insofar as anything had been achieved by this disastrous conflict, and Ayatollah Khomeini angrily described the ceasefire as 'a poisoned chalice'. Iraq's economy was, by any sensible standards, pretty obviously in ruins, with an annual budget deficit of $10 bn and a $75 bn foreign debt, most of it owed to neighbouring Saudi Arabia and Kuwait. But for Western defence manufacturers, frustrated for eight long years in their ambition of making major arms deals with Saddam, the longed-for moment had arrived at last. Just days after the ceasefire was signed, it was announced that Tony Newton, the Trade and Industry Minister, was to lead the UK delegation to the annual UK–Iraq Joint Commission 'to help British companies to benefit from the trade opportunities' that would follow the end of the conflict. Britain already enjoyed the accolade of 'favoured nation' status for its financial assistance to Iraq during the hostilities, and Newton was keen to capitalize on Saddam's goodwill. In November 1988 he closed a deal that made available to Iraq £340 m of export credit in the next year, almost double the £175 m currently on offer.

There was, however, an outstanding problem. Britain's ally in Baghdad was now widely regarded not just as a torturer of political opponents at home and an assassin, by proxy, abroad. He was also a war criminal, guilty of both genocide and crimes against humanity of a type unknown since the First World War. The British government had already faced a series of uncomfortable questions on the subject in the House of Commons, well before Newton's visit. Would ministers take into account, an MP asked, human rights violations by Iraq, including the use of chemical weapons, when considering extending credit to Saddam? The government's official position was stated by Alan Clark, then a junior Trade Minister, in a Commons reply on 4 November 1988:

The Government are concerned by the denial of human rights wherever this occurs, and has consistently made our views clear to the Iraqi government on this subject. We have also made clear to the Iraqi government our condemnation of the use of chemical weapons. We will continue to do so. At the same time, we should not lose sight of the importance of developing political and economic relations with Iraq, and the provision of export credit is a major contribution to this.

This reply was hardly going to worry Saddam, nor did it address the magnitude of the problem. Less than eight months before, on 17 March, Iraqi warplanes had dropped chemical weapons on the Kurdish town of Halabjah, killing between 6,000 and 8,000 people and injuring another 12,000; five months later another chemical weapons onslaught was responsible for the deaths of thousands of people in seventy Kurdish villages in north-east Iraq. In the Bassay Valley 200 families were reported to have been killed. A survivor from the village of Aikmala described a 'yellowish cloud' and a 'smell of rotten parsley or onions. There were no wounds. People would breathe the smoke, then fall down and blood would come from their mouths.' In all, during the campaign against Iraq's Kurdish minority, 3,000 villages and hamlets were said to have been destroyed and half a million people moved to detention camps elsewhere in Iraq, while 100,000 others fled to Turkey or Iran.

On 30 November 1988 Sir Geoffrey Howe responded to evidence in a Channel 4 *Dispatches* programme that mustard gas had been used on the Iraqi Kurds, including a soil analysis carried out by a chemical analyst. 'We have proclaimed the evidence of CW (chemical weapons) use compelling, but not conclusive,' said the Foreign Secretary. Other authorities took a stronger stand: the US Senate Foreign Relations Committee was later to report 'overwhelming evidence that Iraq used chemical weapons on Kurdish civilians', in attacks that violated the 1925 Geneva Protocol on Chemical Weapons. In addition, Iraq was almost certainly guilty of violating the 1948 Convention on Genocide. At a conference in London in March 1989, a year after the attack on Halabjah, the Labour MP Ann Clwyd said that 'the terror practised by this state is systematic and all-encompassing. In the arena of crimes against humanity, Saddam Hussein and his henchmen score a first.' That very week, the conference heard, two women had been publicly hanged in a square in Baghdad and their bodies left on view as a warning to others.

The Americans, meanwhile, were no more moved than the British government by reports of murder and atrocities emerging from Iraq. On the contrary, still implacably hostile to Iran, they were eager to exploit the business opportunities created by the ceasefire. In June 1989 representatives of twenty-five American companies, accompanied by an American Senator, arrived in Baghdad for a meeting of the US–Iraq Business Forum. They included the Presidents of

Westinghouse, Brown & Root, Kellogg and Bell Helicopter. Together, their companies had grossed $500 bn in sales in the previous year, and they were 'warmly received' by senior economic ministers, the Foreign Minister and Saddam himself. The President, dressed in a smart business suit, listened and made notes for two hours at a meeting with the tycoons on 7 June, as the delegation Chairman, Mr Abboud from the First City Bank of Texas, boasted about their track record. His group represented the US banking, oil, construction and food production sectors, he said, and their total wealth was sufficient to make them the third largest economy in the free world. They were able to speak directly to senior officials in the American government, and had done so when Congress was considering sanctions legislation on chemical weapons in 1988. US exports to Iraq stood at $600 m in 1986, were currently worth $1.5 bn, and Abboud's group hoped to see them double in two years.

What happened next was reported in a confidential report from the US Embassy in Baghdad to Washington. Saddam, the American Ambassador recorded, suddenly 'made a curious excursion into the human rights field'. Astonishing his visitors, who had presumably been briefed not to mention this awkward subject, he announced that Iraq 'deserves credit from the whole world for its human rights record' – an assertion that the Ambassador described, with ample justification, as 'extraordinary'. Revealing a previously unsuspected sense of irony, Saddam went on explain that the purpose of this exemplary record was 'to comfort money' – to reassure foreign capitalists who might be persuaded to invest in Iraq. No one, according to the Ambassador's report, challenged his brazen untruths, leaving the impression that the tycoons, like others before them, found their meeting with Saddam just as reassuring as he had intended.

Four months later, it was the turn of another British minister to set off on the well-worn route for Baghdad. The government in London was increasingly anxious about Saddam, but once again the problem was not human rights. The purpose of the visit by John Wakeham, the Energy Secretary, was to discuss Iraq's inability to keep up payments on its loans, a subject that the Americans had also raised during their meeting. Saddam was almost £80 m in arrears, and a meeting of the Joint Commission in London in December accordingly reduced credit for the following year to £250 m. That same month, on 14 December, the government was once again publicly challenged to explain why, in view of Iraq's human rights record, it was still prepared to trade with Saddam. Lord Trefgarne, a junior Trade Minister, argued that cutting off trade relations would mean the loss of 'many opportunities to convey our views on other matters'. Ignoring the fact that his government's representations had thus far had no visible impact on the regime, he used precisely the same justification that the American Embassy in Baghdad had cited as long ago as 1973: the fact that 'Iraq is sitting on oil reserves second only to those of Saudi Arabia'. It's oil, stupid, as the Old Haileyburian did not go on to say.

The British government had by now got itself into a position where it was extending credit to an attested bad payer who also happened to be a war criminal, to buy goods he could not afford, including arms, at a time when he was beginning to make threatening noises towards a neighbour, Kuwait, to whom he was also deeply indebted. ('We did not just arm his forces, we paid for them into the bargain,' observed Robin Cook, then the shadow Trade and Industry Secretary, at the time the Scott Inquiry was set up.) Yet whatever reservations ministers expressed in public, and there were not many, a very different discussion was going on in private. In essence, what happened in a period of nearly two years after the ceasefire in 1988 was a struggle between three government departments: the Foreign Office, which wanted to maintain the existing restrictions on arms sales to Iraq, and two other ministries – Defence, and Trade and Industry – which lobbied hard to have them relaxed or abolished. The key player in this battle was Alan Clark, first as a junior Trade Minister from 1986 to 1989, then at the MoD, where he was Minister of State for Defence Procurement. According to an MoD official, whose observations were recorded at a meeting on 7 March 1990 – towards the end of the saga, which ended in a victory for Clark – the minister was 'gung-ho for defence sales'. Only a little less enthusiastic was Lord Trefgarne, with whom Clark swapped jobs and ministries in the summer of 1989. Ranged against them was the Foreign Office Minister William Waldegrave, briefed and supported by FCO officials.

In essence, the argument was what to do about the Howe guidelines in view of the cessation of hostilities in the Iran–Iraq war. Clark, when he moved to the MoD, tended to support his old department when Trade Ministers objected to refusals of export licence applications for defence-related goods to Iraq. Waldegrave, who thought that relaxing restrictions on arms sales might well undermine the fragile ceasefire in the Gulf, 'found himself exposed and attacked on two flanks' by his ministerial colleagues. His view that removing the restrictions 'would give a green light to arms suppliers' was countered by MoD officials who complained, in a briefing prepared for Clark, that 'the guidelines are penalizing our exports over a wide range of equipments'. In 1989 export licences for Iran worth £70 m and for Iraq worth £20 m had been turned down – and, they added plaintively, 'our competitors are cashing in'. The figures did not include the prospect of selling Hawks to Iraq, a project BAe was still hoping to revive, even though it had been blocked by ministers as recently as July that year, or other deals debarred from being put forward by the Howe guidelines.

Clark scored his first victory as early as December 1988, when ministers agreed that there should be 'a more relaxed interpretation for both countries (but with no publicity)' – backbench MPs were, after all, continuing to ask awkward questions about Saddam's use of chemical weapons, his human rights record and his attempts to build nuclear weapons. This did not satisfy Clark, and the Cabinet agreed in February 1990 to re-examine policy on exports to both Iran and Iraq, a decision that led to the preparation of a lengthy document known as the 'Iraq Note'. This was a briefing drawn up for a meeting on 19 July 1990, chaired by Douglas Hurd, who was by now Foreign Secretary, summarizing the arguments for keeping the guidelines, relaxing them or abandoning them altogether. The case for the latter was simple: trade, trade, trade. But what is so instructive about the Iraq Note is the way in which it confirms that ministers had no illusions about the kind of regime they were dealing with. It reported that Iraq 'continues to experience severe payment difficulties'; it revealed that the Export Credits Guarantee Department was currently exposed to the tune of £1 bn on contracts with Iraq, while Saddam had failed to make payments of £120 m due on short- and medium-term credits. It also recognized Saddam's military ambitions, covert as well as openly expressed:

Iraq's position as a major military power in the Middle East has been confirmed and reinforced by the Gulf War, and she is plainly determined to extend the range of her military capabilities. Her nuclear weapons programme could lead to an operational capacity in the second half of the 1990s. She already has an advanced chemical warfare (CW) capability, as demonstrated during the Gulf War, and is fast progressing towards a biological warfare (BW) capability ... She aims to be self-sufficient by obtaining transfers of technology to set up factories, initially to assemble defence equipment, and later to manufacture it. The Hawk aircraft ... are one example of this; another is communications equipment. Iraq is also involved in a wide range of missile and space development projects.

The ministerial meeting to consider the Note was attended by Peter Lilley, Secretary of State for Trade and Industry, his junior minister Trefgarne, Clark for the MoD, Waldegrave for the FCO, and Richard Ryder, Economic Secretary, on behalf of the Treasury. As well as the economic arguments in favour of relaxing or abolishing the guidelines, the ministers were presented with a Foreign Office background paper that reminded them, among other things, that 'the nature of the Iraqi regime has not changed. It is repressive and belligerent. It has an aggressive policy of arms procurement, and development of its own missile and nuclear weapons capabilities.' As well as threatening the stability of the entire Middle East, Iran and Iraq, the FCO briefing pointed out, 'continue to have human rights records among the worst in the world'. It listed arbitrary arrests, suppression of political dissent, torture and summary execution as 'regular occurrences' in both countries.

In the circumstances, the ministers present at the 19 July meeting could not later claim that they had not been warned about the potential consequences of their decision. Yet their recommendation to Mrs Thatcher, swayed by the argument in the Iraq Note that Britain was currently losing out on business with Iraq valued at £170 m, was to relax the Howe guidelines. They also concluded that a delay of several weeks in implementing the policy would be prudent, because of reasons mainly to do with Iran – the old urge to appear even-handed again – when the change could be 'presented publicly in the context of the Government's concern for regional stability in the Middle East'. The ban on 'lethal equipment' was to stay, but this category would be drawn more narrowly so as not to prevent sales of 'weapons platforms including aircraft', theoretically giving the green light to an export licence application from BAe for its notorious Hawks.

The only thing that remained to do was to convey the ministers' recommendation to the very top, which Hurd did in a letter to Mrs Thatcher. Her Private Secretary, Sir Charles Powell, replied a week later, signifying that she was happy with the decision. Everything was now in place for a new era in trade relations between Britain and Iraq. After years of frustrating restrictions, British defence companies would be able to bid for contracts in a new climate that was broadly in favour of trade rather than overly concerned with what Iraq might do with its purchases. Whether they ever got round to telling Saddam the good news is unclear, for their efforts on his behalf were now overtaken by events. British ministers, like their American counterparts, were about to discover that their anxiety about Islamic fundamentalism in Iran had led them into a spectacular misjudgement about a much more immediate threat. Precisely a week after Mrs Thatcher agreed to relax the Howe guidelines, effectively signalling her government's approval of the regime in Baghdad, disaster struck. On 2 August 1990 the ungrateful Iraqi dictator justified all the warnings about him offered over the past decade by human rights activists, military experts and the British Foreign Office. Assuming that the West had given him carte blanche to do as he liked, Saddam Hussein ordered his troops across the border and invaded Kuwait.

Postscript: Margaret Thatcher was replaced as leader of the Conservative Party and Prime Minister in December 1990. She later became a life peer, as did Douglas Hurd. John Major, who succeeded Thatcher as Prime Minister, led Britain to victory against Saddam but later lost the May 1997 general election. Alan Clark gave up his House of Commons seat in 1997 but returned after a by-election; he died of a brain tumour in 1999.

In spite of being driven out of Kuwait in 1991, Saddam Hussein was still President of Iraq ten years later. He also persisted in his attempt to develop weapons of mass destruction, in the face of economic sanctions, UN weapons inspections and a little-reported Anglo-American bombing campaign that is alleged to have killed more than a hundred civilians and disrupted oil pipelines. The Iraqi people grew steadily more destitute, without access to adequate supplies of food or basic medicines. In 1996, the World Health Organization reported that infant death rates had increased by 600 per cent between 1990 and 1994. The figures are hotly disputed, but Dr Peter Pellett, Professor of Nutrition at Massachusetts University, who served on three UN food and agriculture missions to Iraq, delivered this verdict in 2000: 'All recent food and nutrition surveys have reported essentially the same story: malnourished children . . . increased mortality, and general breakdown in the whole fabric of society.'

PART TWO

The Policing of Private Life

4

Fooling the People

Parnell's amours were undignified, but not nearly so discreditable as some of mine! But he has been exposed, so must pay the penalty in this most hypocritical and virtuous land.

— EARL OF DURHAM

You know, I get a migraine headache if I don't get a strange piece of ass every day.

— PRESIDENT JOHN F. KENNEDY TO BOBBY BAKER

Not so many years ago, the worst thing that could happen to a woman was to become pregnant outside marriage. Single women who had babies were ostracized, sacked from their jobs, forced to give up their children for adoption and even incarcerated in mental hospitals. 'Having an illegitimate baby was worse than murder,' I was told by a woman who adopted the child of one such union in the early 1960s after the birth mother, abandoned by her lover, ended up in prison. Another woman, Joyce Bennett, described how she was deserted by her boyfriend when she became pregnant in the 1930s, just before the Second World War; he enlisted in the RAF, without telling her about his plans, and left her to face the consequences alone in a rural community. After the child was born, Joyce approached the local vicar about having her daughter christened. He informed her that she would have to be 'churched', an old-fashioned ritual to cleanse her sins. This is what happened:

I was taken by him to the front pew and I had to kneel down as he was reading these passages out. There were parts of it that I had to repeat, about how awful it was that I committed the sin of having a baby and I wasn't married. I can't remember the exact words but I know it felt as if I had committed a criminal sin . . . It seemed to me that it was all my fault and nothing to do with the father of the child. Even today I can feel the pain and disgrace of having to tell him I was sorry I'd got this baby. I wasn't sorry, not afterwards, because she was a ray of sunshine in my life.

This kind of heartlessness would have been a normal reaction towards unmarried mothers at the time, so much so that few people would have questioned the way Joyce Bennett was treated. Girls who 'got into trouble' dreaded telling their boyfriends and parents, and shotgun weddings were common; sex and shame were inextricably linked, at least as far as women were concerned. And while social attitudes to marriage and cohabitation have relaxed dramatically, the connection has yet to be definitively broken, especially in the US. Homophobia is, in some Southern and Midwestern states, endemic and lethal; evangelical churches, like the one Bill Clinton belongs to, batter their congregations with denunciations of adultery and fornication. This historical legacy produces many paradoxes; one of them is that pornography is a multi-million-dollar industry, from the respectable *Playboy* end of the market to the most explicit hardcore videos, yet it sometimes seems as though the only immoral acts generally agreed upon by the population at large are sexual ones. To accuse someone of being immoral rarely suggests that he or she manufactures landmines, cheats on tax returns or makes money by doing insider deals on the stock market; even Mother Theresa happily accepted donations from a convicted American fraudster. These twisted values were graphically demonstrated in Central America in the early 1980s, when an evangelical Christian, General Efrain Rios Montt, seized power in Guatemala and presided over a counter-insurgency campaign in which thousands of people were murdered; at the same time, Rios Montt appeared regularly on television, inveighing against the twin evils of alcohol and fornication. This is known, in some circles, as getting your priorities right.

Immorality, according to the *Concise Oxford Dictionary* (eighth edition, 1990), means behaviour that is 'morally wrong' – we hardly need a dictionary to tell us that – but with a telling rider, 'esp. in sexual matters'. To emphasize the point, the lexicographer has added two synonyms, 'depraved' and 'dissolute', both of which are normally used to indicate sexual misconduct. Indeed, 'dissolute' is defined, in its own separate entry, as 'lax in morals, licentious', while 'licentious' is glossed (with pleasing circularity) as 'immoral in sexual relations'. (The tenth edition, 1999, removes the reference to sex. Things have improved, but only very recently.) The same point, that immorality is first and foremost about sex, is made even more strongly in the *New Oxford Dictionary of English* (1998), where 'immoral earnings' are defined as 'earnings from prostitution'. There is something of a time lag here, in that attitudes to women in the sex industry have become less censorious in recent decades, thanks largely to the critique made by feminism; prostitution tends to be regarded more as an economic choice forced upon poor women than, as it was in the nineteenth century, evidence of gross moral turpitude. (Victorian doctors seriously debated whether there was a congenital disposition towards this way of life, some of them going so far as to suggest that women who turned to prostitution had abnormally large clitorises, an argument that would rightly get very short shrift nowadays.) On the contrary, it could be argued that making a living this way is more honest than fraudulently claiming state benefits, an activity that is probably more widespread but tends to be regarded as cheating rather than actively immoral. What is striking is that both the dictionary definition and the popular understanding have remained so narrow when there are dozens of ways of earning money – selling torture equipment to repressive regimes, paying starvation wages to children in developing countries, breeding animals for vivisection, to name just three – which are far more offensive than the transactions involved in prostitution. The phrase 'living in sin' is another anachronism: it was defined in the *Concise Oxford Dictionary* in 1990 as living together 'without being married'. This suggested that around a third of the population were sinners, even if they were vegetarians who worked for AIDS charities, wore plastic shoes and invested only in companies that did not test their products on animals.

We might go so far as to argue that any history of morality is above all else a history of sex, of the private conduct of individuals and the State's attempts, usually in tandem with the Church, to control it. When we exclaimed in horror as the Taliban executed homosexual men in Kabul by crushing them beneath a specially constructed wall in a football stadium, or criticized the Saudis for flogging women in public for committing adultery, we tended to forget that it is only comparatively recently that some sexual acts between consenting adults ceased to be criminal offences in Britain and the US. Anal *and* oral sex between people of the same sex were illegal in the United States until 1961. Most states have now decriminalized sexual activities between adults in private, but both continued to be a crime for homosexuals in six states, including Clinton's home state of Arkansas, in the 1990s. The moral absolutists who pour forth a non-stop series of pronouncements that vilify not just paedophilia but extramarital sex, homosexuality, contraception and abortion – anything, in fact, other than penetrative sex aimed at procreation between two heterosexuals married to each other – are merely repeating a refrain whose origins reach back at least 2,000 years. Perhaps the most breathtaking example in recent years was in September 2001, when an evangelical preacher went on television and blamed the terrorist attacks of 11 September on 'the pagans, and the abortionists, and the feminists, and the gays and the lesbians'. The Rev. Jerry Falwell, a Baptist minister, attacked people who were trying 'to secularize America', saying: 'You helped this happen.' He later apologized.

When plays, paintings or other cultural artefacts are accused of obscenity, it is almost always because of erotic elements in their composition. Sometimes violence is involved as well, but this is far from essential; works as diverse in style and intention as the entire opus of the Marquis de Sade, Radclyffe Hall's groundbreaking lesbian novel *The Well of Loneliness*, D. H. Lawrence's pompous erotic fable *Lady Chatterley's Lover*, Bertolucci's movie *Last Tango in Paris*, Robert Mapplethorpe's photographs and Howard Brenton's play *The Romans in Britain* have all been targeted at various times by people who objected to their depictions of sexuality. The combination of sex and religion is particularly combustible; in 1976 the editor of *Gay News* was privately prosecuted for the archaic offence of blasphemous libel after publishing James Kirkup's poem, 'The Love that Dares to Speak Its Name', in which a centurion fantasizes about having sex with Jesus Christ after he is brought down from the cross. (It was ironic that, in secular modern Britain, sex and Jesus were apparently more taboo than they were in the second century, AD, when the gnostic Gospel of Philip had him kissing Mary Magdalene on the mouth.) Such objections are not raised only by Christians. When Muslims in Britain and abroad took violent exception to Salman Rushdie's novel *The Satanic Verses*, their accusation of blasphemy was grounded in a scene set in a brothel called the Curtain, where twelve prostitutes impersonated the wives of the Prophet, a piece of characterization that offended them not as a slur on the women's reputation but as an insult to his.

In each case, it was sex that caused offence, regardless of whether it was Hall's famous evasion as her cross-dressing protagonist finally slept with her inamorata – on this occasion, she wrote coyly, they 'were not divided' – or Brenton's graphic on-stage portrayal of homosexual rape. The moral majority – for people like Mary Whitehouse, self-appointed guardians of the nation's morals, always claim to be speaking on behalf of a much larger, though strangely mute, constituency – objects to consensual homosexuality and sex outside marriage as much as it does to sado-masochism, fetishism and sexual violence; it objects as vehemently to scenes in movies in which naked actors cheerfully caress each other as to depictions of rape and sexual murder. In Mapplethorpe's case, his photographs of naked black men were judged as offensive as his studies with S & M overtones, leading to threats to withdraw funding from galleries in the United States that exhibited his pictures; in Britain a university library that stocked an illustrated book on his work was raided by the police and threatened with prosecution until wiser counsels prevailed, possibly influenced by the fact that the photographer had been honoured with a posthumous exhibition at the highly respectable Hayward Gallery on London's South Bank. What is striking about the censorship aspirations of these self-appointed moralists, whether they seek to ban Dennis Potter's television plays or explicit pop lyrics like Frankie Goes to Hollywood's 'Relax' – refused airtime by BBC Radio 1 in the early 1980s because it was about premature ejaculation, a decision that simply accelerated its progress to number one in the singles chart – is that their remit is so narrow; *petit bourgeois* to the core, perpetually affronted by sex, they have little to say about vastly more important moral questions such as racism, arms sales or the unequal distribution of wealth. (It could be argued that their real target is pleasure, which is why they demonize relatively harmless recreational drugs like cannabis as stridently as representations of the erotic.)

In the United States, it is often the people who crusade noisily against so-called sexual immorality who are also in favour of the right to carry guns, upholding patriarchal family values and the right to defend them by lethal force. There is an extraordinary degree of moral confusion here, vividly expressed in the pronouncements of the National Rifle Association, the powerful lobbying organization led by the actor Charlton Heston, and in a bumper sticker popular among gun-owners: 'God, guns and guts made America great – let's keep all three'. The absence of irony in this linkage of the ownership of weapons with Christianity is striking, even though it is evident that absence of effective gun control regularly leads to the transgression of one of the religion's core commandments, 'Thou shalt not kill.' The result is that the pre-eminent state in the modern world is currently plagued by massacres on an almost medieval scale; there is even a slang term – 'going postal', from the number of postal workers who have done it – that describes the actions of a disgruntled employee who guns down colleagues and bystanders before turning the weapon on himself (my choice of pronoun is, of course, deliberate).

Each year 32,000 Americans die from wounds inflicted by guns, in incidents that include murder, accidents and suicides; these shootings involve, on average, 12 children and teenagers per day. Besides deranged individuals, guns are easily available to right-wing militias whose neo-Nazi convictions are a direct threat to the State; the terrorist bombing of a federal building in Oklahoma City, which was originally blamed on Muslim fundamentalists, turned out to be the work of Timothy McVeigh, a home-grown extremist. While the political Right targets the government, the religious Right bombs abortion clinics and has assassinated doctors who are willing to carry out this legal operation.

The barbarism of these citizens is in turn reflected in the legalized violence of the State, which stands among the top four in the world when it comes to the use (more correctly, abuse) of the death penalty. In contemporary America, where politicians do not get very far unless they make a public and preferably lachrymose commitment to God and family values, 656 people have been executed (at the time of writing, though the figure is rising inexorably) since the death penalty was reinstated by the Supreme Court in 1976. For many European critics, who have demonstrated outside the country's embassy in Paris and protested to the US Ambassador in Berlin, America's use of capital punishment strikes down its claim to be a civilized society; the most god-fearing country in the world, in this respect, is also one of the most barbaric. It is on the statute books of 38 of the 50 States. They apply it with varying degrees of enthusiasm and place the US in a select group of countries – along with the repressive states of China, Iran and Saudi Arabia – when it comes to the judicial murder of its own citizens; these countries together accounted for 85 per cent of all the executions recorded worldwide by Amnesty International in 1999. In that year the US almost equalled Saudi Arabia (103) in bare numbers, sending a total of 98 people to die in the electric chair, gas chamber or by lethal injection, while more than 3,500 others – mostly impoverished black men, some of them convicted on dubious evidence whose unreliability is now being exposed by DNA testing – languished on death row. (By contrast, and demonstrating the higher value placed on white lives, 80 per cent of the crimes for which they were convicted involved white victims.) Among the most recent victims is a depressed working-class mother found guilty of killing her children, a woman who would, in a civilized penal system, have been referred for mental health reports and psychiatric treatment. It is almost certainly the case that a high proportion of the convicts on death row are innocent, victims of America's racist justice system – one African-American, currently on death row, has appealed against his sentence on the grounds that his lawyer was asleep for long periods during his trial – while its record on killing child offenders is the worst in the world. There have been 13 executions of defendants under the age of eighteen – the age of adulthood recognized by most international treaties – since 1990. Few Americans, no matter how god-fearing, object to the use of the death penalty or to the savage conditions in penitentiaries, where the use of leg-irons and intrusive body searches is commonplace, as is homosexual rape and the fear of HIV transmission. A study of seven men's prisons published in December 2000 suggested that 21 per cent of the inmates had been pressured into having sex, while 7 per cent had been raped. Human Rights Watch believes as many as 140,000 men may have been raped in American prisons. The small groups of protesters who gather outside prisons during the run-up to executions, and the dedicated lawyers who work *pro bono* on behalf of men on death row, are heavily outnumbered in a populace that regards judicial murder with enthusiasm.

Canny politicians reflect the popular mood, taking every opportunity to demonstrate their support for the ultimate sanction. During his unsuccessful bid for the presidency in 2000, Vice-President Al Gore admitted only that a large number of mistakes in application of the death penalty would make him 'uncomfortable', implying, bizarrely, that he could accommodate one or two. At around the same time, Gerald Kogan, former Chief Justice of the Florida Supreme Court, acknowledged that he had 'serious doubts' about the guilt of 28 people put to death in the state while he sat on the court. Yet in May that year, Jeanne Shaheen, Governor of New Hampshire and a left-wing Democrat, vetoed a vote in the state legislature to abolish the death penalty, the first time a state has given up this power since the Supreme Court reinstated it. Shaheen, a keen Clinton supporter, was being spoken of at the time as a possible running-mate for Al Gore and was not prepared to endanger her political prospects over the small matter of human rights; Gore's Republican opponent, Texas Governor George W. Bush, came from a state that was responsible for no fewer than 227 executions, a third of those that have taken place in the US since 1976. (The process accelerated considerably after Bush became Governor in 1995; by the summer of 2000 he had presided over no fewer than 140.) Democrats have not forgotten the example of Michael Dukakis, the Massachusetts Governor and would-be Democratic presidential candidate who suffered a disastrous drop in poll ratings because of his support for a state programme of weekend leave for prisoners serving life sentences – making him 'soft on crime' – and his opposition to the death penalty. Taking this lesson to heart during his own campaign for the presidency in 1992, Bill Clinton refused to intervene, in his capacity as Governor of Arkansas, to prevent the execution of a brain-damaged black man, Ricky Ray Rector, whom his home state was about to execute. As a journalist later revealed, Rector's incapacity to understand what was happening to him was exposed by his request, during his last meal, to be allowed to put part of his pudding aside to eat later. When Clinton failed to pick up a specially installed hot line in the gubernatorial mansion and grant clemency, the uncomprehending Rector was dispatched by lethal injection. His aide, Stephanopoulos, later wrote that he would have been proud if Clinton had intervened, 'but the devil on my shoulder whispered that we were handing the Republicans a huge issue'. As President, a year later, Clinton revealed his continuing enthusiasm for crudely retributive forms of justice when he reacted furiously to the murder of American soldiers in faraway Somalia. 'We're not inflicting pain on these fuckers,' he complained to his advisers. 'When people kill us, they should be killed in greater numbers.' (The deaths of the Americans, part of a UN peacekeeping force, had disastrous consequences not just for Somalia but for all future operations, including Kosovo, in which US forces became involved during Clinton's presidency, a subject I shall return to in Chapter 9.) In 1998, three days after he was forced to appear before a grand jury inquiring into his affair with Monica Lewinsky – and volunteered to explain himself to the nation on TV the same evening – Clinton launched missile strikes on Afghanistan and the Sudan, two countries accused of sheltering the Muslim terrorist Osama bin Laden. As later events were to demonstrate, these assaults completely failed to curb the activities of international terrorists.

A moral position? Only in terms of the primitive morality of the Old Testament, with its insistence on punishments of exact equivalence: 'Life for life, eye for eye, tooth for tooth, hand for hand, foot for foot,' as Exodus puts it. (In August 2000, by the way, the Islamic regime in Saudi Arabia made history by applying this principle literally: an Egyptian, Abdel Moati Abdel Rahman Mohammed, aged thirty-seven, had an eye surgically removed after being convicted of throwing acid in another man's face.) It is a telling commentary on late-twentieth-century notions of morality that a politician from the liberal wing of a centre-left party should expend so much energy on concealing his sex life while ordering lethal missile strikes on innocent foreigners and flaunting his commitment to a form of punishment that has been outlawed right across Europe. (Even Turkey, which continues to use torture, is a *de facto* abolitionist state.) Nor is there any doubt about the racist nature of American justice, a terrible blot on the record of a nation whose commitment to human rights dates back to its moment of creation, the Declaration of Independence in 1776. In a country with the highest incarceration rate in the world, 1 in every 20 black men over the age of eighteen is in prison. In 5 states, the figure is between 1 in 13 and 1 in 14. The overall rate of imprisonment for black men accused of drugs offences is 13 times higher than for whites, even though 5 times as many whites use drugs. In 10 states – Illinois, Wisconsin, Minnesota, Maine, Iowa, Maryland, Ohio, New Jersey, North Carolina and

West Virginia – black men are sent to prison at rates 27 to 57 times higher than whites.

This extraordinary moral blindness at the heart of American politics is no accident, nor is it an affliction that affects only the United States. Tony Blair's first Home Secretary, Jack Straw, repeatedly played to a reactionary audience in Britain, making decisions that were profoundly shocking in their refusal to acknowledge difficult moral issues. In February 2000, when it emerged that some of the passengers on a hijacked Afghan airliner at Stansted Airport were going to ask for political asylum from the barbaric Taliban regime, Straw announced in Parliament that they would be removed from the country before they had had the opportunity to submit formal applications. How misguided he was to do so emerged months later, when some of the passengers were granted asylum on the grounds that they had a well-grounded fear of persecution if they returned to Afghanistan. But Straw's premature announcement had a dire effect, lending a kind of legitimacy to right-wing populists who cared nothing about well-documented human rights violations. For several days, tabloid newspapers competed to produce the most racist comments and one of them, the *People*, even printed a form for readers to send to the Home Secretary, demanding that he 'kick the Afghan asylum-seekers out'; no fewer than 13,000 readers, equally oblivious to conditions in Kabul and Britain's obligations under international law, complied. It was only much later, after 11 September, that the plight of Afghan refugees suddenly became a major international issue. On another moral issue, the use of recreational drugs, the Blair government followed the American lead by insisting on absolute prohibition and appointing a drugs czar, a gimmicky response to the fact that millions of people would like to see the drug laws liberalized. The failure of this approach was tacitly admitted by Straw's successor as Home Secretary, David Blunkett, when he relaxed the law on cannabis in October 2001. What prohibition has achieved is the lumping together of substances whose effects are very different and the encouragement of a flourishing criminal industry that itself wrecks lives. In one instance, Colombia, it has encouraged a bloody and protracted civil war between the government, left-wing guerrillas and powerful drugs cartels.

Events like these are not merely an inevitable consequence of confining discussions about morality to the sphere of private life and sexual relations. It has been, for centuries, a positive benefit for ruling elites, placing an unspoken restriction on discourse that permitted the rampant *im*morality of so many of their decisions and actions – from the Crusades to colonialism, from corruption to State trafficking in opium – to go unchallenged. Not that the rules on sexual conduct were ever intended to apply to people of their sort; their prerogative was to frame and enforce them, not to observe them. It was the great mass of ordinary people who offended these codes at their peril, and were punished accordingly with shame, ostracism and imprisonment, as I shall describe in detail in the next two chapters. In Renaissance Italy, successive Popes were notorious for their enthusiastic enjoyment of favourites of both sexes; in Restoration England, Charles II handed out titles to the illegitimate children borne by his mistresses, whom his disapproving but powerless subjects sometimes booed in the streets. The situation for the upper classes – their male members, at any rate – was not that they should eschew adultery, homosexuality or pederasty, but that they should not cause a public scandal. When they did, a rapid assessment was made of the degree of damage that had been inflicted, followed either by a cover-up or – in a minority of cases – a decision to throw the unlucky miscreant to the wolves. This created a useful smokescreen, persuading the middle and lower classes that the rules were not just for them, and acted as a warning to other elite men to keep their extramarital sexual adventures under wraps.

A textbook example is Charles Stewart Parnell, the Irish Home Rule campaigner whose career was wrecked by his involvement in a divorce in 1890. For almost a decade Parnell had been living more or less openly with a woman called Katharine O'Shea, who was separated from her husband, and they had had two children together. The affair became a scandal only when Katharine's husband, Captain William O'Shea, gave up his attempt to extort money from the couple in return for silence and initiated divorce proceedings. Parnell married Katharine as soon as she was free, but died a year later, aged only forty-five. At a time when marriage was regarded as a sacrament, and divorce an affront to God, Parnell's readiness to carry on a lengthy affair with a married woman was undoubtedly a risky venture. Yet his relationship with Katharine was well known among his colleagues, and his 'sublime indifference' to what other people thought, in the words of a modern historian, was reflected in his preference for spending time at home with her in Eltham rather than at the House of Commons. And if Parnell displayed extraordinary recklessness in ignoring the social conventions of his time, it has to be said that it was matched by the generosity of his contemporaries in not using his private life against him; they permitted his ruin only at the very end, when it was clear that publicity could no longer be avoided and Parnell's career could not be salvaged.

As the third Earl of Durham suggested in his private correspondence at the time, Parnell's behaviour was not unusual. Well-connected men with unconventional sexual tastes got into trouble only if they were unusually careless or flaunted their behaviour – Lord Byron, for example, who fled the country in 1816 when his marriage broke down, after hinting heavily about his indulgence in taboo sexual practices, such as homosexuality and incest. Byron was one of the first celebrities in the modern sense, creating his own myth and allowing himself to be destroyed by it. Men from the lower classes of society were more vulnerable, as the suicide in 1903 of the distinguished soldier Sir Hector Macdonald, hero of Omdurman, vividly demonstrates. Macdonald was a Scottish crofter's son who rose through army ranks to become Commander-in-Chief, Ceylon, in 1902. When he was accused of involvement in a paedophile ring early in 1903 – among others things, he was caught in a railway carriage at Kandy with four Sinhalese boys, probably during a session of mutual masturbation – he was advised to return to England to avert a scandal. In March, a few days after an interview with Edward VII, Macdonald set off on the return journey to Ceylon. While he was in Paris, the *New York Herald* revealed that far from covering up his activities, the

Governor had laid charges against him and he would be court-martialled on arrival; Macdonald shot himself in the Hotel Regina, apparently following advice offered a few days earlier by the King. It is hard to resist the conclusion that Macdonald's working-class origins worked against him, or that he was not sufficiently versed in upper-class codes of behaviour to protect himself. As Colin Spencer points out in his history of homosexuality, 'the rich, if caught, could generally avoid the situation by bribery or influential connections; besides, they had their own clubs and a network of discreet pimps to furnish them with lads from the working class'.

Throughout history, a white male ruling elite – what twentieth-century feminists would later characterize as patriarchy – assumed that access to women and girls (or boys, depending on taste) was a perk of the job. They also assumed, correctly for the most part, that their wives, servants, social peers and professional colleagues would join them in a conspiracy of silence. So effective were the barriers they erected around their privacy that 200-year-old scandals are still being unearthed and causing shockwaves: in 1998 DNA testing finally established the truth of the long-standing claim that Thomas Jefferson, co-author of the American Declaration of Independence, had fathered at least one child with his mixed-race slave, Sally Hemings. Jefferson's famous preamble, quoted to this day by human rights activists, would appear to make his position on slavery – *against* slavery – absolutely clear: 'We hold these truths to be self-evident, that all men are created equal; that they are endowed by their Creator with certain inalienable rights; that amongst these are life, liberty and the pursuit of happiness.' Yet he not only owned slaves but kept Hemings as his concubine. The allegation, first made in Jefferson's lifetime, was dismissed as malicious gossip and largely ignored by historians. But tests on Jefferson's and Hemings's descendants proved paternity in one case, and suggested it was likely in another four – an example of modern science finally catching up with early-nineteenth-century hypocrisy. In Britain, as in the fledgling United States, double standards started at the very top: the male line of the British royal family, required as a matter of duty to marry foreign princesses they barely knew, routinely picked up and discarded mistresses. Among the best known are Mrs Fitzherbert, who underwent a morganatic marriage with the future George IV, and Mrs Jordan, a successful actress who financially supported the future King, William IV, when he was still a spendthrift duke. This tradition was enthusiastically carried on by Edward VII, whose many liaisons included affairs with Lillie Langtry and Alice Keppel, while Edward VIII was unusual not in having a mistress, an American divorcee named Wallis Simpson, but in renouncing the throne in order to marry her. When Prince Charles wed a certified virgin, Lady Diana Spencer, in 1981, he soon revived his affair with a married woman, Camilla Parker Bowles – Alice Keppel's great-granddaughter – apparently unmoved by the possibility that his besotted young wife might find his behaviour surprising, let alone objectionable.

The nineteenth-century statesman Lord Palmerston employed the code 'fine day' in his diary whenever he successfully propositioned a woman, sometimes using the phrase as often as five times a week; one of his extramarital liaisons lasted twenty-eight years. Another eminent Victorian, W. E. Gladstone, described by a historian as 'almost unique among nineteenth-century prime ministers' because of his fidelity to his wife, was famous for his nightly excursions to rescue prostitutes, an activity that was notably unsuccessful and caused so much guilt that he used to flagellate himself. Lord Rosebery's sexual orientation has been questioned because he 'behaved oddly during the [Oscar] Wilde trials' and acquired a villa in Naples, 'which looks suspiciously like a typical ploy of late-Victorian upper-class married men who were attracted to other males'. Wilde himself took extraordinary risks, suing his lover's father for libel when he accused him of 'Posing as a Somdomite!' – neither spelling nor broad-mindedness was the Marquess of Queensberry's forte – even though he habitually enjoyed sex with rent boys, some of whom appeared as prosecution witnesses at his own subsequent trials. Two British leaders during the First World War, H. H. Asquith and David Lloyd George, had extramarital affairs, with Venetia Stanley and

Frances Stevenson respectively; Lloyd George was distracted from his duties, at a crucial moment in the hostilities, by the news that Stevenson, his secretary and mistress, was pregnant. Eleanor Roosevelt, the most famous and admired First Lady before Jacqueline Kennedy, discovered early in her marriage to Franklin Delano Roosevelt that her husband was having an affair with her social secretary, Lucy Mercer. The couple came close to divorce in 1918, but FDR's mother and political advisers talked them out of it, realizing the impact it would have on his career. Eleanor agreed to act as FDR's wife in public, but the relationship with Mercer continued throughout his presidencies and she was with him at the time of his final collapse in 1945. Dwight D. Eisenhower, who succeeded FDR, very nearly divorced his wife Mamie when he fell in love with his Irish driver in London, Kay Summersby, during the Second World War. She was about to join him in Washington in 1945 when he changed his mind, fearful of the impact of divorce on his political career, and refused to see her again. Summersby, like many other mistresses of powerful men, was abandoned and heartbroken, while her ex-lover thrived. Perhaps the most affecting victim of all these liasions was Mrs Jordan, who died in poverty in France in 1816, five years after her royal lover (by whom she had ten children) tired of her. It is a striking fact that, in the majority of these relationships, the women came off much worse than their lovers.

The Eisenhowers were replaced in the White House in 1961 by the politician who broke all previous records when it came to extramarital affairs, John F. Kennedy. While the couple appeared strikingly modern, and outsiders were fascinated by the First Lady's appearance, Kennedy was as much a sexual predator as his political heir, Bill Clinton. Kennedy boasted about his sexual appetite, shocking his bodyguards with the orgies that took place in the White House when his wife was absent. His affair with Marilyn Monroe, whom he seems to have passed on to his younger brother Bobby, the Attorney-General, when he tired of her, was only one of many he conducted with young wannabes from Hollywood. What is astonishing – or a reflection of the brothers' accurate judgement that an exposé of their behaviour was unlikely to be written by the complacent Washington press corps, nor believed if it was – is that they did not moderate their sexual appetites after the Profumo affair. Perhaps *the* pre-eminent sex scandal of twentieth-century British political history, mythologized since in films and books, it destroyed the career of John Profumo, Secretary of State for War in Harold Macmillan's government. Profumo had become involved with a young woman, Christine Keeler, who worked as an upmarket prostitute and included a Soviet diplomat among her clients. Profumo's relationship with Keeler was unwise, to say the least, given that Captain Eugene Ivanov was Assistant Naval Attaché at the Russian Embassy in London and rumoured to be a spy; the minister was alarmed enough to lie about the relationship in the House of Commons, a piece of folly that quickly led to his resignation and retirement from public life.

In Washington, Kennedy followed the scandal closely, aware that two of the peripheral players, Maria Novotny and Suzy Chang, posed a threat to his own administration. The FBI gnomically instructed its agent in London to 'keep bureau fully and promptly informed of all developments with particular emphasis on any allegation that US nationals are or have been involved'; the bureau almost certainly knew that Kennedy had taken Chang to dinner at a restaurant in New York when he was a Senator, while Novotny was later to claim that both she and Chang had slept with him. But Kennedy's name did not come up, and once again it was the minor players in the drama who suffered most: Keeler was sentenced to nine months in prison for perjury, while an osteopath called Stephen Ward, who leased the cottage in which Keeler worked, committed suicide. Profumo's reputation revived in the 1980s when it was revealed that he had spent his years of disgrace quietly working for charity.

I have already mentioned the minor scandals that brought about the resignation of David Mellor, a minister in John Major's government, and Bob Livingston, who stepped down as Speaker Elect of the House of Representatives in December 1998. Livingston was a collateral casualty of the Starr investigation, finding himself in the spotlight at a moment when the sexual conduct of politicians was under particularly close scrutiny. Gary Hart, a contender for the Democratic presidential nomination in 1988, scuppered his chances by challenging a journalist to produce evidence of his liaison with a young woman named Donna Rice – which the reporter did, on a yacht appropriately named *Monkey Business*. Ron Davies, Secretary of State for Wales in Tony Blair's first Cabinet, resigned instantly as a minister when he realized that a bizarre series of events that led to him being robbed and kidnapped on Clapham Common in south London, a well-known cruising area for homosexual men, was about to become public knowledge.

The common factor in most of these recent scandals is a sea-change in the media, especially the tabloid press, which created a very different situation from the one Kennedy had to deal with. Driven by prurience and an assumption that the private conduct of public figures is always the subject of legitimate inquiry, the pursuit of politicians with irregular personal lives became almost a national sport in the final decade of the twentieth century, with one public figure after another held up to ridicule for their extramarital liaisons. Robin Cook, Blair's Foreign Secretary after the 1997 general election, lost much of his political clout when he succumbed to government pressure and left his wife to marry his mistress; Cook made his decision at an airport, as he was about to go on a family holiday, when the Prime Minister's Press Secretary informed him that his affair with his secretary was about to be revealed in a tabloid newspaper. Yet Cook did not have to give up his job, and there were signs that, in a changing moral climate, sex was moving down the list of activities that was capable of inflicting serious damage on political careers, turning instead into a cause of intense but temporary embarrassment for men in public life. Blair's first Cabinet reflected the increasing openness about sexual diversity in Britain, containing one minister who had publicly declared he was gay, the Culture Secretary Chris Smith, and two others whose orientation was widely known though not strictly in the public domain. Several

MPs in the new Parliament declared their homosexuality, rightly assuming that the public was relaxed about what they did in private, as long as it did not involve lying or double standards; Ron Davies's belated admission, several months after his resignation as Welsh Secretary, that he had suffered psycho-sexual problems was greeted with widespread sympathy.

Indeed, there was some evidence that the continuing assumption that sex posed the biggest threat to a political career was blind-siding politicians to other forms of inadvisable behaviour. Peter Mandelson, who had always asserted quite reasonably that his sexual orientation was his own business, was forced to resign from the Cabinet in December 1998 when a newspaper revealed he had borrowed £373,000 before the general election to buy a house in Notting Hill. The loan came from another soon-to-be minister, Geoffrey Robinson, whose business dealings eventually came under investigation by Mandelson's own officials at the Department of Trade and Industry. Neither man declared the obvious conflict of interest until it was exposed by the *Guardian*, whereupon both resigned their portfolios. It certainly looked, at the time, as though Mandelson's defensiveness about his homosexuality had blunted his awareness of the career implications of other types of transaction. His offence was judged trivial enough – or his relationship with the Prime Minister sufficiently close – to permit his return to the Cabinet less than a year later, in the sensitive role of Northern Ireland Secretary. (The circumstances leading to Mandelson's second resig-nation, in January 2001, were less clear, and he vigorously protested his innocence of the charge of an absence of candour on his part in the Hinduja passport affair.) But the very fact that he and Robinson had to resign at all was a sign that morality, at the end of the twentieth century, was changing its meaning. Politicians, like the rest of us, were discovering that there were more pressing things to worry about than sex, even if it happened to be outside marriage and with a partner of the same gender. This was nothing short of a revolution, and one that had been centuries in the making, as we shall see in the next two chapters.

5

The Body Enclosed

The chastity of women is of all importance, as all property depends on it. — DR JOHNSON

A woman who has lost her honour, imagines that she cannot fall lower, and as for recovering her former station, it is impossible; no exertion can wash this stain away. — MARY WOLLSTONECRAFT

The eighteenth century was, par excellence, the age of privatization. Not in the modern sense of selling off publicly owned utilities but in a much more fundamental way: what passed into private ownership was land and bodies. On the first count, countryside that for centuries had been open to all, whether for village festivals or the use of smallholders who needed extra pasture for their livestock, was fenced off and became the inviolable property of wealthy individuals. As a direct result, the landscape changed dramatically, and so did the lives of millions of people who lived upon it. The appropriation was carried out legally, through a series of Acts of Parliament, and it meant that farm labourers who used to supplement their meagre income by turning out their hens, pigs and geese to graze at no cost on common land were no longer able to do so. The rich benefited enormously, which is why they resorted to legislation so often: there were 64 Enclosure Acts between 1740 and 1749, 472 between 1770 and 1779, and 574 – the peak – during the first decade of the nineteenth century. But the effect on the rural working class was catastrophic. Families who had depended on access to common ground became landless trespassers. 'The poor man was rooted out, and the various mechanics of the villages deprived of all benefit of [the land],' wrote Thomas Bewick, an engraver and writer from Newcastle who was himself the son of a small farmer. 'An amazing number of people have been reduced from a comfortable state of partial independence to the precarious position of mere hirelings, who when out of work immediately come on the parish,' observed the Revd David Davies, Rector of Cookham, Berkshire, in 1795. New boundaries – ditches, hedges and walls – not only created a more ordered vision of the countryside but acted as a visual reminder of the power of landlords to exclude outsiders from territory over which they now exercised sole rights.

Whatever their other effects, and historians are still debating their impact on agriculture, the Enclosure Acts are regarded as a significant step in the creation of a modern society. What is less frequently remarked upon is the way in which a comparable process of enclosure was acted out in the eighteenth century on bodies, primarily on women's bodies. The effect was to divide women into two classes: wives, who were indubitably the property of their husbands, and unmarried or abandoned women who, not belonging to one master, ran the risk of being regarded as the collective property of all. The link between the ownership of land and the ownership of women was not accidental; just as the wealthy wanted control of vast estates, they also wanted certainty about the sons and heirs who would inherit the property they had gone to so much trouble to secure. At a time when blood tests to establish paternity had not yet been dreamt of, and no one knew about DNA, this was hardly the easiest goal to achieve. But what the ruling elite could do, and did with extraordinary thoroughness, was take more effective control of women's bodies. They did it by outlawing all forms of marriage except one that was formal and indissoluble, except by Act of Parliament – and naturally they made sure that even this perilous and expensive escape route was not open to women. The parallels with the appropriation of land are compelling, in that several existing laws came to be used, or new ones were passed, that denied access to wives to all but their husbands and extracted financial penalties from outsiders – literally trespassers, under the bizarre law of 'criminal conversation' – who managed to breach the marital stronghold. Mary Wollstonecraft, author of *A Vindication of the Rights of Woman*, was quicker than most to perceive that her century was obsessed with private property, and the baleful effect of that obsession on women. 'From the respect paid to property flow, as from a poisoned fountain,' she wrote in the *Vindication* in 1792, 'most of the evils and vices which render this world such a dreary scene to the contemplative mind.' (She was also painfully aware of the liminal status of women who, like herself, gave birth to a child outside the protection of wedlock.) That this happened at all, reducing wives to the status of slaves and making other women acutely vulnerable to seduction and abandonment, is bad enough. But the white male elite that required absolute power over both women and property in England also managed to disguise its intentions, arriving at a deal with the Anglican Church that gave rights over private life to clerics in return for guarantees about legitimacy and inheritance. This was perhaps an instance of expediency coinciding with inclination, in that capitalism has rarely been prepared to look its malign effects squarely in the face. But it also restored the status of the Church as moral arbiter, a role that had been steadily eroded over the sixteenth and seventeenth centuries as ecclesiastical courts went into decline (resulting, *inter alia*, in the effective decriminalization of adultery). Now, thanks to new legislation in the middle of the eighteenth century, the Church resumed its traditional role: whatever moral code the emerging modern state was about to espouse would be shaped exclusively, and oppressively, by the Christian religion.

The first triumph of this powerful coalition was to elevate a method of securing and passing on property into a moral principle, while the historical baggage brought by the Church – including, of course, its cult of female virginity – combined with the secular notion of women as chattels to produce discriminatory punishments for offenders. The most clear-sighted observer of this process was Wollstonecraft, who argued that the very existence of morality was undermined by making it synonymous with a woman's sexual reputation. 'It has long since occurred to me,' she wrote, 'that advice respecting behaviour, and all the various modes of preserving a good reputation, which have been so strenuously inculcated on the female world, were specious poisons, that encrusting morality eat away the substance.' This vivid image reveals Wollstonecraft's understanding that linking morality and sex was not just a burden on women but destructive of the wider moral order – a lesson that would not even begin to be taken to heart until the second half of the twentieth century.

The piece of legislation that enclosed the female body as tightly as any tract of land was Lord Hardwicke's Marriage Act of 1753. It was already the case, as Sir William Blackstone expressed it in his *Commentaries on the Laws of England*, that 'by marriage, the husband and the wife are one person in law; that is, the very being or legal existence of the woman is suspended during marriage, or at least is incorporated and consolidated into that of the husband; under whose wing, protection, and cover, she performs everything.' Before the Hardwicke Act, however, couples benefited from the long-standing confusion that existed around the various forms of marriage. One of them – contract marriage, frequently consisting of no more than a verbal agreement between a man and a woman – was notoriously difficult to prove, sometimes prompting costly disputes over property but also providing an escape route for discontented spouses. Then there were clandestine marriages, entered into without parental approval and frequently involving an elopement. Such arrangements were legally binding if conducted by a clergyman, offering young lovers a means of marrying in the face of opposition; they were sometimes the only bearable alternative for an heiress whose father or guardian was pressing her to accept a suitor of his choice. This is exactly what happened to Lady Mary Wortley Montagu, who wrote bitterly that 'people in my way are sold like slaves, and I cannot tell what price my masters will put on me'. She meant daughters of the aristocracy, and she avoided an arranged marriage with an unappealing candidate, selected by her father, by eloping with someone else. Many of these ceremonies were conducted perfectly legally by clergymen who had been incarcerated for debt, who were able and willing to marry couples, for a fee, with no questions asked, at any hour of the day or night. And while historians disagree about the numbers, some couples simply lived together and were accepted by their families and friends as husband and wife. Their children were baptized and treated no differently from legitimate offspring, but the spouses could and sometimes did go their separate ways at some point. While it would be wrong to claim much in the way of rights for women in the period before the passing of the Hardwicke Act, there *was* sufficient uncertainty about who was legally married to create a fluid situation, in which women in irregular unions were not automatically looked down upon.

The Hardwicke Act, and the moral discourse that underpinned it, changed all that. In future, the only marriages that had legal force were those carried out by a clergyman in a church or chapel in daylight hours. Banns had to be read in advance, alerting anyone with an interest in preventing the wedding, and no one under the age of twenty-one could marry without parental consent. How seriously the bill's drafters took the need for State control of marriage is demonstrated by a clause that was eventually dropped, stipulating the death penalty for anyone who officiated at an unlicensed wedding; wiser counsels prevailed and the penalty was reduced to transportation for a mere fourteen years. The only way out of a bad marriage, other than a separation that prevented either spouse marrying again, was for the husband to go to the enormous cost of obtaining a parliamentary divorce – a procedure that included a full trial, held in public, with testimony of the most intimate kind about the wife's sexual conduct. Her adultery, confirmed by two witnesses, was the only ground that was likely to be successful in dissolving the marriage, conditions so onerous on both men and women that they prompted a battle for easier divorce that would rage for two centuries. Even so, there were sufficient parliamentary divorces to scare MPs and peers into a belief that women were still not fully under patriarchal control. Four attempts were made, between 1771 and 1809, to introduce punitive Bills that would prevent divorced women marrying their lovers – though not, of course, divorced men marrying their mistresses. The justification put forward was simultaneously moral – 'the statute laws against immorality have lost their edge', as one pamphlet arguing in favour of the change put it – and frank in its acknowledgement of the primacy of property. In a climate in which the dire effects of the Hardwicke Act were already being felt, the Bills were rejected, but the Church was still trying to enact identical legislation as late as 1856, when a bishop sought to add a clause to the first Divorce Bill ensuring that wives who escaped their marriages would be unable to marry again.

What has not yet been sufficiently acknowledged, when modern commentators discuss the history of marriage, is the state of total subjection in which wives were placed from the middle of the eighteenth century onwards. Women who were trapped in unhappy marriages, often arranged by their parents if an inheritance was at stake, had more to contend with than their inability to get a divorce. What was required of them, according to Wollstonecraft, was 'slavish obedience' to their husbands, an inequality that led to her scandalous observation that wives were 'legally prostituted' in marriage. The effects, she concluded, were dire for both parties: 'Whilst [women] are absolutely dependent on their husbands they will be cunning, mean and selfish; and the men who can be gratified by the fawning fondness of spaniel-like affection have not much delicacy, for love is not to be bought; in any sense of the words, its silken wings are instantly shrivelled up when anything beside a return in kind is sought.'

Wollstonecraft's elevated sentiments about heterosexual love prefigure the purity campaigns of some nineteenth-century feminists; it is hardly an exaggeration to say that, faced with the degraded circumstances in which unprotected women (and especially prostitutes) were forced to live, some prominent Victorian women retreated into a state of denial about female sexuality. But the radical, dissenting circles in which Wollstonecraft moved understood all too well that wives were dependent on their husband's benevolence and vulnerable to their malice: wives who ran away from a violent marriage, and unlucky women whose husbands had tired of them, could be kidnapped, held against their will and – in the very worst cases – confined to a lunatic asylum. Until 1774, when it became illegal to incarcerate a patient in a lunatic asylum without a doctor's order, there was nothing to prevent a malicious husband shutting up his wife with genuinely disturbed patients for the rest of her natural life. The historian Lawrence Stone describes this phenomenon in stark terms:

One of the most terrible fates that could be inflicted upon a wife by a husband was to be confined, sometimes actually in chains, in a private madhouse far from her friends and unknown to them, where she might linger for months or even years. The mere threat of such confinement, which was frequently used by angry husbands in the eighteenth century, was enough to strike terror. In eighteenth-century England, this fear hung over every wife, just as it did until recently over every political dissident in Russia.

Even when the law on asylums was reformed, there was nothing to prevent a husband kidnapping his wife and locking her up at home for the rest of her natural life – a fate that, we might speculate, as Jean Rhys did in her novel *Wide Sargasso Sea*, was imposed on Mr Rochester's 'mad' first wife in *Jane Eyre*. (As late as 1840 a judge ruled that a husband was entitled to lock up his wife to prevent her running away with her lover.) At a time when male control of female sexuality was absolute, a similar threat hung over single women who lost their reputations, as Wollstonecraft recorded:

I cannot avoid feeling the most lively compassion for those unfortunate females who are broken off from society, and by one error torn from all those affections and relationships that improve the heart and mind. It does not frequently even deserve the name of error; for many girls become the dupes of a sincere, affectionate heart, and still more are, as it may emphatically be termed, *ruined* before they know the difference between virtue and vice, and thus prepared by their education for infamy, they become infamous. Asylums and Magdalens are not the proper remedies for these abuses. It is justice, not charity, that is wanting in the world!

Given the punitive moral climate of the times, it is hardly surprising that the institutions for the reformation of prostitutes, to which Wollstonecraft refers in this passage, were called Magdalens. But even if wives escaped the threat of imprisonment, they were still subject to legal forms of domestic violence. A legal decision in 1782 established that a husband was entitled to beat his wife with a stick no thicker than his thumb, while an even earlier judgment by Sir Matthew Hale established that rape in marriage was not a crime. In that sense, the growing importance placed on romantic love can be seen as cosmetic, a means of disguising the harsh reality of women's lives in which 'the cult of the family merely created doll's houses for women to live in within a man's world, underlining men's grip on the rest of society', according to the historian Roy Porter. How little they were trusted or valued is revealed by the law relating to children, which gave very few rights to mothers. In the second half of the eighteenth century, a wife who committed adultery was likely to find herself an outcast whose punishment might include never seeing her children again; even nursing infants could be snatched from her breast.

According to the morality that prevailed at the time, this was as it should be. Respectable men seduced servants and enjoyed the services of prostitutes, habits that might stimulate gossip but did not incur the terrible penalties that their wives and daughters rightly feared when the least stain adhered to their reputations. Clarissa Harlowe, eponymous heroine of Samuel Richardson's novel, declared she had lost her honour when she was abducted, imprisoned and raped – a reaction mocked by Wollstonecraft, who pointed out the excessive scruples of any creature 'who could be degraded without its own consent!' Yet Clarissa's estimation of the consequences of her rape was accurate – and would remain so until the late twentieth century, when the suspicion that attached to victims of sexual violence ('she asked for it') came under concerted feminist onslaught. A woman who had been raped or seduced was almost certain to fall into prostitution, as Wollstonecraft herself pointed out: 'Losing thus every spur, and having no other means of support, prostitution becomes her only refuge, and the character is quickly depraved by circumstances over which the poor wretch has little power, unless she possesses an uncommon portion of sense and loftiness of spirit. Necessity never makes prostitution the business of men's lives; though numberless are the women who are thus rendered systematically vicious.'

Apart from Wollstonecraft's, few other voices were raised against the sexual double standard. Her friend, the writer Thomas Holcroft, boldly put forward the rational argument against the indissolubility of marriage in his novel *Anne St Ives*: 'Of all the regulations which were ever suggested to the mistaken tyranny of selfishness, none perhaps to this day have surpassed the despotism of those which undertake to bind not only body to body but soul to soul, to all futurity, in despite of every possible change which our vices and our virtues might effect.' Such views flew in the face of a moral code whose bedrock was the notion of lifelong fidelity to a single partner.

Reform of the marriage laws proceeded at a snail-like pace, even though the misery they caused incompatible spouses, particularly wives, quickly became obvious. Wollstonecraft's one-time pupil, Margaret King, married the Earl of Mountcashell at the age of nineteen to escape from an unhappy home life. Her father, the Irish peer Lord Kingsborough, had married his wife Caroline when she was only fifteen; the couple quarrelled frequently, with Lady Kingsborough accusing her husband of persistent ill-treatment, and separated in 1789, when Margaret was seventeen. The pattern was repeated in Margaret's life: in 1803, after giving birth to eight children, she eloped with her lover, George Tighe, and was obliged, like other aristocratic women whose marriages collapsed not just in acrimony but in scandal, to live abroad. Adopting the pseudonym 'Mrs Mason', she had two daughters with Tighe – some compensation for the children she had been forced to leave behind but her social ostracism was complete. Even when she lived in Pisa, she kept well away from nearby Florence, where there was a flourishing expatriate community that would undoubtedly have refused to receive her. Almost twenty years later, in a letter to the poet Shelley, whose radical views on marriage were well known, Lady Mountcashell complained bitterly about the hypocrisy of the English, which had caused her so much misery.

Her contemporary Claire Clairmont, the clever and ambitious stepsister of Shelley's second wife, Mary, suffered even more cruelly from laws that gave mothers no rights to their children. Her only daughter, Allegra, fathered by Lord Byron during a brief and unsatisfactory affair, was taken from her by the poet and placed in a convent in Italy, twelve miles from Ravenna. As not just a woman but an unmarried mother, Claire could only plead with Byron for access to her child and to be consulted about how and where she should be brought up; Byron was entirely unsympathetic to her claims, dismissing her as 'a damned bitch' and refusing to answer her letters. 'If Clare [sic] thinks that she shall ever interfere with the child's morals or education, she mistakes; she never shall,' he wrote angrily to a friend in 1820. Encouraged by the sympathetic 'Mrs Mason', Claire made frantic plans to kidnap her daughter, which came to nothing. In 1822 her worst fears were justified when Allegra died at the convent after several days of fever, aged five years and three months. Byron tried to have the child buried at Harrow Church in west London, next door to his old school, but the Rector objected to a headstone or any other memorial on the grounds that she had been a bastard. Allegra was interred just inside the door of the church, but without a tablet to mark the place or her identity.

By 1800 the double standard was so firmly in place that the lawyer Thomas Erskine could claim, in a speech in the House of Commons, that adultery was the worst crime that could be committed, in the knowledge that his audience would understand that he was referring to *female* misconduct:

All other injuries, when put in the scale of . . . the crime of adultery . . . are as nothing. Is there any other private wrong which produces so many public consequences? The sanctity of marriage, of a contract which is the very foundation of the social world, is violated – religious and moral duties made a sport of – the peace and happiness of families utterly broken up – the protection of daughters destroyed, and their character, though innocent, disparaged in opinion by their mother's dishonour.

What was already beginning to happen in the eighteenth century was the loading of marriage, and especially wives, with a huge moral responsibility, a process that accelerated as the effects of unregulated capitalism became apparent. Against this background, attempts to rescue wives from their state of abject servitude, and to give them rights to their children, took years of patient campaigning. In 1839, after a woman named Caroline Norton shocked legislators with her account of her husband's lawful abduction of their three children, the law was changed to allow the courts to give custody of children up to the age of seven to their mothers. (Norton later became one of the leading lights in the campaign to change the law to give wives rights over their own property, after her husband absconded with hers – an all-too frequent story in Victorian England.) A Divorce Act was finally passed in 1857, and one of its innovations was to allow custody of children up to the age of fourteen to be awarded to their mothers. Naturally, the Act allowed a husband to divorce his wife solely on the grounds of adultery, but not vice versa; a husband who was 'a little profligate', in the words of one of the Act's supporters, should not be penalized in the same way as an adulterous wife, who was required to demonstrate an additional ground such as cruelty or desertion. And even if wives who had themselves committed adultery succeeded in obtaining a divorce, they were told by a judge as late as 1862 that they should on no account expect to have access to their children, an unfairness that was not corrected for another eleven years.

What these modest reforms reflected was a refinement of the idea of wives as property, adding a moral dimension to the uncomfortable role they already occupied. As the landless poor congregated in overcrowded conurbations, where they lived in slums while prostitutes openly patrolled the streets, the demand on respectable women to be the moral centre of the universe became all the more pressing. What was so clever about this shift was that its coercive intent was less transparent *and* it required women to play an active role in their own oppression. Thus in the nineteenth century the middle-class home, and especially the bodies of the women who resided in it, came to be regarded not just as a refuge for husbands but as the very *locus* of morality. This was, according to the historian John Tosh, a response to what was perceived as the widespread collapse of moral values in the market-place. Capitalism, colonialism, the opium trade: fortunes were waiting to be made, but not by men who were morally squeamish or overly concerned with ethics. This was a century in which children were put to work in factories and sent up chimneys, in which workers routinely suffered from dreadful industrial diseases like the so-called 'phossy jaw', caused by phosphorus, which gradually ate away the jaws of women who worked in match factories. Britain went to war with China from 1839 to 1842, and again in the 1850s, when the Chinese government objected to the importation of opium by the British, a trade that netted the East India Company £3 m a year; countless Chinese were addicted, but the trade paid for the governing of India, and the British were not minded to give it up. The UK abolished the slave trade in 1807, and slavery itself in 1833, yet maintained until 1919 a form of indentured labour in its colonies that 'seemed to many like a variant of slavery and which involved an international maritime trade in humanity not dissimilar to the old slave trade'. (In North America it took four years of civil war, from 1861 to 1865 and one of the bloodiest conflicts of the nineteenth century, to abolish slavery.)

The muscular ideal of manhood that middle- and upper-class boys were taught to aspire to in their British public schools prepared them for entry into this heartless modern world: adolescents were encouraged to value the traditional attributes of warriors – physical strength, loyalty to comrades, emotional numbness – in the name of a militant form of Christianity, preparing them for the privations of a career in the armed forces, the colonies or the City. Middle-class Victorian men, says Tosh, looked to their homes – their domestic space – to offer a moral vision of life that would make them better human beings: 'In keeping with the current elevated notions of womanhood, the custodians of the moral flame were the women of the home – perhaps a mother or a sister, sometimes a favoured daughter, but most often the wife, who was seen as owing a sacred duty to her husband in this respect.' The demand was, in some instances, overt. Archibald Tait, headmaster of Rugby School, wrote to his fiancée, Catherine Spooner, in 1843: 'Oh my dear girl, I do look to you to be my good Angel . . . you shall stay & hinder me, with God's help, from being worldly.' This is, in a sense, another manifestation of the familiar nineteenth-century notion of separate spheres, which held that men had been endowed by God with the talents and skills needed in the public world of commerce, government, the armed forces and the law, while women had gentler natures, better suited to child-rearing and domestic management. It imposed on middle-class women a form of innocence that was synonymous with ignorance, restricting their education to what was needed in the home and protecting them from worldly knowledge, especially in sexual matters. What it certainly did not allow for was an awareness on the part of adult women of their own sexual needs, less so even than in the late eighteenth century, when Wollstonecraft scolded her peers for what she saw as their selfish pursuit of pleasure. Unfortunately for many young wives, perhaps even the majority, the chief method of preserving their supposed purity was to keep them in complete ignorance of sex, and the functions of their own and their husbands' bodies. The shock some of them received on their wedding nights reinforced the middle-class erotophobia whose outlines were already discernible in some of Wollstonecraft's pronouncements in the 1790s – unsurprisingly, in view of so many women's experience in the Victorian period and the association of sexual pleasure with 'fallen' women. A hundred years after publication of the *Vindication*, some of the bolder women writers of the day were beginning to expose these hidden sexual horrors in their fiction, just as novelists in the mid century had tackled domestic violence (*The Tenant of Wildfell Hall* by Anne Brontë) and the anguish of mothers separated from their children (Charlotte Brontë's *Shirley*, *East Lynne* by Mrs Henry Wood). The novelist Margaret Oliphant tackled the theme of female ignorance and male insensitivity in 'A Story of a Wedding Tour', published in 1898. Her heroine, Janey, is 'a very lonely little girl, without parents, almost without relations', who is quite unprepared for her initiation into sex – into becoming what twentieth-century feminists would call a sex object – on her honeymoon:

I am afraid that Janey, being young and shy, and strange, was a good deal frightened, horrified and even revolted, by her first discoveries of what it meant to be in love. She had made tremendous discoveries in the course of a week. She had found out that Mr Rosendale, her husband, was in love with her beauty, but as indifferent to herself as any of the persons she had quitted to give herself to him. He did not care at all what she thought, how she felt, what she liked or disliked . He took it for granted that, being his wife, she would naturally be pleased with what pleased him, and his mind went no further than this.

Mr Rosendale 'overwhelmed her with caresses from which she shrank in disgust, almost in terror'. The theme of rape in marriage – still quite legal, of course – was even more starkly addressed in 'Virgin Soil', a short story published in 1894 by George Egerton (the male pseudonym of Mary Chavelita Dunne). Married to an older man at the age of seventeen, Florence returns to visit her widowed mother five years later for the first time since her wedding; she is changed beyond recognition, her skin sallow and her eyes burning resentfully in their sunken sockets. Her husband Philip is in Paris, with his current mistress, a circumstance that comes as a terrible shock to her mother – and an enormous relief to Florence. What is so revealing about the story, apart from its frankness, is the way in which the two women tussle over who bears the moral responsibility for everything that has gone wrong; even as advanced a thinker as

Egerton is unable to rid herself entirely of the notion that it is the duty of women to set and maintain standards of male sexual conduct. For the mother, the fault lies with her daughter, whom she berates for her failure to save Philip from 'such a shocking sin'. Her daughter replies with an angry, impassioned repudiation of the central tenet of Victorian matrimony: 'Bosh, Mother, he is responsible for his own sins, we are not bound to dry-nurse his morality.' Marriage, she says, in what may well be a deliberate echo of the *Vindication*, is 'legal prostitution' – it is 'one long crucifixion, one long submittal to the desires of a man I bound myself to in ignorance of what it meant'. But it is her mother's failure to warn her what to expect from sex, not her husband's brutal enforcement of his conjugal rights, that she regards as the origin of her plight: ' "You gave me not one weapon in my hand to defend myself against the possible attacks of man at his worst. You sent me out to fight the biggest battle of a woman's life, the one in which she ought to know every turn of the game, with a white gauze" – she laughs derisively – "of maiden purity as a shield." ' The evocation of the hymen, the frangible membrane that guards the entrance to a woman's vagina, is startling. Egerton makes it clear that Florence believes she has been cheated into surrendering her virginity to a man she finds loathsome, instead of waiting for a lover for whom she could feel 'the white fire of love or passion' – a daring recognition, for its time, that women also feel desire. Egerton's heroine, who eventually decides to leave her husband rather than kill him, may represent an extreme of female experience at the end of the nineteenth century. But the cherished ignorance of wives and the worldly knowledge of prostitutes was another aspect of the century's doctrine of separate spheres, one that relentlessly pitted women against each other.

There could be no greater contrast to the Victorian home, whether it was presided over by the sexually anaesthetized 'angel in the house' or a young wife haunted by what she regarded as her secret, nightly degradation at the hands of her husband, than the anonymous and often dangerous city streets in which thousands of gaudily dressed prostitutes sought out clients. (Nor is it a coincidence that the prototype serial killer, Jack the Ripper, made these vulnerable women his target among the crowded tenements of London's East End.) As in any system of crude binary opposition, each could be said to depend on the other, a proposition acknowledged by the Victorian commentator W. E. H. Lecky, who characterized the prostitute thus: 'Herself the supreme type of vice, she is ultimately the most efficient guardian of virtue.' He meant that the existence of prostitutes protected decent women from the repugnant sexual demands their husbands might otherwise make of them – a proposition flatly contradicted, as we have just seen, by women's fiction of the time. But they certainly depended on each other in another sense, which is to say that the so-called vileness of one enhanced the suffocating virtue of the other. If wives were idealized, infantilized and desexed, the exact opposite happened to prostitutes, who were discussed in the latter half of the nineteenth century in terms that equated them with animals and/or carriers of disease. When Mary Higgs visited a brothel in Oldham at the end of the nineteenth century, intent on 'saving' some of its inhabitants, her account revealed mingled fascination and disgust: 'Round the fire was a group of girls far gone in dissipation, good-looking girls most of them, but shameless; smoking cigarettes, boasting of drinks or drinkers, using foul language, singing music-hall songs, or talking vileness.'

Higgs's portrait is almost benign compared with other Victorian depictions of prostitutes. A Royal Commission that reported in 1871 described them as 'miserable creatures' who were 'masses of rottenness and vehicles of disease'. Admiral Edward Hawker, in a report entitled A *Statement of Certain Immoral Practices Prevailing in HM Navy*, could scarcely conceal his disgust at the conduct of prostitutes and their sailor-clients: 'Let those who have never seen a ship of war, picture to themselves a very large and low room with 500 men and probably 300 or 400 women of the vilest description shut up in it, and giving way to every excess of debauchery that the grossest passions of human nature can lead them to, and they see the deck of a gun ship upon the night of her arrival in port.'

Hawker's anxiety was about health as well as morals. Rates of venereal disease were lower in the navy than the army, where by 1864 one in three sick cases was suffering from sexually transmitted infections like gonorrhoea and syphilis. Five years later, a medical officer reported that 7 per cent of the patients who sought treatment at poor-law institutions, hospitals and dispensaries in London were suffering from VD in one form or another. But this does not give a full picture of the class distribution of the diseases. A modern historian, Judith R. Walkowitz, has suggested that 'syphilis was endemic to the civilian population in Great Britain in the Victorian and Edwardian periods and that it was most prevalent among men of the upper and middle ranks and among the casual laboring poor'. This picture of syphilis ravaging men of all classes comprehensively demolishes the notion that 'immorality' was confined to the urban poor; it also exposes the fraudulence of the doctrine of separate spheres, in the sense that the most sexually continent Victorian wife was vulnerable to exactly the same diseases as the prostitutes her husband visited without her knowledge. The chain of infection linked working-class men and women, and middle-class husbands and their wives, a reality that was strenuously denied by the authors of the 1871 Royal Commission. They stated unequivocally that 'there is no comparison to be made between prostitutes and the men who consort with them. With the one sex the offence is committed as a matter of gain; with the other it is the irregular indulgence of a natural impulse.' The clients' behaviour, according to this formulation, was regrettable but not unnatural; the women were mercenary, which was much worse.

The solution to the VD problem was, to an all-male House of Commons, simple and obvious: lock up diseased women. In 1864 an Act of Parliament was passed that allowed for the arrest and forcible examination of women who were suspected of being prostitutes, and their detention for up to three months in certified 'lock' hospitals if they were found to be infected. (There was no obligation under the legislation to do anything about their syphilitic or otherwise diseased clients.) The Contagious Diseases Acts – two others followed, giving the authorities even more power over women, in 1866 and 1869 – applied only to specified garrison and dockyard towns, including Plymouth, Portsmouth, Chatham, Dover and Sheerness, but they sent shudders of horror through the ranks of educated women. When Florence Nightingale read a draft of the first Act, she was astounded. 'I don't believe any Ho of C [House of Commons] will pass this bill,' she wrote to Harriet Martineau. 'Any honest girl might be locked up all night by mistake by it.' She was right about the effects of the Act, but wrong in her estimation of the fair-mindedness of the legislature. The second Act provided the police with even greater discretionary powers to pick up any woman, not necessarily a prostitute, suspected of promiscuous behaviour. The third extended the period of detention for diseased women to a maximum of nine months. In 1873, according to the *Shield* – a journal originally set up in South Shields, a port on South Tyneside, to campaign for the repeal of the Acts – a retired prostitute was hauled into court in Dover solely because she had been seen out late at night, walking on the beach. The powers invested in the police were so draconian that working-class women, especially those who had personal experience of how the Acts worked, joined the chorus of protest. One articulate young woman, Mary Ann Godden, was reported in the *Dover News* in 1870 to have protested after her detention that 'women were now treated as white slaves'; in Southampton, in 1871, a local vicar organized a petition, which was signed by 116 prostitutes, protesting against police brutality. The extent to which working women were at the mercy of arbitrary moral judgements about their character was demonstrated in 1875 by the case of Mrs Percy, a widow who supported her three children by entertaining soldiers at the army camp in Aldershot with what approximated to a music hall act. Although they had no evidence that she was a prostitute, the police demanded that she and her sixteen-year-old daughter should submit to physical examinations under the Act, and harassed her when she refused. Faced with the loss of her income, Mrs Percy protested in a letter to the *Daily Telegraph*, then committed suicide by throwing herself into the

Basingstoke Canal. Josephine Butler, the dedicated social reformer who, with the Liberal MP James Stansfield, led the campaign to repeal the Acts, recorded in a letter the experience of a woman who had been forcibly examined: 'It is awful work; the attitude they push us into first is so disgusting and so painful, and then these monstrous instruments – often they use several. They seem to tear the passage open first with their hands, and examine us, and then they thrust in instruments, and they pull them out and push them in, and they turn and twist them about; and if you cry out they stifle you . . .'

These medical inspections were a form of sexual assault, carried out on women who had so thoroughly lost their reputations that they were no longer regarded, under the law, as having a right to bodily integrity.* They represented the brutal but logical conclusion of a process that began, as I suggested at the beginning of this chapter, more than a century earlier, when the State embarked on its mission to assume absolute control of women's bodies. With middle- and upper-class wives safely enclosed in their luxurious homes – an earlier version of what the American feminist Betty Friedan would one day describe somewhat hyperbolically as the 'comfortable concentration camp' of suburban existence – women who did not aspire to or were unable to obtain male protection were now subject to an altogether bleaker form of confinement. This is not what twenty-first-century politicians mean when they talk nostalgically about Victorian values, but it is the dark underside of the bustling, ordered household popularized in TV programmes like *Upstairs, Downstairs*.

The Contagious Diseases Acts remained on the statute books for more than two decades and were finally repealed, after a long and bitter campaign, in 1886. Prostitutes, and women suspected of occasionally earning money this way, were still disparaged, but they

---

* At the beginning of the next century, the authorities reached a similar conclusion about the suffragettes. Aristocratic and working-class women alike were subjected to the brutality of forced feeding; Sylvia Pankhurst's graphic account of being over-powered by warders while metal instruments and a tube were forced down her throat describes, in effect, a species of oral rape.

had at least regained some rights over their own person – unless, of course, they also happened to be married women. Ironically, in a culture that claimed to value marriage so highly, wives had to wait much longer than unmarried sex workers to obtain the right to bodily integrity. The Married Women's Property Acts of 1870, 1874 and 1882 – the fact that there were three of them shows how difficult it was to get a parliamentary majority for a Bill giving wives substantial rights – began to correct a long-standing injustice by giving wives some control over their belongings. But the underlying assumption – that a wife's body and property were irreversibly vested in her husband – proved stubbornly resistant to change. This was demonstrated once again in 1888, when a woman who had left her husband was seized and imprisoned in a relative's house while he pursued a court case against her. Three years later, when another separated wife was kidnapped on the street by her furious husband, the courts were finally shocked enough to outlaw the practice.

One of the many social changes precipitated by the First World War was an expansion of the idea of what constituted women's work, although the notion that their wages were secondary – pin money – was to endure for some decades, with significant financial consequences; indeed, the concept of wives (and women generally) as chattels – property rather than property-owners – was sufficiently strong even in the second half of the twentieth century to become one of the principal targets of the feminist movement that emerged from the sexual revolution of the 1960s. Nowhere was this more evident than in the sphere of money, where women continued to encounter extraordinary obstacles when they tried to assert owner-ship, whether of houses or their own incomes. As late as the 1970s women were routinely refused mortgages and loans, even if they had earnings in their own right, or were granted them on special conditions, usually requiring the signature of a male guarantor. This ambiguous status was underlined on tax forms, archaic documents that required a wife's income to be shown on her husband's return unless she declared that she wished to have a separate assessment, a move unusual enough to cause raised eyebrows. This meant, of course, that husbands automatically knew how much their wives earned, but a wife had neither privacy for her own financial affairs nor the right to be told her husband's income – a preposterous situation that became untenable when it was pointed out that Britain's first woman Prime Minister, Mrs Thatcher, was technically supposed to declare her salary on her husband's tax form. The injustice was finally corrected in the late 1980s, by one of Mrs Thatcher's Chancellors (a man, inevitably), giving wives full control over their finances for the first time in history. There was, however, one more step to be taken before they acquired unconditional rights over their bodies. In 1991, with a palpable air of embarrassment, the House of Lords ruled that rape in marriage would in future be a criminal offence. It had involved two and a half centuries of protest and struggle, but at long last women had been liberated – even if they could not yet claim to be on absolutely equal terms with men – from the physical and legal restrictions imposed on them under cover of Christian morality. Mary Wollstonecraft could hardly have guessed, when she analysed the de facto enclosure of women's bodies and souls in 1792, that it would take such a painfully long time to undo.

6

Back to the Future

A local authority shall not – (a) intentionally promote homo-sexuality or publish material with the intention of promoting homosexuality; (b) promote the teaching in any maintained school of the acceptability of homosexuality as a pretended family relationship

– SECTION 28, LOCAL GOVERNMENT ACT 1988

We will not stand back and allow a politically correct minority to undermine the position of marriage in society and deter-mine morality for the majority. We did not vote for it, we're not having it.

– BRIAN SOUTER, SCOTTISH BUSINESSMAN AND
SUPPORTER OF SECTION 28

It was not just female sexuality that was closely scrutinized and policed in Victorian society, as we have seen in the previous chapter. Although men's private sexual conduct usually escaped critical com-ment, as long as they paid lip-service to the Christian ideal of monogamy, there was an exception to this rule; no sooner had they been given a name by the Hungarian doctor Karoly Benkert in 1869 than homosexual men began to occupy an ever larger place in the imagination of moralists and legislators. Although the word did not come into popular use until the early twentieth century, the fact that it was coined at all is evidence that gay sex had begun to exist as a category – and a problem. Unnatural, vile, heinous, revolting, unbalanced, neurotic, decadent: each of these adjectives was applied at various times in the Victorian period to male homosexuals – when, that is, god-fearing men could bring themselves to speak of them at all. This was perhaps inevitable in a society organized for and ruled by the heterosexual paterfamilias, whose desire and its female object constituted not just the norm but the only legitimate expression of sexuality. There is a direct link between their misogyny towards any woman who was not an obedient wife and mother and the Victorians' increasingly overt homophobia: gay men, prostitutes and unfaithful wives all posed a threat, in different ways, to the project of regular production of legitimate offspring. This reality is revealed by the tone of the discourse employed against gay men, which identified homosexuality as a moral problem but also categorized it as *degenerate*, an adjective that derives in part from the Latin noun *genus*, meaning race. The challenge apparently posed by homosexuals to the project of breeding an imperial race was compounded by the way in which their very existence exposed a contradiction in the prevailing masculine ideal; with its emphasis on male comradeship and bonding, the Victorian notion of manliness was drawn from a foreign culture where male homosexuality had been common and discussed openly by intellectuals, a fact that could hardly have been unknown in a country where the scions of aristocratic families were steeped in classical literature. The fact that the British education system relied so heavily on Latin and Greek authors, with their relaxed and even enthusiastic attitudes to man–boy love, meant that the British ruling class perpetually teetered on the brink of detonating its own much stricter mores, which is why the male homosexual had to be externalized and persecuted. He also, by transcending class boundaries – a major issue in the trials of Oscar Wilde – threatened a kind of social miscegenation that was wholly unacceptable in a country acutely anxious about maintaining existing boundaries. In an empire at the height of its power, invulnerable according to its own rhetoric but perpetually anxious about revolts and incursions into its territory by rival powers, it is easy to see how gay men came to represent the enemy within – a sort of cancer eating away at the otherwise healthy body of Britannia. (The popularity as an imperial icon of Britannia, with her strikingly muscular body, may have expressed an unconscious anxiety about gender on the part of a self-styled warrior nation whose titular head was a dumpy widow in black. Indeed, her popularity peaked during the Queen's final decade, achieving its zenith during the Diamond Jubilee celebrations in 1897.) It was unfortunate for homosexual men that their sexuality should have tapped into so many of these unacknowledged vulnerabilities, ensuring that they acquired a weight of meaning for the Victorians that was quite disproportionate either to their numbers or the challenge they represented – remember that many gay and bisexual men, including Wilde, were in fact married – to the heterosexual family.

A new breed of doctors, popularly known as sexologists, was on hand with a medical model that appeared to confirm the status of homosexuality as not just a perversion but a disease. Richard von Krafft-Ebing played a key role in this process, in his famous *Psychopathia Sexualis* (1886) and in a later book where he was frank about the danger posed by homosexuals. In *The Deviant Sexual Male Before the Court of Justice* (1894), he wrote: 'Such degenerates have no right to existence in a well-regulated bourgeois society, and they have no gift for doing so. They endanger society to a high degree and they do so as long as they live. Medical science has found no way to cure these victims of an organic disturbance. They should be put away for life; however, they should not be branded as criminals – they are unfortunates, deserving pity.'

A volume entitled *Degeneracy* (1898), in a contemporary science series edited by Havelock Ellis, characterized homosexuals as 'moral imbeciles' and 'degenerate lunatics'. Freud was more judicious in his *Three Essays on the Theory of Sexuality* (1905), weighing the evidence that homosexuality was 'an innate indication of nervous degeneracy' and concluding that the facts were against the diagnosis. He pointed out that 'inversion [homosexuality] is found in people who exhibit no other serious deviations from the normal' and also in people 'who are indeed distinguished by specially high intellectual development and ethical culture'. Yet the disease model, whether it was understood literally or figuratively, as a disorder of mind or body, was hugely significant in shaping attitudes towards homosexuality; gay men, at the very moment when they were about to become more visible in *fin de siècle* society, were already associated in the educated mind with morbidity, lunacy and moral decline. It is hard to avoid the conclusion that the visceral loathing of gay sex that resulted in a flurry of hostile legislation in the final decades of the Victorian period was an exercise in projection, the recourse of a society so reluctant to face its internal contradictions and flagrant immoralities that it had to find a scapegoat. Homosexual men were stigmatized as mad and bad – the slippage between actually quite separate categories, even on the part of medically qualified authorities, is striking – and Britain came to have, by the end of the Victorian period, tougher laws against male homosexuality than any other country in Europe. (France, for comparison, had removed homosexuality from its penal code as early as 1791.)

On the face of it, the new legislation looked like a relaxation of the statute it replaced, abolishing the death penalty for sodomy that had been in force in England since the time of Henry VIII. In practice, though, by replacing capital punishment with long prison terms, it ensured that men charged with homosexual offences were more likely to be convicted and punished. In 1861 the Offences Against the Person Act stipulated a minimum penalty for buggery of ten years' imprisonment and a maximum of life, with hard labour. The law was strengthened in 1885, when Henry Labouchère's notorious amendment to the Criminal Law Amendment Bill was passed by the House of Commons: for the first time, *all* sexual acts between men were criminalized, including fellatio and mutual masturbation. The fact that both activities were rife in English public schools, which still educated the vast majority of MPs, confirms the degree to which ideas about class and the unacceptable 'other' influenced the legislation; its target was not teenage Harrovians, who were assumed to grow out of this adolescent phase, but men from the working class who persisted in what was regarded as unnatural vice – and, of course, their well-bred lovers. As Wilde would soon discover, the notion of corruption, in one direction or another, lay at the heart of the legislation.

What is so striking about the new law, in the context of this book, is the way in which it effectively denied gay men a private life: it punished *private* acts, as well as those committed in public, and criminalized even the act of *approaching* another man for sex: 'any male person who, in public or in private, commits, or is a party to the commission of, or procures or attempts to procure the commission by any male person of any act of gross indecency with another male person, shall be guilty of a misdemeanour, and being convicted thereof shall be liable at the discretion of the court to be imprisoned for any term not exceeding two years, with or without hard labour'.

There was an interesting lacuna in the legislation, which is that lesbians were not mentioned. It is often said that the Victorians, including the Queen herself, simply could not bring themselves to believe that it existed; even if this story is apocryphal, feminist historians cite a precedent in 1811, when two women teachers in Scotland were acquitted of a charge of improper sexual contact on the grounds that 'the crime here alleged has no existence'. Given the extent to which heterosexual women were regulated by the State, the omission of lesbians from the amendment seems odd, yet it is almost certainly further evidence that a society that liked to pretend that women had no sexual feelings simply could not imagine women experiencing physical passion for each other. It is also the case that some MPs found the whole idea of lesbianism so perverse that they did not want to alert women to its existence, fearing they might stimulate a curiosity that would not otherwise have existed. Lord Desart, who was Director of Public Prosecutions at the time of Oscar Wilde's trial, certainly took this view in 1921, when there was an attempt to remedy its absence from the statute book. Very few women were lesbians, he suggested, and it would be a mistake 'to bring it to the notice of women who have never heard of it, never thought of it, never dreamed of it'. (Of all the theories about the origins of same-sex love, the notion of heterosexual women becoming inflamed with passion for each other by reading Hansard or parliamentary reports in *The Times* over breakfast is surely among the most far-fetched.)

Astonishingly, MPs passed the amendment criminalizing lesbianism by 148 votes to 53, at a late-night sitting, but it was subsequently overturned by the House of Lords and failed to become law. The timing is interesting: in a society whose male population had just been decimated in the First World War, the brief emergence of lesbianism as a subject of publicly expressed anxiety reflected a broader fear of the growing power of women, whose progress towards full citizenship had accelerated as a result of the role they played during the conflict. It also happened at a moment when gender boundaries were blurred. Women not only looked different in the immediate post-war period, with their newly bobbed hair and boyish figures, but women over the age of thirty who fulfilled certain property qualifications had been granted the vote in 1918, a cautious reform that went some way to achieving the aims of the suffragettes who had terrified polite society before the war. It was clear, even to conservatives, that full admission to the electorate, on the same terms as men, could not be far behind.

If legislators were for the most part uninterested in or wary of lesbianism, the same was not true of the sexologists. 'By the 1920s,' according to one history of women's lives, 'crushes on other women, a too-boyish or mannish style of dress and behaviour, even an "unfeminine" ambition to succeed in a male profession were interpreted as warning signals of sexual "inversion".' The latter was only one of the new names applied to sex between women, most of them codes that kept the practice safely obscure, either by locating it in a classical context that few ordinary women would recognize (Sapphism) or stressing its alien, inhuman origins (Uranism, after the recently discovered planet of that name). But it is instructive that lesbians never achieved the visibility of gay men, confirming the hypothesis that male homosexuality acted as a receptacle for all sorts of anxieties and contradictions about masculinity. Moral panics, which is what the Wilde trials came to represent, occur when there is an urgent need to deflect internal tensions within a hegemonic group; having identified a promising candidate in gay men, all *fin de siècle* society needed was a suitable victim.

What is surprising, in retrospect, is that a man as intelligent as Wilde did not grasp how well he fitted the bill. His imprisonment for acts of indecency in 1895 was a direct consequence of Labouchère's amendment, ten years before, but it was also a catharsis: the public immolation of a celebrity in order to confirm the boundaries of a type of masculinity that was under threat from half a dozen directions. Scepticism inspired by Darwinian science, late-nineteenth-century feminism (the New Woman), the rise of the entrepreneur ('trade'), a new professional class and greater social mobility had all combined to challenge the muscular (and philistine) Christian ideal of the mid century. Wilde's dandyish airs, his disdain for tradition and perverse bons mots neatly embodied aspects of the threat, as the response of the London *Evening News* to his conviction made clear. He was, the paper declared, 'one of the high priests of a school which attacks all the wholesome, manly, simple ideals of English life, and sets up false gods of decadent culture and intellectual debauchery'.

Wilde had certainly been reckless and predatory in his enjoyment of young working-class rent boys, but no more so than some of his heterosexual contemporaries, whose tastes ran to even younger girls and who were willing to pay a premium for virgins. He may well have assumed, wrongly, that his fame would protect him, as it did other men with unorthodox sexual tastes. What he failed to appreciate was that his behaviour pressed all the alarm buttons of a culture that was affronted by any suggestion of effeminacy, that lived in terror of cross-class relationships, and that already regarded homosexuality as dangerously infectious. Wilde was portrayed as a potent source of corruption, passing on his disease to the class above him – his one-time lover, Lord Alfred Douglas, son of the Marquess of Queensberry, whose challenge to Wilde started the witch-hunt – and the one below, young working-class men whose morals were regarded as precarious at the best of times. That he was the victim of double standards was a point forcibly made by the crusading journalist W. T. Stead, whose famous exposé of the trade in girls had been published ten years earlier under the title 'The Maiden Tribute to Modern Babylon'. Stead was a puritan and his language is uncomfortably judgemental, but his argument cannot be faulted:

If Oscar Wilde, instead of indulging in dirty tricks of indecent familiarity with boys and men, had ruined the lives of half a dozen innocent simpletons of girls, or had broken up the home of his friend by corrupting his friend's wife, no one could have laid a finger upon him. The male is sacrosanct: the female is fair game. To have burdened society with a dozen bastards, to have destroyed a happy home with his lawless lust – of these the criminal law takes no account. But let him act indecently to a young rascal who is well able to take care of himself, and who can by no possibility bring a child into the world as a result of his corruption, then judges can hardly contain themselves.

Stead even pointed out that the public tacitly accepted 'the same kind of vice in our public schools. If all persons guilty of Oscar Wilde's offences were to be clapped into gaol, there would be a surprising exodus from Eton and Harrow, Rugby and Winchester.' But Stead, for all his courage, was in a minority. Given the maximum sentence, two years with hard labour, Wilde's conviction marked not just the end of an artistic movement, Decadence, but the branding of the male homosexual as a pariah. Gay men panicked as the news of his conviction spread: Henry Harland, editor of the *Yellow Book* – the avant-garde quarterly was to become another casualty of the Wilde trials – claimed in a letter to the novelist Edmund Gosse that 600 male passengers sailed from Dover to Calais in a single night instead of the expected 60. Wilde himself emerged from Reading Gaol a broken man, his health wrecked by hard labour, hunger, illness and exhaustion. 'He looks well,' the Prison Governor informed Wilde's old friend Robbie Ross, when the playwright completed his sentence. 'But like all men unused to manual labour who receive a sentence of this kind, he will be dead within two years.' Wilde lasted three, which he passed in exile in France. But the treatment meted out to him – in effect, a protracted death sentence – was so savage that its shadow hung over gay men in Britain for decades, persuading some of them to submit to blackmail rather than to risk a similarly harsh fate.

Even Wilde's example was not enough for Britain's triumphalist legislators, who decided to make life even harder for gay men three years after his trial. In 1898 a section against homosexual soliciting was added to the Vagrancy Law Amendment Act, specifically to 'lay hold of a certain kind of blackguard who is unmentionable in society'. At one level, this merely confirms that British society, or the men who continued to shape its identity, had not fully discharged their anxieties. It did of course have hideous consequences, vividly conveyed by court records; in 1911 a London magistrate revived the birch as a punishment for gay sex, and 23 men received sentences of 15 strokes in the next year. If anything, the First World War confirmed and institutionalized homophobia, partly because the close quarters of trench warfare fostered 'unnatural' feelings between men. I am not convinced, as some contemporary psychoanalysts were, that a diagnosis of shell shock resulted from the fact that 'conditions of bonding in the army allowed for the return of repressed homosexual desire'. But the intimacy of army life created conditions in which male homosexuality, in theory the antithesis of warrior culture but in reality its underlying motor, covertly flourished. It is not surprising, in the event, that the period after both world wars saw an intensification of the persecution of gay men: between 1920 and 1924 there were on average more than 60 prosecutions per year in England and Wales for 'unnatural offences', 215 for attempted sodomy or indecent assault and 176 for indecency. Sir Theobald Mathew, who was appointed Director of Public Prosecutions in 1944, subscribed to the theory that many gay men were not genuinely homosexual at all but heterosexuals who had been 'corrupted' by their experience in the armed forces; no admirer of psychoanalytic theories of innate bisexuality, Mathew set himself the grim task of stamping out the practice before it became established in civilian life. As a direct consequence, the State's enthusiasm for interfering in consensual sex acts between gay men increased exponentially: between 1945 and 1955 prosecutions rose from under 800 a year to 2,500, with 40 per cent of the offenders receiving a custodial sentence.

What the prosecutions may have done – the extent to which this is a result of anti-gay legislation is still debated by historians – is shape some of the prevailing forms of gay identity. In effect, homosexual men were denied a private life: unable to meet each other openly, they were forced to develop codes that would be understood and recognized by potential sexual partners, thus affording minimal protection against blackmail; they also needed places to encounter other like-minded men, which encouraged the development of an illicit market-place, exposing homosexuals to exploitation and criminality. Above all – and this is a paradoxical result for legislation that claimed to be concerned with decency – the laws drove secretly gay men out of their usual social milieu and into public places like lavatories, parks and commons in search of sex. In that sense, the legislation achieved precisely the opposite of what was intended, failing to protect heterosexual men from being solicited for sex, as well as rendering gay men vulnerable to police spies and malicious opportunists who recognized the potential of the situation for robbery and/or blackmail. That some gay men continue to use these places, long after male homosexual acts in private were legalized in Britain in 1967, leaves open the question of whether anonymous sex is an integral part of their identity or a habit acquired by gay culture during the decades of State persecution. It seems logical that turning homosexual men into outlaws for such a lengthy period would have long-lasting effects on how they perceive themselves; it may be that decades of illegality continue to have an impact on their vision of private life *and* how they express their sexuality.

For many gay men, the AIDS panic of the early 1980s revived the fear and shame earlier generations of homosexuals had experienced every single day of their lives. (One of the cruellest effects of HIV was to confirm, in the minds of homophobes, the link between male homosexuality and disease. At a time when the extent of heterosexual transmission in sub-Saharan Africa was not yet apparent, AIDS could be and was characterized for a time as a gay plague: metaphor appeared to have become diagnosis.) In the first half of the twentieth century the revelation of homosexual or even bisexual tendencies was almost certain to wreck marriages, families and careers; men threatened with exposure often committed suicide rather than face ruin and almost certain imprisonment. The armed forces were particularly unrelenting, for reasons I have already suggested, as well as being the one place where lesbians faced the same kind of discrimination as homosexual men; while lesbian acts were not illegal in civil society, servicewomen in same-sex relationships were at risk of being court-martialled and dishonourably discharged. In the United States the authorities resorted to extraordinary methods to deal with what they regarded as a threat to discipline and the class system: American soldiers who were convicted of sodomy were sent to military prisons and at one establishment, in Kansas, they were required to wear a big yellow D, for 'degenerate', on the back of their uniforms. Colin Spencer estimates that during the 1930s more than 40 per cent of new admissions to Portsmouth Naval Prison in New Hampshire – designated a 'place of confinement for moral perverts regardless of length of sentence' – were men convicted of sodomy or fellatio. It was ironic that, failing to recognize the source of their homophobia, American military leaders tended to share exactly the same attitudes as their titular enemies; US generals and admirals in the 1930s were as fanatically hostile to gay sex as the Nazi leaders they would soon face in battle. Long before the war, Hitler – who had his own problems with masculinity and homosexuals among his most trusted associates – issued a directive that any member of the Brown Shirts (SA) who committed an offence under Paragraph 175, the German law dating back to 1871 that criminalized homosexuality, should be expelled at once. 'I want to see men as SA commanders,' he wrote, 'not ludicrous monkeys.' (Ernst Röhm, openly gay leader of the Brown Shirts, fell victim to this policy during the Night of the Long Knives in 1934.) The Nazis were obsessed with the so-called purity of the race and their eugenicist motives are evident in the remarks of Himmler, head of the SS, who denounced homosexuals as 'sociosexual propagation misfits' and 'as useless as hens that don't lay eggs'. The Third Reich favoured pink rather than yellow for homosexuals, herding wearers of the pink triangle into concentration camps where, according to Richard Plant, author of a book about the Nazi persecution of gay men, between 5,000 and 15,000 of them died. (Spencer believes the figure is higher, perhaps as many as 50,000.)

The immediate post-war period was no happier for homosexual men in Britain. In spite of having won the war, old notions of Englishness and particularly English masculinity were under threat, and the State responded by hounding its habitual victim of choice, gay men, with unmitigated ferocity. One of Britain's most senior law officers, Lord Chief Justice Goddard, proclaimed that he felt 'physically sick' when trying 'buggers'; his views echoed those of Sir David Maxwell Fyfe, Home Secretary from 1951 to 1954, one of the most illiberal holders of an office that seems to attract authoritarian personalities. A Somerset man, writing in 1958 when police harassment of gay men was at its height, characterized their activities as 'pogroms'; later writers have characterized Britain in this period, as far as gay men were concerned, as a police state. Old-fashioned prejudice was reinforced by widespread paranoia, fed by the Cold War, which encouraged the notion that the alien 'other' was everywhere, in the form of spies, foreigners and – especially in the US – invaders from faraway planets. This is the period of the notorious Roswell incident, when the American government is supposed to have covered up the crash-landing of a space ship in the desert; it is the moment in cinema history that produced such memorable movie titles as *I Married a Communist* (1949) and *I Married a Monster from Outer Space* (1958). What they express is a dread of invasion by creatures who looked normal – just like Communists, homosexuals and the pod people in *Invasion of the Body Snatchers* (1956) – but whose aim was to take over 'our' world and subvert 'our' values. In Britain and the US, panic about Soviet spies became bound up with homophobia, as some of the era's biggest espionage scandals turned out to involve gay men, including the British diplomat Guy Burgess who defected to the Soviet Union in 1951. (His fellow-defector, Donald Maclean, was bisexual.) No gay man was safe. John Gielgud had been knighted in 1953, but Churchill conferred the honour reluctantly, because of the actor's homosexuality. Gielgud was arrested a few months later and charged with 'persistently importuning male persons for immoral purposes'. He was fined and the incident almost wrecked his career. In the *Sunday Express* John Gordon complained about 'moral rot' and urged readers to ostracize people he described as 'social lepers'. Gielgud contemplated suicide, but was supported through the ordeal by fellow-actors, principally Sybil Thorndike and Ralph Richardson, who were appearing with him in *A Day by the Sea*. An attempt by a faction in the actors' union, Equity, to have him thrown out and barred from acting was easily defeated.

Yet the fact that Gielgud survived, if only by the skin of his teeth, should have alerted the authorities to the fact that Britain was now in transition. The Second World War had been much more effective than the 1914–18 conflict in breaking down old attitudes and Gielgud's prosecution came at a moment when the moral climate, super-ficially stable and deeply conservative, was beginning to change. The election in 1945 of a Labour government signalled the high expectations created during the war in working-class people who remembered the bitter disappointment felt by their parents after the First World War; mass education, established by the 1944 Education Act, meant that a college education was now a real possibility, if not for those who actually fought in the war, at least for their sons and daughters; women who had worked during the conflict were discovering that housework did not compensate for a wage packet, no matter how small, and access to a wider circle of friends and opportunities than they experienced as wives and mothers; class barriers were coming under assault, a phenomenon that was vividly embodied in John Osborne's *Look Back In Anger*; immigrants from the colonies were arriving, encouraged by post-war governments that needed a cheap source of manual labour. A combination of radical ideas, including a newly sceptical attitude to authority, and the fact that the old pre-war elite had not managed to re-establish its grip, created a situation in which all sorts of modernizing campaigns, including those to legalize homosexuality and abortion, began to get off the ground.

One of the most significant barometers of change was the trial in 1954 of three prominent men, a case with distinct echoes of the Wilde trial sixty years earlier. The best known of the defendants was Lord Montagu of Beaulieu, who had originally been arrested and charged a year earlier with committing an unnatural offence and indecently assaulting two Boy Scouts. Montagu was acquitted on one charge, after it was demonstrated that the police had tampered with a key piece of evidence, but the jury could not agree on the charge of indecent assault. The homophobic DPP, Mathew, decreed that Montagu should face another trial, and three weeks later the peer's cousin, Michael Pitt-Rivers, was arrested, along with a *Daily Mail* journalist, Peter Wildeblood. They were charged with committing indecent acts with two consenting RAF men, Edward McNally and John Reynolds, highlighting a class difference between the accusers and the defendants that initially recalled Wilde and his rent boys, but that eventually backfired on the prosecution. The suggestion that the defendants were 'so infinitely' the 'social superiors' of their accusers, and that they had seduced them with offers of lavish hospitality, was insulting to everyone concerned; the men's sentences – Montagu got a year in gaol, the others eighteen months, while their accusers were given immunity from prosecution – were regarded as unduly savage and a demonstration of the need for reform.

That same year, the British government set up a committee chaired by the Vice-Chancellor of Reading University, John Wolfenden, to examine the current laws on both homosexuality and prostitution. It reported back in 1957, with the humane and sensible recommendation that 'homosexual behaviour between consenting adults in private be no longer a criminal offence'. Public reaction was polarized, with the *Guardian*, *Observer* and *The Times* offering a cautious welcome to the report, while the *Daily Telegraph* predictably reached for the disease metaphor and warned that legalized gay sex would spread through the population like an infection. But there was at least a public debate and the Homosexual Law Reform Society was founded in 1958, when a group of prominent citizens wrote to *The Times*, calling for the reforms recommended by Wolfenden to be implemented. In 1961 the director Basil Dearden made what is widely regarded as the first mainstream film to deal with homosexuality, *Victim*, starring Dirk Bogarde. In one of his most courageous roles, Bogarde played a married man, a bisexual barrister who defies a blackmailer after his ex-boyfriend commits suicide to protect him. The movie went on general release in Britain but was refused a licence by the American censor on the ground that it was 'thematically objectionable'. In a review that sounded more like evidence of an outbreak of moral panic, *Time* magazine attacked the film for its failure to 'suggest that homosexuality is a serious but often curable neurosis that attacks the biological basis of life itself. The picture at its most offensive is full of sodomites and, what is most offensive, an implicit approval of homosexuality as a practice.'

Yet this was a rearguard action. In 1961 homosexuality began to be decriminalized in some American states and six years later it was legalized in Britain. In both cases, the new laws were probably ahead of public opinion, but their long-term effects can be mapped through the public image of homosexual celebrities. The movie star Rock Hudson desperately concealed his sexual orientation and eventually died of an AIDS-related infection; so did Liberace, who sued for libel and won when the *Daily Mirror* columnist Cassandra implied in a decidedly homophobic article that the entertainer was gay, although he too later succumbed to the effects of HIV. Kenneth Williams and John Inman, by contrast, felt able to shelter under the ambiguous label of camp, while a later generation of performers – Boy George, Holly Johnson of Frankie Goes to Hollywood and the flamboyant comedian Julian Clary – integrated their homosexuality into their stage identity. It was a sign of how much things had changed that the gay singer George Michael, arrested for indecency in a public toilet in a park in Los Angeles in 1998, emerged from the incident with more dignity (and considerably more humour) than the heterosexual actor Hugh Grant, who was widely mocked when he was caught in a car in the same city with a prostitute he had paid to perform oral sex.

None of this meant that homophobia had evaporated in the final decades of the twentieth century, although in Western democracies it was for the most part no longer State-sanctioned. The slang terms for homosexual men, some of them ironically appropriated by gay rights campaigners in an analogy with feminist reclaimings of words like 'bitch', demonstrated continuing anxieties about masculine identity; insults like 'queer', 'poof', 'nancy boy' and 'faggot' expressed an entrenched fear of effeminacy, while others – 'shirtlifter' and 'arse-bandit', for instance – revealed heterosexual fantasies about (and sometimes a repressed wish for) homosexual seduction. Heterosexual culture has never been able to resolve the precise nature of its anxiety about homosexuality – unsurprisingly, since it actually reflects its own uncertainty about what properly constitutes masculinity – and this confusion manifested itself in conflicting propositions. Instead of accepting that gay men were as diverse in character and tastes as heterosexuals, they were stigmatized as insufficiently masculine at one moment and chided for displaying heterosexual traits, especially promiscuity, to an excessive degree in the next. In that sense, recurrent panics about gay paedophilia – periodically the bogeyman of choice in twenty-first-century Britain – deflected attention from the awkward fact that so many child-abusers were both heterosexual and members of the victim's family. This is not to deny that homosexual paedophiles exist, but it is ironic that some of the most prolific offenders whose activities were exposed in the 1990s were not out gay men but Catholic priests and monks, closet homosexuals in a Church that remained implacably hostile to them.

It is in this context, I think, that outbreaks of homophobia in our own time need to be understood, whether they appear in the form of lynchings of gay men or paranoid attempts to exclude them from new definitions of the family. Gay men have been murdered in conservative American states, usually in rural communities where traditional male jobs have disappeared or no longer carry their former status, while the bomb attack on a gay pub in London's Soho in 1999 was carried out by a self-confessed neo-Nazi whose own insecurities were hinted at when he told police he loathed gay men. (What the bomber failed to appreciate is the extent to which gay and heterosexual culture overlap in modern Britain, a fact that meant that one of the three people who died was a pregnant woman who had been drinking with her husband and gay friends.)

But there are few more revealing examples of the anxiety and hostility felt towards gay men by some embattled heterosexuals than a bizarre piece of legislation that was piloted on to the statute books in the dying days of the Thatcher administration. Section 28 of the 1988 Local Government Act is not at first sight an obvious vehicle for homophobic prejudice, but it is in fact an exceptionally potent icon of Christian, pro-family, anti-gay campaigners. It is often remarked, with some justice, that the long period of Conservative rule in Britain from 1979 to 1997 was characterized by the political triumph of the Right and the cultural hegemony of the Left, driving die-hard reactionaries into paroxysms of fury as radical theatre, gay-pride marches and other equally unacceptable manifestations of multiculturalism flourished. Section 28, with its declared intention of forbidding teachers to promote 'the acceptability of homosexuality as a *pretended family relationship*' (my italics) in schools, marked the moment when upholders of Victorian values successfully struck back, reinstating *in law* the heterosexual couple as the most desirable – indeed, the only authentic – model of family life. This is demonstrated by its status as a highly controversial and entirely *unnecessary* piece of legislation, pushed through Parliament in spite of the absence of any credible evidence that teachers were showing gay porn in classrooms or trying to 'convert' pupils to a gay lifestyle. (What it almost certainly did do was inhibit teachers, straight and gay, who might otherwise have helped gay teenagers who feared bullying from their classmates or a hostile reaction from their parents.) That the real function of Section 28 was symbolic rather than practical was confirmed by the hysterical opposition that emerged when Tony Blair's government set about fulfilling an election pledge to repeal it; the determination of the Conservatives, especially a rump of Tory peers in the House of Lords, to preserve a law that had neither identified a problem nor checked an abuse demonstrated its significance as a warning to the Left of the continuing vigour of traditional – and, above all, patriarchal – values. So important was it deemed in Scotland that a dour working-class millionaire, an evangelical Christian who made his money out of the aptly named Stagecoach bus company, poured a million pounds of his own money into a private referendum designed to demonstrate popular support for retaining the legislation. (Two thirds of the ballot papers were not returned in this statistically unsound exercise, in which only one side of the argument was represented; it is interesting to speculate how many hungry children in developing countries could have been fed or vaccinated with the money Brian Souter wasted on this peculiar obsession.) Stripped of its noisy rhetoric, what the campaign to retain Section 28 was demanding was the right to promote the traditional married family among children whose own parents might very well not subscribe to it, turning it into just as much a propaganda exercise as the (unproven) gay proselytizing that the Act was meant to protect them from.

It is no accident that, while the battle over Section 28 was being fought in Westminster and the devolved Scottish Parliament in Edinburgh at the end of the 1990s, the tabloid press was opening up another front: stirring up popular outrage over the prospect of lesbians and homosexual men becoming parents. One of the catalysts for Section 28, back in the 1980s, was a children's book about a small girl living with two gay men, which supporters of the bill flourished as an example of the kind of material they were trying to prevent getting into schools; another moral panic – fuelled by covert hints about paedophilia, as well as the dreadful prospect of gay parents bringing up gay children – was in the making. Yet gay men and women often seemed, when they were interviewed by incredulous journalists, to have given more thought to the question of how to look after children than their heterosexual counterparts; unconventional arrangements, such as a lesbian couple having a child with a gay man, appeared to be just as stable – sometimes more so – than the nuclear family model that was generally agreed not to be working. Themselves the product, more often than not, of heterosexual marriages, gay parents pointed out that their own children were no more likely to grow up gay than their peers who lived with straight parents. They also felt that their willingness to embrace new techniques like *in vitro* fertilization, to overcome their inability to have children via the usual route, was being unfairly held against them; two gay men in Essex, who paid an American surrogate mother to bear twins using a donor egg and a mixture of their sperm, were denounced by the tabloids in terms more appropriate to child abusers. It was even suggested at one point that the babies would not be allowed into Britain, even though both men's names appeared on their birth certificates.

It was impossible to miss the rich irony that the same moralists who habitually criticized single mothers, and unemployed parents living on state benefits on council estates, were now complaining about a stable couple, self-made millionaires – shining examples of Thatcherite ideology, in other words – who had made a conscious decision to have children and were able to provide both a comfortable home and a whole series of nannies. As the arguments raged over Section 28 in the first months of the twenty-first century, it became clear that this very modern family had exposed a new terror among social conservatives: that some gay men, far from being the child-abusers of myth, might turn out to make better parents than those heterosexual fathers who abandon their offspring to the care of impoverished single mothers and the Child Support Agency.

PART THREE

The Peasants' Revolt

7

Sex and Drugs and . . . Children

The 'double' sexual morality which is valid for men in our society is the plainest admission that society itself does not believe in the possibility of enforcing the precepts which it itself has laid down. — FREUD

If we are to escape from the treadmill of sexual fantasy, voracious need of love, and obsessiveness in all its forms, we will have to reinstate our libido in its rightful function. Only then will women be capable of loving. — GERMAINE GREER

Sex and drugs and rock 'n' roll are all my brain and body need. — IAN DURY

Revolutions are always, in a sense, incomplete. Either they are overthrown in turn, or the original instigators quarrel among themselves, or events move them in an unforeseen direction. Their effects reverberate for decades, centuries even, which is why Mao's deputy, Zhou Enlai, on being asked by Henry Kissinger whether he considered the French Revolution a success, remarked that it was too soon to tell. This is as true of revolutions in ideas as it is of the violent disturbances more usually associated with the word, and never more so than in the case of the dramatic social upheaval that took place in the 1960s. In a few short years the sexual revolution challenged traditional marriage, the contract between the individual and the State, and the relationship between men and women.

Although the conditions for change were in place in the 1950s, as I suggested in Chapter 6, at the time it seemed inexplicably sudden; it was as though, shortly after the Beatles' first number one, the generation of post-war babies who arrived at college and art school in the 1960s abruptly discovered that the rules that governed their parents' lives did not suit them at all. Freed from one type of anxiety – that their girlfriends would get pregnant and trap them into marriage – by the contraceptive pill, young men with apparently glittering careers in front of them were confronted with new threats: the Cold War, intensified by the Soviet invasion of Hungary in 1956 and the nuclear arms race, and the steadily increasing military involvement of US forces in South-East Asia. American involvement in Vietnam came to appear, on both sides of the Atlantic, as a cynical attempt by men too old to qualify for military service themselves to sacrifice the younger generation in a neo-colonial adventure most of them either knew little about or profoundly disagreed with. In Britain, where the pointless slaughter of the First World War is an extraordinarily potent symbol to this day, there were obvious parallels as US generals hurled reluctant conscripts into a particularly vicious form of warfare and watched them return in body bags. If this represented their parents' moral code, nineteen- and twenty-year-olds concluded that they wanted no part of it. With Harold Wilson's Labour government broadly supporting the American government – though without acceding to its requests to send British troops to South-East Asia – the anti-war movement energized young people on both sides of the Atlantic.

The two rebellions, political and sexual, quickly became entwined, producing famous slogans like 'Make love not war' and 'Girls say yes to boys who say no'. The latter, a direct encouragement to young women, who were not at risk of being drafted, to do their bit by rewarding resisters with sexual favours, is particularly telling. It even resonated (or was exploited) in Britain, where sex was suddenly characterized as a revolutionary act. This explains why one of the most cogent criticisms of the sexual revolution was to emerge not from the ruling class, outraged as it was by free love and fashions in clothes and dress that consciously held up two fingers to military discipline, but from young women. Supposedly comrades in the revolt against bourgeois values, some of them began to realize that the prime movers and the main beneficiaries were one and the same: men. While sharing virtually all of their ideals, they also recognized what was not being addressed: entrenched attitudes that were soon to bring the phrase 'male chauvinist pig' into everyday use. Revolutionary men who talked endlessly about making common cause with the working class saw no contradiction in asking women to make tea; the British underground newspaper *Black Dwarf* did not produce an issue devoted to women's issues until 1969. These were painful experiences for many of the original activists, whose commitment to sexual liberation coexisted with a realization that the pill had not simply empowered women; sometimes its effect was to make it *more* difficult to refuse sex in circumstances where they felt uncertain or equivocal. Fearing an accusation that they were 'uptight' or 'uncool', they lost sight (if they had ever managed to recognize it in the first place) of their own desire, stranded between the uncomprehending disapproval of their parents on the one hand and the insistent demands of their lovers on the other. (Unsurprisingly, for some women these demands became internalized, accounting for the failure decades later of so many prominent American feminists to condemn President Clinton's abusive relationship with Monica Lewinsky; a classic example, we might conclude, of false consciousness.)

The problem with the 1960s, as far as women were concerned, was that it liberated them from the shackles of marriage, but mostly on male terms. Even this was an advance, for Western culture – unlike Islam, which is at least frank in its recognition of female desire and its terror of it – has always been dishonest about female sexuality. While women are supposed to need less sex and fewer lovers than men, they have always been subject to strict rules that limit both choice and opportunity, amounting to a tacit admission that the opposite could just as easily be true. (The latest combatants to join this particular fray are evolutionary psychologists. Comically unable to agree among themselves, they argue about whether women have a lower sex drive or are actually as promiscuous as men, but for a different purpose – trading sex for offspring, food and protection. What they cannot countenance is the possibility that women have sex because they like it.) Natalie Angier identified this paradox in her book *Woman: An Intimate Geography*, listing the restrictions favoured by different societies: 'Women supposedly have a lower sex drive than men do, yet it's never low enough . . . There is still enough lingering female infidelity to justify infibulation, purdah, claustration. Men have the naturally higher sex drive, yet all the laws, customs, punishments, shame, strictures, mystiques, and anti-mystiques are aimed with full hominid fury at that tepid, sleepy, hypoactive creature, the female libido.'

It is a sad fact that the men who made the sexual revolution were not much interested in the unlimited expression of *female* desire – they were men, after all – but capitalized on an iconoclastic atmos-phere and a breakthrough in reproductive technology in ways that suited themselves. This is not to underestimate the achievements of the 1960s, either in political terms (rendering the Vietnam War unwinnable for the Americans) or in challenging the iconic status of marriage and lifelong fidelity. But that the revolution was unfinished in two important respects is undeniable: too little thought was given to what women might want and, with the exception of a few unconvincing attempts at communal living, often modelled on second-hand reports of Israeli *kibbutzim*, to future arrangements for rearing children. These are, from the standpoint of the twenty-first century, astonishing oversights. It is as if the sexual revolution was entirely for the benefit of childless young people, for the students whose anti-war protests and love-ins created its enduring images: hippie girls with painted faces and flowers in their hair, boys model-ling themselves on phallic icons like Jimi Hendrix. It is hardly surpris-ing that the anti-war movement should have concerned itself with short-term aims, but one of the characteristics of the flamboyant sexuality of the period is that it behaved as if no one would ever grow old. Of course, some of them didn't: the premature deaths of Hendrix, Janis Joplin, Jim Morrison of the Doors, Brian Jones of the Rolling Stones and Keith Moon of The Who confirmed the status of the 1960s as a youth cult; they also served as a metaphor for a widespread reluctance, frankly expressed in the lyrics of The Who's 'My Generation', to imagine the future. What would happen to free love when the people who had benefited from it left campuses and student houses, got themselves careers and mortgages, and decided they wanted children? How would they reconcile their belief in the liberating power of sex, which was hardly conducive to an existence of settled monogamy, with the needs of parents and toddlers? In some senses, we are still living out the consequences of those failures of imagination as that generation – publicly represented by Bill and Hillary Clinton, whose marital difficulties are paradigmatic (though in extreme form) of baby-boomers who did not think far enough ahead – reaches middle age.

For the moment, what was clear was that the arrival of reliable contraception had put paid to the constant anxiety women of child-bearing age used to feel about their bodies: the revolution provided the rhetoric, the pill allowed it to be put into practice. Critics might suggest that the result was merely to bring into the open what had hitherto been secret, which is to say male promiscuity, and to allow working-class boys to share the sexual privileges that had always been enjoyed by the ruling class. Yet the pill provided real benefits to women, even if they were sometimes obscured by the excuse it offered men not to worry about contraception, an opportunity most of them jumped at. The technology to prevent unwanted pregnancies, which earlier generations had merely dreamed about, was now a reality – and, crucially, under female control. Rubber condoms had been available for well over a century, but their impact was nothing like as great; their use had in the past been associated with prostitution, they did not provide such a high degree of protection and – a major drawback – they required male cooperation. No longer need women fear, as my paternal grandmother did, the sexual demands of husbands who ignored their protests that they already had too many children (eight surviving infants in her case, plus numerous stillbirths and miscarriages). The long-term impact was truly revolutionary, altering the way women thought about their sexuality, even if they eventually switched to other forms of contraception. Sexual politics, a term that had only just been invented, would never be the same again: whether scientists and drug companies perceived it at the time, it is clear that the chief justification for lifelong fidelity vanished when the first pill prescriptions were handed over the pharmacy counter.

Unless a wife was actively intent upon deceiving her husband, she could now have other sexual partners without the risk of introducing another's man's child into the family unit; unmarried women could have a succession of boyfriends, as discreetly as they liked, without the fear of repeated pregnancies. Why should people of either gender limit themselves, as many women and some men had in the past, to a single partner whose sexual performance remained an unknown quantity until after the marriage vows had been exchanged? Ironically, it was just around this time that the nature of marriage itself was undergoing a significant change, mostly unremarked except in dry statistical tables. Couples who married at the end of the 1960s went through much the same ceremony as earlier generations but faced a radical alteration to the meaning of 'till death us do part'; when they promised to stay together and remain faithful to each other, it might mean for fifty or sixty years, a prospect very different from the one that faced their newly wedded grandparents. The cause was increased longevity, the effect startling: according to Lawrence Stone, the median length of a marriage in England in the seventeenth and eighteenth centuries was between twenty and thirty years for the aristocracy, twenty for the poor, a situation that did not change much until well into the twentieth century. My maternal grandfather, a merchant seaman, died suddenly in 1937 after a minor operation, leaving my grandmother a widow in her early forties, with four school-age children to bring up. The Clintons, by contrast, married in 1975 and celebrated (if that is the right word) their twenty-fifth wedding anniversary when they were in their early fifties, with the prospect of another twenty-five years of each other's company to look forward to.

Just at the moment when the notion of lifelong fidelity to a single partner was coming under ideological challenge, demographics quietly intervened to make traditional marriage seem even more onerous. Yet young women in the sixties and seventies, especially those outside the intellectual and metropolitan elites, were slow to give up the protection marriage seemed to offer, along with its many disadvantages. The pill alone could not remove the stigma that still attached to women who had numerous partners, even among men who regarded themselves as progressive – an injustice that would be addressed by the feminist movement that came into being as a reaction to the masculine bias of the sexual revolution. (In extreme form, this attitude was embodied by a notorious remark made by a Black Panther leader in the US, who claimed that the proper place for women in the revolution was 'on their backs'.) Indeed, some young women found themselves in a new version of the old double bind: pressured by their boyfriends to have sex, but in danger of getting an old-fashioned 'bad' reputation if they complied. 'My awareness of women's subordination arose from the sexual humiliation still evident in terms like "promiscuity", "nymphomaniac" and "slags",' the feminist historian Sheila Rowbotham recalled in her memoir of the 1960s, *Promise of a Dream*. How they could escape from this trap was about to be addressed in a series of groundbreaking texts that created a much more radical discourse than *The Feminine Mystique*, which appeared in 1963 and is widely recognized as the founding text of modern feminism. Its author, Betty Friedan, spoke to a generation of college-educated American women who were already married and living in the suburbs before the upheavals of the 1960s; she denounced what she called their 'mounting sex hunger' in terms that would have struck a chord with supporters of the Victorian social purity movement. Only three years after Friedan burst into print, much more exciting and explicitly political ideas were stirring in Britain, eloquently expressed in Juliet Mitchell's article 'Women: The Longest Revolution' in the *New Left Review*. Germaine Greer, a clever Australian living in the UK, caught the mood of the moment in her book *The Female Eunuch* in 1970, urging women to overcome their inward-directed sexual disgust and famously suggesting that they might consider tasting their own menstrual blood. This was a moment when feminist critiques suddenly seemed to pour out, deconstructing the old morality *and* patriarchy in texts that included *Sexual Politics* by Kate Millett, *The Dialectic of Sex* by Shulamith Firestone and *Patriarchal Attitudes* by Eva Figes. Greer assured her readers: 'Women do have sexual desires and if it is a function of normal mental health development and good breeding to destroy it, let us try some abnormal mental development, rejecting our breeding. If marriage and family depend on the castration of women let them change or disappear.'

The counter-reaction was not long in coming. The Vatican, which was quick to see the implications of both the new reproductive technology and the sexual politics that was beginning to go with it, issued an encyclical, *Humanae Vitae*, in 1968, banning all types of contraception apart from 'natural' (which is to say unreliable) methods such as limiting intercourse to a woman's 'safe' period. What was at stake here, not to put too fine a point on it, was one of the papacy's traditional means of social control: shame. As long as women followed the pontiff's advice and refrained from using effective methods of contraception or abortion, extramarital sex would continue to carry with it the 'punishment' of an unwanted pregnancy. (I heard this link made explicitly when I was promoting the American edition of my book *Misogynies*. During a phone-in on a radio station in Washington DC, an evangelical Christian called to protest that pregnancy was God's way of punishing women for sex outside marriage. He rang off when I asked him why there was no equivalent sanction for men, and whether it was healthy to think about babies in this way.) That the Roman Catholic Church should have taken this line is predictable, given its historical record of misogyny, but it must also have perceived that giving women control over their fertility, in developed countries where the papacy was already losing its authority, would drastically cut the number of children brought up in the faith. The Vatican's continued existence depends on indoctrinating children from a very young age, and it understands the threat posed by congregations limiting the size of their families. In this self-interested sense at least, the papacy was far-sighted, yet it proved unable to enforce its ban on contraception. In Spain and Italy the birth rate eventually fell below replacement level, while Italian voters defied the Pope to support legal abortion and divorce in landmark referenda. In attempting to deny women control of their fertility, the Vatican lost the plot and, in Western Europe, much of its influence.

What does require an explanation is why lifelong monogamy has continued to be promoted as the desirable model for adults. As recently as May 2000, a spokesman for the Archbishop of Canterbury, Dr George Carey, restated the position of the Church of England as follows: 'Lifelong marriage or lifelong celibacy are the two options commended by the Holy Scriptures and by the tradition of the Church.' At one level, this simply illustrates the degree to which Anglicanism has fallen out of step with the way people live, a point forcefully made by the status of its future head, Prince Charles, a divorced man who says he has no plans to marry his current partner, herself a divorcee. Their relationship is one of the few modern things about the Windsors, yet it is still the case that the moral argument for keeping sex inside marriage was revived with renewed force after the 1960s, this time in a form that suggested that restraint was desirable *for its own sake*. Popular culture provided another kind of reinforcement, celebrating romantic love in movies like *Love Story*, the 1970 adaptation of Erich Segal's sentimental novel, which promoted the notion of passion transcending even death. (What gave the book a gloss of modernity was the way in which its much repeated slogan – 'Love means never having to say you're sorry' – validated the hippie mantra of refusing to recognize responsibility for hurting someone else's feelings.) Children whose parents separated and divorced continued to be unusual enough to cause whispered comments, especially if their mother was involved with another man; the old discourse was sufficiently durable for advice about 'saving themselves' for marriage to continue featuring in girls' magazines and parental advice to young women. I remember being puzzled and embarrassed when a schoolfriend's mother warned us both in the early 1970s about not allowing men to 'go too far'; an identical instruction seems to have impressed the future Princess of Wales, Lady Diana Spencer (born in 1961), who told her biographer, Andrew Morton, that she knew she had to preserve her virginity for her future husband. 'She was surrounded,' recalled a friend, 'by this golden aura which stopped men going any further, whether they would have liked to or not, it never happened. She was surrounded somehow by a perfect light.'

Few modern teenagers consider their virginity a route to secular sainthood, even if the revelation that Diana and her inner circle talked in these terms suggests that the quasi-religious fervour that manifested itself after her sudden death should not have been as unexpected as it appeared at the time. Yet we have moved, in a comparatively short number of years, from a situation in which most brides were assumed to be virgins when they married, as Diana Spencer's uncle egregiously certified her to be at the time of her engagement in 1981, to one in which some sexual experience is taken for granted in young adults. It is not so long since older women talked disapprovingly of brides who were 'not entitled' to wear white, such an otiose requirement that it is hard to believe it was ever taken seriously. (Another friend of mine, who left college in her first term when she discovered she was pregnant, bowed to her family's wishes and wore a lemon-yellow dress at her hastily arranged wedding.) These days, it is not uncommon for the ceremony – if there is one at all – to follow a period of cohabitation, perhaps even the birth of a child, as was famously the case of the pop star Victoria Adams and her footballer boyfriend, David Beckham, in 1999. These relaxed attitudes owe everything to the 1960s, even if, like many feminist theories, they have become so mainstream as to obscure their origins. That they were once part of an experiment, and one that did not always run smoothly, is reflected in a section of Rowbotham's memoir in which she discusses her relationship with her then partner: 'We had both found that our relationship did not preclude being attracted to other people – but that we still wanted to stay together. We had not explicitly called it an "open relationship", but the idea was already around on the left. This was to work all right in practice, but sometimes the emotions got more bumpy than our rational calculations had assumed they would.' Open relationships have been much mocked, mainly on the grounds that they were so often asymmetrical – a licence for one partner, not always the man, to be promiscuous while the other suffered in silence. They were also easier to maintain in a pool of young adults, most of them unmarried and without children, than for people who had reached their thirties and forties and had young families. What they have developed into in the twenty-first century is, for many adults, one form or another of serial monogamy: an acknowledgement that desire cannot and should not be limited to a single relationship, replaceable only when one partner dies.

In that sense, the lives of millions of ordinary people have outpaced public discourse, creating anomalies and inconsistencies that have not fully been faced. This is in part due to the continued existence of an established Church, and its disproportionate influence on ceremony and ritual, even though the vast majority of us do not belong to it. In the year 2000, the number of people attending Anglican services each Sunday fell below one million, in a population of 60 million. Those couples who still choose to get married in Britain, a little under 300,000 a year, commit themselves to a lifelong relationship, and there is no reason to believe that the aspiration, in the majority of cases, is anything other than sincere. But nearly half of them break their promise, and the marriage ends in separation and divorce; an unquantifiable number remain married but commit adultery, to use an old-fashioned term, and conceal the deception from their spouses. Is this immoral behaviour? Or evidence that the unrealistic expectations that remain an integral part of marriage make hypocrites of us all?

In recent years, there have been attempts to reconsider both ceremony and structure, so that weddings may now take place outside churches and register offices, while the left-leaning think-tank, Demos, has come up with a proposal for ten-year renewable marriage contracts. That this debate has been so long in coming is astonishing; we are only just catching up with Freud, who recognized the innate instability of monogamy in the first half of the twentieth century. 'As a rule, second marriages turn out better,' he observed coolly in 1931, flying in the face of not just Christian doctrine but Platonic philosophy, which characterized the search for love as a quest for each person's missing half, and was thus the origin of the romantic notion that there is just one Mr or Miss Right for everyone. But what made Freud's thinking on this subject so advanced was the way in which, as early as 1908, he understood that the conventional morality that demanded sexual fidelity was merely a cover for hypocrisy and social control. In an essay provocatively entitled ' "Civilized" Sexual Morality and Modern Nervous Illness', he went so far as to suggest that the former, far from being beneficial, was a significant cause of the latter. He considered the prohibition on sex outside marriage unworkable, condemning couples to 'spiritual disillusionment and bodily deprivation', a gloomy prospect that men were allowed to compensate for through the double standard. For women, Freud believed, the outcome of monogamy was even worse, its disappointments causing 'severe neuroses which permanently darken their lives'. A young woman had to be 'very healthy if she is to be able to tolerate [marriage], and we urgently advise our male patients not to marry any girl who has had nervous trouble' before the engagement.

The bleakness of Freud's vision is startling, and almost certainly influenced by his own frustration as a middle-class husband and father of six children. Free of religious superstition, unlike most of his peers, he was able to acknowledge the pivotal role of desire among human emotions, the damage created by its repression and the hypocrisy that demanded that denial. His pessimism stems, in part, from his recognition that the only solution he could think of, safe and 'dignified' contraception, was still several decades away, but he was not prepared to subscribe to the fiction that monogamy is either natural or easy to sustain. What he could not foresee was that the pill would arrive at a moment when the status of women was undergoing rapid change, hugely complicating the picture. Its development in the post-war period coincided with an alteration in the economic conditions of women, dramatically enlarging their choices; no longer entirely dependent on their husbands, they also benefited from an expansion of the welfare state that transformed the prospects even of non-working wives whose marriages had broken down.

The change in outlook, in a relatively short space of time, is startling. If we track female self-esteem through popular culture, it moves from the swooning, masochistic lyrics sung by Dusty Springfield in the 1960s – 'You Don't Have to Say You Love Me' and 'I Just Don't Know What to Do with Myself' – to the self-confident declarations of Madonna and Macy Gray in the final decades of the twentieth century. What their songs reflect, among other innovations, is a willingness to make sexual and emotional demands and a readiness to strike out alone, if necessary; Whitney Houston declared that 'I'd rather be alone than unhappy' in her eve-of-millennium hit, 'It's Not Right, But It's Okay'. By the end of the 1980s, according to government figures that turned conventional wisdom on its head, three quarters of the fast-rising divorce rate in Britain was accounted for by wives seeking to end unsatisfactory marriages; there is no doubt that the figure revealed discontent with those men who remain untouched by the discourse of feminism and its reordering of domestic life. In that sense, the popularity of Princess Diana is explained in no small degree by identification: her biography – love, marriage, betrayal, disillusionment and divorce, followed by a dramatic reinvention of the self – assumed the role of ur-story for millions of women who observed it unfold with intense interest.

Sensibly, some of the organizations that used to offer marriage guidance have begun to offer a service that helps couples to decide whether they want to stay together, in an attempt to reduce the acrimony that often accompanies the breakdown of a relationship. This is a big step forward: we have ample evidence that serial monogamy is not just the last resort of the discontented but a recognition of the role played by passion, love and novelty in human existence. What is astonishing is that these were ever regarded as moral issues at all, as though restricting sexual relations to one other person was somehow a reliable index of goodness. Some of the wickedest people to influence the course of the twentieth century were happily married and, as far as we know, monogamous: Pinochet, Enver Hoxha, Nicolae Ceaușescu. Coercive sex is, rightly, a crime, whether it takes the form of rape or trafficking in women from Eastern Europe, many of whom are deceived into prostitution or forced into it by poverty. But most of us are not vengeful dictators, serial killers or intent on deliberately defrauding our partners; how we order our private lives – who we have sex with, who we live with, and for how long – has nothing to with Manichaean notions of good and evil. (Indeed, I would argue that the Vatican's obsession with sex as the locus of morality has led it into an indefensible and deeply immoral position on AIDS; its continuing refusal to countenance the use of condoms is, in Catholic countries where HIV is prevalent, tantamount to a death sentence.) Human emotions change over time; few of us have the same best friend throughout the course of our lives; our feelings towards siblings and parents alter, much as we would like them to stay the same; so, if we are honest, do our feelings towards lovers and spouses. This is not to undervalue the power of love; on the contrary, it acknowledges both its importance and the fact that most of us experience it more than once in our lives. This has always been recognized, in limited form, insofar as widows and widowers have been allowed to remarry even in non-divorcing societies, for companionship in old age but also for love. Some individuals do remain in love with one person throughout their lives, forswearing all others even if the object of their affections dies or is otherwise unavailable. Even so, the extent to which this is a voluntary choice has been exaggerated; many of the women who did not marry after the First World War had no alternative, as a consequence of the acute shortage of marriageable men caused by the conflict. But love and passion are for the most part involuntary, which is one of the reasons they continue to fascinate and astonish us, and to inspire novels, songs, poetry and plays as well. It is completely illogical, in the circumstances, to suggest that a monogamist is morally superior to someone who has had more than one passionate relationship in the course of his or her adult life.

On the contrary, the dishonesty about sex and love that was imposed on us until very recently has had dire consequences, ensuring that marriages end in a welter of guilt and recriminations that sour future contact and turn joint responsibilities towards children into a battleground. A culture that denies adults the right to separate, morally if not legally, also denies them mechanisms for doing so; friends and family, invited to witness a couple's public commitment to one another in the first place, often act unthinkingly as society's enforcers, urging the couple to 'try again' or 'think of the children'. These exhortations raise a vitally important point, the welfare of children when their parents divorce or separate, though not in the sense that is usually intended. We are only just beginning to acknowledge that there is a far more cogent argument for asking people to make long-term commitments to their *children* than for trying to make reluctant adults stay together. What this requires, in Maureen Freely's incisive phrase, is 'a separation of our attitudes about marriage and our attitudes about parenthood'. This is particularly timely in Western Europe, at a moment in history when a substantial number of people are deciding against or unable to have children; in future, it seems likely that adults will have different kinds of relationships in the course of their lives, some involving children and others not. It could be argued that, for too long, our culture's obsession with relationships between adults, formal marriage and the attendant horror of divorce (or separation in the case of couples who live together) has actively worked against making proper arrangements for children. When couples do not know how to part honourably and are encouraged to blame each other even by well-meaning friends and family, it is hardly surprising if their future relations as joint parents, rather than present spouses, do not receive sufficient attention. Yet that is where their moral obligation lies: it is perfectly reasonable to insist that parents take responsibility for sons and daughters at least until they are grown up, whether this is done through formal contracts, in which each parent undertakes to do certain things, or informal agreements. It is almost certainly the case that many separating parents would welcome the clarity this would bring to their circumstances; most of us know couples who have split up, and in some cases moved into new relationships, yet made amicable arrangements for joint care of their children. The nexus of step-families that is thus created resembles a pattern familiar in the nineteenth century, except that second and even third families now come about more often through choice, not accident or premature death.

The alternative is to make divorce more difficult and force couples to stay together, what the conservative commentator Melanie Phillips calls 'putting muscle back into marriage'. In some cases this is literally what happens when relationships go wrong: one in four British women, according to a government survey published in 1999, have been physically assaulted by their partners; two women a week are murdered by current or previous partners. The silence on this subject has been broken only recently, when campaigners for abused women persuaded a series of well-known figures, including the Labour MP Glenda Jackson and Sheryl Gascoigne, ex-wife of the footballer Paul Gascoigne, to speak in public about the violence they had experienced from partners. The boxer Frank Bruno, the former England cricketer Geoffrey Boycott and several prominent footballers have been accused of beating up their wives or girlfriends; Boycott lost his appeal in a French court against his conviction for assaulting an ex-lover.

Is this what we want to return to? A situation where a wife (or indeed a husband) has to plead with a judge to escape from a miserable and possibly violent relationship? There can be little doubt that the pressure on couples to remain together makes the situation worse, delaying a separation until tempers are running dangerously high. A more serious objection to serial monogamy, made by some feminists as well as conservative theorists, is that it works to the advantage of men. The statistics suggest there is some truth in this argument: men seem to find it easier to remarry than women, with

36.2 per cent of widowed and divorced men going on to marry again, compared with 17.8 per cent of women. While some of those women may choose to remain single, the figures reflect an imbalance in the population: in 1996, the latest year for which figures are available at the time of writing, divorced women outnumbered divorced men at every age; by the time they reach 65, there are around 125 divorced women for every 100 divorced men. This is explained, in part, by the freedom men have to seek out younger partners, although there is scant evidence for the popular view that this preference is biologically determined. Both sexes are attracted by youth and beauty, but men have at present the advantage of greater prestige and resources, allowing them to make this choice even though it tends to be the case that many women age better – another blow for conventional wisdom, which holds that the opposite is true and has not yet recognized this egregious example of male projection. It is a striking fact that successful women, from Mae West and Georgia O'Keeffe to Madonna, choose younger men as their partners, a route that more women would follow if they could.

Another inequality between the sexes is expressed in what we might call the numbers game, especially in tabloid culture. That celebrities like Mick Jagger are regarded with awe and envy for their supposed tally of lovers is nothing new; the tradition stretches back to Mozart's *Don Giovanni*, in which Leporello's famous solo 'Il catalogo è questo' celebrates his master's conquests. But a thicket of pejorative language lies in wait for any woman who replicates this behaviour: 'slapper', 'dog', 'slag', 'bitch' and the ubiquitous rap insult 'ho' (whore). When the Singaporean actress Grace Quek went to Hollywood and reinvented herself as the porn star Annabel Chong, she quickly became infamous for a video in which she had sex 251 times in 10 hours, a marathon that would have drawn admiring gasps if the genders were reversed. Even when she subsequently made a frank and by all accounts harrowing film exposing the porn trade, Quek was dismissed as pathetic and self-deluding; in a final insult, the documentary was unfavourably compared to *Boogie*

Nights, the cheerless commercial blue movie about a male porn star with an unusually large penis.

What can we do about this? Turning the clock back is neither a serious nor a desirable option, even though centuries of prejudice about female sexuality and women's role in the family is not going to disappear overnight. We are in a transitional period, which is rarely a comfortable experience, but we should not be frightened into thinking that the old certainties or present imperfections are our only choices. In the short term, it would help if government ministers admitted that much of their rhetoric about family life is grounded not in morality but economics. The nuclear family is a stable, attractive unit in terms of tax and benefits, keeping down the cost of a welfare system that otherwise has to support single parents and their children. It is understandable that in Britain, where a third of annual government expenditure is absorbed by the social security system, Chancellors of the Exchequer should regard it nostalgically. Yet single parenthood cannot be wished away. Between 1971 and 1994 the proportion of families headed by a lone mother in Britain rose from 7 per cent to 20 per cent. Nearly two fifths were single, and around the same number were divorced. There is no question that declining rates of marriage, single parenthood and the growing number of never-married people in the population – in London, for example, around a third of the city's inhabitants are single – also lead to higher housing demand and duplication of resources.

One long-term goal must be to ensure that both parents take the needs of existing children into account before producing second families. The Child Support Agency was set up to tackle the problem of parents, most of them fathers, who are unable or unwilling to support their children when they move on to a new relationship, but its adversarial style and notorious incompetence have done little to change cultural attitudes, or to benefit single parents rather than the Exchequer. But there are steps that could be taken to help existing lone-parent families, beginning with a concerted attempt to address the scandal of discrimination in the workplace, which means that any family with a female breadwinner is at an automatic disadvantage. The differential is startling: average gross earnings for men in full-time work in April 1999 were £23,000 a year, and only £16,000 for women, giving men a substantial financial advantage. By the middle of the 1990s nearly two thirds of single parents lived in rented accommodation, indicating that they could not afford or were unable to get a mortgage, compared with only a quarter of other families with dependent children. There is a startling correlation between poor exam performance and families (single and two-parent) with low incomes: in 1998 only a fifth of children whose parents were in unskilled manual occupations got five GCSE passes at grades A to C, compared with two thirds of children from professional and managerial classes. This is bad news for the three million children who, according to a government report published in May 2000, live below the poverty line in Britain. It should also be borne in mind when considering what to do about the country's high rate of teenage pregnancy, the worst in Europe, which is not evidence of rampant immorality but of social deprivation, low self-esteem and the bleak expectations of teenage girls from poor working-class families. Fourteen-year-olds tend to have babies either as a result of ignorance – not knowing about contraception or how to use it effectively – or because they cannot realistically imagine any other role for themselves.

Ignoring the link between single parenthood and poverty is akin to arguing, after the American Civil War, that black people were better off under slavery. Eradicate bad housing, insist on equal pay, improve state education, encourage the ambitions of school leavers, and single parenthood might take on a less alarming hue. But the really important point is that what is often characterized as 'family breakdown' is actually something else entirely: a stage in the process of redefining the family. We are evolving new forms of living together, a fact obscured by the distorting effect of poverty and its disproportionate impact on single-parent families. All around us, people have already begun to create new webs of relationships and obligations, which is why I remarked at the beginning of this chapter that the sexual revolution that started in the 1960s was still working itself out. It has taken years to think about where women and children fit into that framework, and begin to adjust it where we perceive it to have failed. We hear so much about the problems associated with divorce and serial relationships that it is easy to forget that we have come a very long way in four decades, liberating love and sex from an inflexible structure whose terms were handed down from above. We have come to understand that how we organize our relations with other adults is not a moral question, as our parents and grandparents were led to believe, but a practical one, as long as the needs of children are given due weight. That women are having to do this in circumstances that mean they are sometimes at a disadvantage is undeniable, but it is no more than an argument for further change. The old double standards are being abandoned and replaced with a recognition of the importance of passion between adults and its unpredictability. It is a triumph for honesty and the human spirit over the ingrained hypocrisy of a morally bankrupt *ancien régime*.

8

Globalize This!

This is no longer about left versus right; it's about the bottom against the top. — PROTESTER AT WTO SUMMIT, SEATTLE

Not since the student demonstrations of 1968 has the arrogance of power been so boldly confronted.
— HILARY WAINWRIGHT

If you want to change the world, you have first to be able to imagine it. — MICHÈLE ROBERTS

It took almost everyone by surprise, including politicians and the media. When world leaders arrived in Seattle for a routine summit of the World Trade Organization, scheduled to start on 30 November 1999, they had little idea that thousands of protesters were converging on the city with a very different purpose in mind. The WTO is a relatively new organization, set up in 1995 to replace the General Agreement on Tariffs and Trade, and it is a fair bet that there were millions of people around the world who, until Seattle, would not have been able even to say what its initials stand for. So where did it come from, this colourful and unexpected explosion of anger? There was no simple answer to this question, as demonstrators with the broadest of aims, nothing less than to bring down capitalism, marched shoulder to shoulder with trade unionists who were worried about the effect of foreign imports on their jobs, greens protesting about the impact of free trade on the environment, and people from developing countries who saw attempts to bring their working hours and conditions into line with the prosperous North as a backdoor method of taxation. The protesters' targets included cruel methods of farming, the fur trade, damage to rainforests, sea pollution and over-fishing, genetically modified food, the EU's agricultural policy, US domination of the trade talks and, incongruously, the Starbucks coffee chain, a rapidly expanding company whose innocent-sounding mission to deliver *caffè latte* to the masses suddenly came to symbolize the globalizing tendencies of American culture. If the world leaders huddled inside the conference centre were astonished by the vehemence of the protests – those who managed to get there in their environmentally unfriendly limousines, that is, as the streets of downtown Seattle came to a complete halt – so were viewers around the world, watching the amazing scenes on their television screens. Was capitalism more vulnerable than anyone had previously imagined, especially coming so soon after the supposedly invincible tiger economies of Asia found themselves in deep trouble only a couple of years before?

As well as the events in Seattle, there were smaller N30 demonstrations – the abbreviation derived from the date – in France, India and Australia. In London, fighting between police and demonstrators erupted outside Euston Station, prompting fears of civil disobedience on a scale not seen in Britain since the poll tax riots in 1990. But the most eye-catching scenes were staged, deliberately and after months of planning, outside the WTO Summit. It was a carnival of protest in which the more imaginative demonstrators dressed up as undertakers bearing the coffin of world humanity, murdered by corporate greed; Lesbian Avengers marched bare-chested with slogans scrawled on their bodies; and animal rights activists paraded in sea-turtle costumes, complaining that a recent WTO ruling on fishing nets threatened the amphibians with extinction. They talked to anyone who would listen about liberty, democracy, human rights and the global damage inflicted by the WTO's single-minded commitment to getting rid of barriers to trade, offering what was, in effect, a crash course in how this previously obscure organization affects our everyday lives.

They pointed out that unelected members of its panels have the power to overturn decisions taken by elected governments, as they did in 1998 when EU countries were compelled to accept American hormone-treated beef; the EU had banned the use of synthetic hormones thirteen years before on health grounds, a prohibition confirmed in 1996 by a unanimous vote in the European Parliament, but member governments had no choice but to comply with the ruling. They talked about the organization's indifference to the suffering of animals, recalling that in 1997 the EU had to drop its proposed bans on cosmetics tested on animals and fur from wild animals caught in barbaric legtraps; these prohibitions would have been contrary to WTO rules. Nor, said the protesters, would the EU be able to ban cheap imports of eggs from battery chickens in the US if it went ahead with a ban on battery cages in its own territories. Meanwhile human rights campaigners expressed their alarm over the WTO's opposition to economic sanctions, claiming that the international boycott that helped overturn the apartheid regime in South Africa would be illegal today. 'The WTO speaks only for corporations and has become a global coup against democracy,' declared People for Fair Trade, one of the groups that coordinated the demonstrations. 'It is the dismantling of democracy disguised as a trade pact.'

'All the WTO's money and power and influence wasn't enough to move all those concerned, committed people out of the way,' declared Sam Corl, designer of a website set up by the Ruckus Society, a group of environmentalists from Berkeley, California – once the hub of 1960s student activism and the anti-war movement – who train volunteers in non-violent direct action. Yet there were also disagreements among the demonstrators, highlighting the inevitable contradictions within such a heterogeneous movement; the battles were not just between North and South, although that was one of the most significant schisms, but between groups with conflicting agendas. This state of affairs was dramatically enacted in front of the cameras when angry American steelworkers dumped foreign imports in the harbour and green activists promptly rushed to fish them out. There was anxiety too about the violent attacks on property carried out by a minority of demonstrators, which threatened to undermine the stunning overall success of the protest. But when the city authorities responded by sending heavily armed 'Robocops' on to the streets to tackle peaceful protesters as well as looters, they handed a propaganda triumph to their opponents.

The police had by then, it is safe to assume, accessed the main N30 website, with its clarion call: 'May our resistance be as transnational as capital.' Perhaps influenced by Marx's famous observation that capital has no country, the demonstrations were living proof of an emerging politics that insists that, if the authoritarian tendencies of multinational corporations and their client governments are to be resisted, the movement against them also has to be international. This was certainly true of the way the Battle of Seattle, as it came to be known, was organized; it was both a model for future actions – notably at the EU summit in Gothenburg in June 2001, and the G8 meeting in Genoa a month later – and a warning to police, elected governments and authoritarian regimes alike of what they are up against. The principal tool in the run-up to the summit was the internet, as 1,200 groups from 85 countries drew up a manifesto calling for a moratorium on any further dismantling of trade barriers. The degree of organization was formidable, with websites offering not just details of where and when to assemble but lists of hotels near the convention centre that offered group discounts. Others displayed a map of the world, inviting protesters to click on individual countries to find out the time and location of smaller events, saving huge amounts of money on international telephone calls. While the cyberspace slogans of groups like Anarchy Now! inevitably caught the attention of the media, much of the planning was done quietly by lobby groups based in Washington and Geneva, turning information technology, which has done so much to foster globalization, into a formidable weapon *against* capitalism. Twenty months later, when Italian police raided the Diaz school in Genoa, arresting and beating up protestors, news and pictures of the event were on the internet within hours, placed there by a collective of independent journalists and film-makers calling themselves Italia Indymedia. Their reports prompted protests from foreign governments and criticism of the police action by Italian magistrates. No wonder governments around the world have become increasingly jumpy about the potential of a medium that allows people who are geographically dispersed to communicate – to warn, inform and set up actions – with each other in seconds. Some brutal regimes, notably China and Saudi Arabia, are trying to limit access to the internet in a blatant attempt to control dissent – in the Saudi case, supposedly in order to ban 'material that corrupts or harms our Muslim values, tradition, and culture', but actually to protect one of the most secretive and authoritarian governments in the modern world. Even in Britain, a Labour government officially committed to freedom of information quickly set about passing legislation compelling internet service providers to install technology that would allow the security services to monitor and read private and company e-mails, a measure condemned in the normally restrained *Financial Times* as a power 'that Joseph Stalin would have used with relish'. It announced in November 2001 that the Freedom of Information Act, described by a Tory MP as 'feeble', would not be implemented until January 2005, more than four years after it reached the statute book.

What are they so afraid of, the people who govern us? The realization, most likely, that millions of us believe we have been let down; that even in countries with elected governments, and leaders who declare themselves practising Christians, the rich go on getting richer and big business calls the shots. Traditional morality has done little to prevent this redistribution of wealth in the wrong direction: as recently as June 2000 the World Health Organization confirmed that the gap between rich and poor is widening. The transfer of money and resources from the bottom to the top, and from South to North, was a global phenomenon in the final decades of the twentieth century: in 1960 the gap in terms of wealth between the world's top 20 per cent and bottom 20 per cent was 30-fold; four decades later it is more than 75-fold. The new millennium opened shamefully with 1.2 billion people, a fifth of the world's population, living in poverty. Protesters picked on the WTO to highlight this injustice because its commitment to free trade is all too likely to increase the gap; it is globalization writ large, in theory no more than the collective will of its 134 members but dominated, in practice, by the US, the EU and Japan. At Seattle this conflict came into the open when India's Minister of Commerce protested that his country and others from the developing world were being excluded from key rounds of negotiations. Slow to recognize what was going on, the Americans had arrived at the summit with a controversial, self-interested agenda and, tactlessly, a negotiating team that included more lawyers than are to be found in some developing countries. One of their aims was to head off any attempt to regulate the trade in GM organisms, which the US bio-tech industry has invested in so heavily, by opposing a Biosafety Protocol that would permit individual governments to ban food imports if they believed they posed a danger to health. And the Americans might well have got their way, if the protests outside the hall had not led to the summit being abandoned: round one to the demonstrators.

It is becoming clear that the WTO has fallen foul of a new kind of movement, one that draws its inspiration and tactics not from conventional political parties but from pressure groups, single-issue campaigns and grass-roots protests. Some of its components have been visible since the 1980s, principally in the form of the green parties that flourished across Western Europe, especially in Germany, where they achieved a remarkable degree of electoral success; in the US the Green Party candidate in the 2000 presidential election, Ralph Nader – consumer advocate turned environmentalist – polled as high as 9 per cent in key western states such as California during the campaign, sufficient to alarm the Democrats' candidate, the then Vice-President Al Gore, who paraded his own green credentials at every opportunity. Other recruits cut their teeth on local projects, campaigning against nuclear bases or raising money to support the population of occupied East Timor; lobbying the manufacturers of powdered milk to cut back on exports to developing countries or trying to prevent the construction of a bypass in an area of outstanding natural beauty; they have often attracted scorn from sections of the media, who have characterized individual protesters as 'tree-huggers', New Age travellers or impractical idealists. The events at Seattle, however, marked the moment that these disparate campaigns finally appeared to cohere against a common enemy, revealing the extent to which they have both a common agenda and a set of ethical standards that stand in opposition to free-market forces. Their determination and tactics alarmed governments and large corporations, which are used to riding rough-shod over what they have always regarded as crackpot obsessions; both ministers and the tycoons who run multinational companies have suddenly realized they might have to take the challenge seriously, or at least give the appearance of doing so. This development was all the more unexpected because one of the distinguishing features of the protest movement is a passionate involvement with issues that old-fashioned politicians have mostly failed to identify, or have begun to address belatedly, even on the Left. It is impossible to imagine Mrs Thatcher (as she then was) wasting much time on measures to protect the ozone layer, let alone worrying about the fate of wild animals, even though opinion polls have since demonstrated overwhelming public support for a ban on hunting with dogs. Previous Prime Ministers, including the 1960s Labour leader Harold Wilson, were too easily seduced by new technology – or, to be fair, did not have access to the kind of information about damage to the planet that is now available to any literate citizen. These days, by contrast, British politicians such as Michael Meacher and John Gummer have been trying to place the environment at the top of the agenda, especially since the Kyoto Summit; in June 2000 Meacher welcomed a report by a royal commission on environmental pollution that recommended a 60 per cent cut in carbon dioxide emissions in the UK over the next half century. This would require drastic changes to how we live, including a carbon tax on energy to reduce demand for electricity and a much greater reliance on wind, solar and wave power. It is a challenge to individuals as much as government, especially in view of the latter's reluctance to make ordinary people face the stark truth about the damage done by emissions from private cars to human beings and the environment; the haze of pollution visible on certain days over big cities is its visible product and the cause of many premature deaths from respiratory disease. The British government's own White Paper, *A New Deal for Transport*, admitted that 'up to 24,000 vulnerable people are estimated to die prematurely each year, and similar numbers are admitted to hospital, because of exposure to air pollution, much of which is due to road traffic'. Ministers have not, thus far, shown much appetite for taking the measures necessary to bring down these shocking figures, and even appeared reluctant to justify high rates of fuel tax when confronted by angry demonstrators in September 2000. But Sir Tom Blundell, Chair of the Royal Commission on Environmental Pollution, declared starkly: 'Recklessly causing large-scale disruption to climate by burning fossil fuels will affect all countries. It is the poorest that would suffer most. We cannot expect other nations to do their part in countering this threat – least of all if they are much less wealthy – unless we demonstrate we are serious about it.'

Such statements are in dramatic contrast to what is happening in the US, where energy is still regarded as cheap and plentiful. Successive American governments have shied away from the problem, allowing petrol prices to remain absurdly low and doing little to encourage cuts in its use; the country lacks the kind of public transport system necessary to change people's habits, and shows no sign of trying to develop one. It is only very recently that a handful of commentators have begun to question the political consequences – especially in the Middle East – of America's dependence on oil. Al Gore's commitment to green issues did not preclude his serving as Vice-President in an administration that, even after Seattle, continued to oppose restrictions on GM foods; the US fought a fierce rearguard action against the Biodiversity Protocol but lost the argument when, at a meeting in Montreal on 29 January 2000, more than 130 nations signed the historic document: round two to the demonstrators. Five months later, the WTO upheld a French ban on asbestos imports from Canada, the first time in more than 200 trade disputes that it refrained from striking down measures to protect the health of humans or animals. The EU, which represented the French government, claimed that asbestos exposure killed 2,000 people in France each year and thousands more across Europe. Canada complained that the ruling would damage its £75m asbestos industry, which employs 2,500 people in Quebec, but it was welcomed as a landmark by the WTO's critics. It showed, they said, that the organization was no longer overriding environmental and public health concerns in the name of free trade: round three to the protesters.

Yet what is going on here is not simply a struggle between the free market and protectionism, or between wealth and poverty, although it has elements of both. It is about the very nature of freedom, a moral debate in which the definition imposed from above by the strident capitalism of the 1980s – Reaganomics in the US, Thatcherism in Britain – is finally being challenged from below. It is not merely a matter of the old Left finally beginning to regain its confidence after years in the wilderness, although that is happening, but of thinking in new ways and listening to new voices, whether they belong to human rights campaigners, animal rights activists or ethnic minorities whose claims have previously been ignored. The language too is fresh and invigorating, not an exchange of insults between Left and Right but a debate about universal standards and how they should be applied around the world. The overarching philosophy is that the 'freedom' trumpeted by Western leaders in the second half of the twentieth century was little more in practice than an absence of restraint on capital: a licence for rich men (and a few women) to get even richer by moving money about, exploiting vulnerable labour forces and irreplaceable natural resources, and then abandoning them to suffer the consequences. The victims of the free-market economy are to be found at Bhopal in India, at Seveso in Italy, in the uranium mines of Namibia, in the opium fields of Afghanistan, in sweatshops in the East End of London, in mass graves in East Timor and other outposts of the crumbling Indonesian empire, in the asbestos mines of South Africa and the diamond fields of Sierra Leone; anywhere in the world, in fact, where the opportunity to make money has been placed above all other considerations. It is a specious doctrine whose effect has been to *restrict* the liberty and rights of human and non-human species all over the globe.

Ironies, we are beginning to see, abound in this upside-down universe. As trade barriers tumble, the governments of affluent countries are struggling to close their doors to immigrants and asylum-seekers, even from regimes as repressive as China and Iraq; the developed world demands the freedom to buy cheap goods from the Indian subcontinent, but erects insurmountable barriers against the people who make them at a fraction of European or American wages. The middle classes in developed countries are discovering the freedom to work on short-term contracts, without pensions or sick pay, and for unsocial hours that damage private life. Around the world, 250 million children aged between five and fourteen have the freedom to work and support their families, instead of going to school and enjoying a normal childhood. In Central and Eastern Europe, recently privatized industries, often owned by members of a gangster mafia, have the freedom to pollute the environment but ordinary people do not have a corresponding freedom not to drink contaminated water or breathe filthy air. In supposedly civilized countries, human beings have the freedom to experiment on monkeys, cats and dogs, sometimes merely to protect consumers from irritating ingredients in cosmetics, while the subjects of these experiments have no rights at all. Wild animals, even our closest relatives such as bonobos and chimpanzees, have the freedom to live in smaller and smaller areas as their natural habitat is destroyed and their numbers are decimated by the trade in bush meat. And we have all experienced the freedom to live in a world whose existence is threatened by nuclear weapons, while a flourishing trade in Western-produced arms kept dictators like ex-President Soeharto of Indonesia in power for decades and has encouraged mutually hostile neighbours, such as India and Pakistan, to develop nuclear missiles.

The result may be a 'free' world, in the narrow sense employed by right-wing economists, but it is neither stable nor just. If its critics appear to have a huge and ambitious agenda, nothing less than an attempt to redraw the moral atlas, then that reflects the scale of the problems they are addressing – and marks a significant break with the legitimized greed and political pessimism of the late twentieth century. In the run-up to Seattle, organizers of the N30 protest demanded an audit of the WTO's impact on marginalized communities, democracy, the environment, health and human rights – a rollcall, in effect, of people and concepts that were overlooked during the developed countries' love affair with the free market. Add animal rights to the list and it becomes a manifesto on behalf of the disenfranchised and the dispossessed, a coming-together of causes that itself represents a kind of globalization, although not one that CEOs of multinational corporations would welcome or comprehend.

We are entering a world in which all kind of groups have themselves broken a long silence, emerging as advocates for causes that were not recognized or taken seriously a couple of decades ago. In the US and Western Europe the disabled are lobbying governments and claiming rights, instead of meekly accepting the largesse of well-meaning benefactors who think they know what is best for them. In Russia and Ukraine, law students are helping the residents of resort towns on the Black Sea to bring court cases against polluters, the power stations and sewage-treatment plants that pump radionuclides and human waste into their traditional fishing grounds. In Britain anxiety about cross-pollination from GM crops, which may introduce artificially modified genes into the wider environment, has prompted Greenpeace and other campaigners to take direct action on farms where trials are being carried out. In Italy, where opposition to capital punishment is particularly strong, protesters in Rome have taken to illuminating the Colosseum every time a death sentence is commuted or overturned in the US. One American on death row, Joseph R. O'Dell III, was adopted by the city of Palermo in Sicily and his body flown there for burial after the sentence was carried out in 1997; his tombstone records that he was 'killed by Virginia, USA, in a merciless and brutal justice system'. In Australia the government is finally returning vast tracts of land to the aborigines who were brusquely evicted from it by the first white settlers, although its policy towards refugees has attracted world-wide criticism. In East Timor the inhabitants are struggling to re-create civil society after twenty-four years of brutal occupation by the Indonesian Army, which burned and looted as it withdrew in 1999 in the wake of a historic referendum in which the population voted overwhelmingly for freedom. Some of these causes have already struck a chord around the world, while others are at first sight strange and unfamiliar to anyone who has not heard the arguments. The Great Ape Project challenges the very notion of what it is to be human; it demands civil rights – the right to life, and freedom from cruel, unnecessary experiments and degrading treatment – for primates such as chimpanzees and bonobos, which share almost 99 per cent of our genes and display the intelligence of a four-year-old human child. Supporters of animal rights have produced horrifying accounts of experiments conducted on live animals in American laboratories, including chimpanzees deliber-ately infected with diseases such as hepatitis C and different strains of HIV; some of these apes grew up in captivity with more benign owners, who taught them sign language and, disastrously, to trust human beings. The primatologist Jane Goodall, who has studied the primates for many years at the Gombe Reserve in Tanzania, describes chimpanzees as 'beings who look into mirrors and see themselves as individuals, who mourn companions and may die of grief, who have a consciousness of "self". Don't they deserve to be treated with the same sort of consideration we accord to other highly sensitive beings – ourselves?' An American lawyer, Steven Wise, who teaches animal rights law at Harvard, argues that just as human beings – aborigines, European Jews, Rwandan Tutsis and Burundian Hutus – become victims of genocide when their rights are ignored, so do animals, often to the point of extinction. 'The entitlement of chimpanzees and bonobos to fundamental legal rights will mark a huge step toward stopping our unfettered abuse of them, just as human rights

marked a milepost in stopping our abuse of each other,' he has
written. (These advocates of animal rights should not be confused
with the movement's fringe, where a passion for animals appears to
coexist with a virulent misanthropy, to the point of threatening
scientists who experiment on them with death.) What these campaigns have in common is the priority they give to rights rather than
profits, conservation rather than exploitation, self-determination
rather than lives directed (and ruined) by the whims of dictators or
their twenty-first-century analogue, the billionaires whose individual
wealth exceeds the gross national product of many poor countries.
That they are not voices crying in the wilderness can be seen by some
early successes, such as the Jubilee 2000 campaign to reduce the
indebtedness of developing countries, even if the promised relief has
been too slow in coming. The British Chancellor of the Exchequer,
Gordon Brown, promised in September 1999 that it would happen
in a matter of weeks, but nine months later only five countries –
Uganda, Bolivia, Mozambique, Tanzania and Mauritania – had
received any relief at all; Tanzania had had its annual debt payment
of £162m cut to £150m, a reduction of only £12m, and no country
had seen its entire debt cancelled. In the US, Congress was severely
criticized after it held up the American government's promised
contribution of $600m in debt relief. Then, as the deadline set by
debt campaigners was about to expire in December 2000, Brown
announced that the British government was to renounce its right
to interest payments on £1 billion owed by developing countries.
This brought the number of countries assisted by Britain to 41,
although Jubilee 2000 pointed out that the UK was only one among
many creditors.

If one single subject is at the top of the new moral agenda, it is the
urgent need to redistribute wealth, globally and within individual
countries. The populations of some developing countries are being
devastated by a combination of poverty, ethnic conflict and AIDS:
Alan Lopez, coordinator of the WHO's epidemiology team, reported
in 2000 that 'healthy life expectancy in some African countries is
dropping to levels we haven't seen in advanced countries since

mediaeval times'. The WHO's league table of life expectancy in 191 countries shows that children born in 1999 in the healthiest countries, Japan and Australia, could expect to live 74.5 and 73.2 years respectively. The US is rated twenty-fourth, and the link with poverty is demonstrated by the team's shocking conclusion that some groups, such as native Americans, rural African-Americans and the inner city poor, 'have extremely poor health, more character-istic of a poor developing country rather than a rich industrialized one'. (It is worth pointing out here that six months before the end of Clinton's presidency, the American government predicted a budget surplus of $1.87 trillion over the next ten years. The *International Herald Tribune* described the sums pouring into the US Treasury as 'staggering', yet the outgoing President announced that he intended to earmark most of this unimaginable sum not for social projects but that exciting ambition, paying off the national debt.) Ill health and weak economies go hand in hand in Eastern Europe, which has not yet recovered from its domination by the old Soviet Union; the Russian economy in particular has performed disastrously in the absence of a Marshall Plan to assist it through the difficult transition from one-party state to democracy and capitalism. Russian men can expect to live 56.1 years, compared to 66.4 for Russian women, a discrepancy explained by male depression and alcohol abuse, which lead in turn to high rates of accidents, violence and heart disease. The figures are similar for the struggling economies of the former Soviet republics, with male babies able to expect only 58.5 years of healthy life in Ukraine and 56.2 in Belarus.

But all ten countries at the bottom of the table are in sub-Saharan Africa, where AIDS-related illnesses are now the leading cause of death. The dry figures tell a story that is nothing short of a catas-trophe: they range from Ethiopia, where life expectancy for babies born in 1999 was 33.5, to Sierra Leone, where it was a bleak 25.9. The syndrome killed 2.2 million Africans in 1999 compared with 300,000 AIDS deaths ten years previously. Governments cannot possibly tackle this terrible epidemic while they are burdened with huge levels of debt – and, in the case of Sierra Leone, torn apart by a civil war in which the West was reluctant to intervene directly until the British government belatedly sent troops in spring 2000. Nor can they get to grips with the special health problems experienced by women, which mean that a woman living in Africa is 200 times more likely to die from complications in pregnancy; there are half a million maternal deaths worldwide each year, 99 per cent of them in developing countries. The causes are unsafe abortion, haemorrhage, infections, high blood pressure and obstructed labour; between a quarter and a third of all deaths of women of reproductive age are due to complications in pregnancy or childbirth. Overall, the WHO says that women suffer more from the consequences of poverty than men, making up 70 per cent of the world's poor population. Twice as many women as men are among the world's 900 million illiterates, and malnutrition is significantly higher among women in South Asia, where almost half the undernourished people in the world live. (By contrast, obesity has reached epidemic proportions in the United States, where over-consumption of the world's resources, from fossil fuels to high-fat, high-protein food, has become an integral part of the American way of life. Britain, sadly, appears to be following suit.) Meanwhile, women in developing countries have to work harder for lower wages, receiving on average between 30 and 40 per cent of what men get for comparable work, even though male wage rates are already shockingly low compared with the developed world.

The governments of prosperous countries in north-western Europe have a particular moral obligation to address these problems, not just because they are in part a legacy of colonialism but because they are increasingly hostile to what they contemptuously call 'economic migrants'. The phrase has become a universal term of abuse, when what it really signifies is that impoverished Africans, Afghans or Albanians are attempting to follow the logic of the free market in their own terms; instead of welcoming these eager converts to capitalism, Fortress Europe cowers behind ever more xenophobic legislation, but none of the measures taken so far has deterred the trade in illegal immigrants. Their desperation to get to Western

Europe can be gauged by the extraordinary risks they are prepared to take. In June 2000, customs officials in Dover opened the back of a lorry on the hottest night of the year and discovered the dead bodies of 58 Chinese crammed inside: 54 young men, mostly in their twenties, and 4 young women perished in the airtight container. Only 2 men survived. Politicians from all parties rushed to express their shock and outrage over this horrific event, but it was left to the *Guardian* to point out the paradox behind it: 'Had the 58 immigrants survived and been exposed in the back of the truck, there would have been nothing but condemnation for the "bogus asylum-seekers" and calls for their deportation as quickly as possible.'

This tragedy occurred at a time when Tony Blair's government was spending a miserly 0.23 per cent of GNP per year on foreign aid, less than a third of the target of 0.7 per cent recommended by the UN. By the end of 2001, it had risen to 0.31 per cent. Meeting the UN goal would release another £4bn into the overseas-aid coffers every year, and make British policy on immigrants look a little less shabby. It is also happening at a moment when the countries of Western Europe are expecting a significant drop in their indigenous populations, due to very low birth rates, and will need to let in foreigners if they are to keep their economies functioning; the terror of being 'swamped', as the racist jargon has it, is more a reflection of an unconscious fear of the outsider than a reality. But knowing that this fear exists, and how easily it can be tapped by unscrupulous politicians, means it is all the more important – as well as morally essential – for governments to act on poverty at home, where successive administrations have allowed the gap between rich and poor to become a breeding-ground for racism. It is an unpleasant fact that people who already feel themselves excluded from their own society by poverty are unlikely to react with generosity towards foreigners whose language and customs they do not understand and who appear, although it is seldom really the case, to be receiving preferential treatment. This is the background to a horrifying upsurge of racism in Western Europe at the turn of the century, including in France and Austria, where right-wing parties made alarming electoral gains; there was dismay throughout the EU in 1999 when Austria's far-right Freedom Party, then led by Jörg Haider, joined Chancellor Schüssel's coalition government.

The UK followed the worldwide trend of the rich getting richer in the final decades of the twentieth century, thanks to the aggressive free-market policies of Mrs Thatcher and her successor as Prime Minister, John Major: at the beginning of the 1970s the incomes of the richest 10 per cent were 3 times higher than the poorest 10 per cent; by the end of the 1990s, they were 4 times higher. By 1996, 1 per cent of the population owned 20 per cent of the wealth, estimated at £388 bn; over half the total wealth of the UK was owned by a mere 10 per cent of the population. The British government's own Office of National Statistics reported that three million children were living in poverty in 1998, a state of affairs broadly confirmed in a report from the UN children's agency, Unicef, in June 2000, which estimated that one in 5 children in the UK were existing below the poverty line – a worse situation than in Turkey, Poland and Hungary. It also said that the number had trebled in twenty years – thanks again, Baroness Thatcher – and suggested that the combined effects of the Labour government's welfare measures and the minimum wage were nothing like enough to fulfil Tony Blair's pledge to eradicate child poverty. His second general election victory in 2001 was more a reflection of the absence of a convincing alternative than a resounding vote of confidence.

So what we have, at the beginning of the third millennium, is a situation in which elected governments in prosperous Northern countries, principally the US and the European Union, are too mean even to look after their own poor, let alone the millions in Eastern Europe, Asia and Africa. Ironically, it is those nations with the strongest Christian traditions that have failed most signally to accept their responsibilities and whose current efforts, under pressure from human rights campaigners, charities and radical think-tanks, are being exposed as too little, too late. Nor is it an accident that it is the Scandinavian countries, with their strong secular and social democratic traditions, that have the lowest levels of child poverty in the developed world: Sweden (2.6 per cent) and Norway (3.9), compared with Britain (19.8) and the US (22.4). These urgent economic questions were overshadowed, temporarily at least, by the terrorist attacks of 11 September. Some supporters of the war against terrorism even argued that the protests against globalization had been exposed as irrelevant by the much more immediate threat to stability posed by al-Qaida. Yet the surprisingly rapid success of the bombing campaign against the Taliban revealed a political vacuum at the heart of the anti-terrorist policy, as well as the limits of this type of military action. Cooler voices began to be heard, insisting that the two phenomena – economic domination by a handful of rich nations and the rise of fascism in the Middle East and Asia – were inextricably linked. Even enthusiastic supporters of globalization, such as the British Chancellor Gordon Brown, acknowledged that it was not necessarily a force for good. 'Managed badly,' he said in November 2001, immediately after the WTO talks in Qatar, 'globalization will leave whole economies and millions of people in the developing world marginalized. Managed wisely, globalization can and will lift millions out of poverty and manage to get them on to the high road to a just and inclusive global economy.' Critics such as George Monbiot were less sure, arguing that the structure of the WTO favours the concerns of wealthy economies. But there was a new mood among the poorer nations, who successfully insisted during the Qatar meeting that governments should be able to override drug company patents during health emergencies in order to supply AIDS victims, for instance, with cheap medicines. The trade declaration that emerged from the talks included a recognition of 'the marginalization of least-developed countries' and a commitment to finding a solution to Third World debt. Even if the motive of the richer nations was self-interest, it represented a belated admission that poverty and inequality have to be at the top of the international agenda if the world is to be made a safer place.

Never Again: The Continuing Quest
for Justice

*Any man's death diminishes me, because I am involved in
Mankind.* — JOHN DONNE

*Whereas the soldier, as the legitimate bearer of arms, had to
be prepared to die for his country, the international soldier/
policeman risks his or her life for humanity.*
— MARY KALDOR

*Man's capacity for justice makes democracy possible; but man's
inclination to injustice makes democracy necessary.*
— REINHOLD NIEBUHR

For my generation, which had not yet been born when it happened,
the Holocaust was a dark, brooding presence throughout childhood
and adolescence. It overshadowed my parents' accounts of the
Second World War, when my mother worked in a munitions factory
in Coventry and my father served in the British Navy, stationed for
four years in Freetown, Sierra Leone. He witnessed great loss of life
in savage conditions as his ship accompanied Atlantic convoys,
carrying essential food supplies to Britain, but his accounts of naval
battles seemed to belong to a different order of conflict from what
had happened to the Jews. As the horrifying testimony of death-camp
survivors surfaced in books and newspapers, I could not understand
why more had not been done to save them. The Nazi policy of
genocide was so shocking that, for a time, it obscured the fate of

other victims – political opponents of the regime, 'gypsies' and homosexuals – whose suffering has been documented much more recently; in a recent book, Wolfgang Benz characterizes the persecution of Roma and Sinti as 'the other genocide' and puts the death toll at a minimum of 200,000 and a maximum of perhaps half a million. Those unfamiliar foreign names, Auschwitz and its Polish equivalent Oswiecim, Dachau, Sachsenhausen, Bergen-Belsen, Majdanek, Buchenwald, Theresienstadt, Chelmno/Kulmhof, Sobibor, Treblinka, quickly came to represent unimaginable horror; I felt physically sick when I saw photographs or film footage from the extermination and concentration camps, and was haunted by accounts of the medical experiments carried out on inmates by Josef Mengele at Auschwitz-Birkenau. I was also aware of and puzzled by the fate of Anne Frank, the German Jewish girl who died in one of the camps after her family's hiding place in Amsterdam was betrayed to the Gestapo. Why had the Frank family's flight from Germany stopped in Holland, which was so clearly under threat of Nazi invasion? Years later I went to the house where they had hidden, now a museum, and realized that Anne's parents had been all too well aware they were at risk and made desperate attempts to reach the safety of the US. They lived at a time before the UN Universal Declaration of Rights had been drawn up and ratified, including Article 14, which states unequivocally that 'everyone has the right to seek and enjoy in other countries asylum from persecution', but it is clear that they were what we would now call asylum-seekers. And, like many of their modern counterparts, their pleas for sanctuary were ignored or refused. This indifference to the plight of the persecuted astounded me when I first encountered it, but in recent years, as Western Europe has closed its doors ever more firmly to refugees, it has come to seem less incomprehensible. It is sobering to reflect that some of the readers who are still being moved by Anne's diaries, more than half a century later, would not be so compassionate if they were required to pay higher taxes to support her family. One of the difficulties posed by modern invocations of the Holocaust is that sympathizing with its victims has become what is now called a low ticket, a statement of anti-racist credentials that does not require action, especially in countries whose present policy towards asylum-seekers verges on crude xenophobia.

In the intervening period, I also became aware of the controversies still raging around the Holocaust, particularly the question of knowledge: who knew about the camps, when they knew, and how they responded. Aerial photographs taken by the Allies showed the railway line to Auschwitz; they even showed huge numbers of Jews descending from the cattle trucks. Yet no attempt was made to bomb the railway line, which would at least have disrupted the grim human transports. As I was writing this book, another damning piece of evidence emerged in the shape of more documents declassified in the US, almost sixty years after the events they refer to; they show that the British government knew in advance about the Nazis' plans to deport Roman Jews in 1943 but did nothing to warn them. At 6 a.m. on a Saturday morning 8,000 people, including children, were dragged from their beds; around 1,000 of them were to die in Auschwitz. The plan had been revealed in a German radio message transmitted ten days earlier, on 6 October, and intercepted at the British code-breaking centre at Bletchley Park. The message from German headquarters in Rome to Berlin reads: 'Orders have been received from Berlin by Obersturmbannführer Kappler [the German Police Attaché in Rome] to seize and take to northern Italy the 8,000 Jews living in Rome. They are to be liquidated.' Coded messages usually took five or six days to decipher and the documents show that MI6 knew what was about to happen, but did nothing. (They could, for example, have transmitted coded warnings by radio, alerting the Roman Jews and giving them a chance to escape, as Winston Churchill did in 1941 when he mentioned a similar threat to Russian Jews in time for some of them to avoid the round-up.) A historian, Timothy Naftali, claimed that 'the Jewish question was not foremost in the minds of the people who saw this material' and that the British government tended to the view that reports about the treatment of Jews were exaggerated. The priority given to the subject can be gauged by a note written a year earlier by Sir Stewart

Menzies, head of MI6, requesting a subordinate to put together a dossier of police messages relating to the Holocaust for the Foreign Office. 'This work need not, of course, be given high priority,' Menzies added laconically.

It was attitudes like this, and their dreadful consequences, that led so many people to declare, at the end of the war, that nothing like the Holocaust should be allowed to happen again. The blood-stained history of the second half of the twentieth century demonstrates how difficult that aspiration has been to put into practice: the Stalinist purges and show trials in the USSR that are thought to have claimed more victims than the Holocaust; the 1.7 million Cambodians murdered by Pol Pot; the massacre of 200,000 people by the Indonesian Army in East Timor; genocide in Rwanda in 1994; the ruthless suppression of democracy in Burma; the shooting of unarmed dissidents by the Chinese government at Tiananmen Square; and the relentless destruction of Grozny, the Chechen capital, by Russian forces; all these atrocities attest to the difficulty of intervention in the face of the ruthless abuse of power. Tragically, even those governments that might have been in a position to intervene, or at least bring influence to bear, showed little enthusiasm for doing so unless their direct interests were perceived to be under threat; the liberal democracies have as bad a record in the second half of the twentieth century of giving aid and succour to tyrants – Pinochet, Soeharto, Mobutu, the Shah of Iran, the nasty Fahd dynasty in Saudi Arabia – as countries with unelected leaders. We have already looked in Chapter 3 at the machinations of successive British and American governments as they tried to sell arms to Saddam Hussein; the fanatical attempts of the Reagan administration to overthrow the elected Sandanista government in Nicaragua landed it in a baroque arms deal, covertly selling weapons to its old enemy Iran, in order to finance the Contras; Tony Blair's government caused an outcry when the police in London exceeded their powers to prevent human rights protesters upsetting the Chinese President during a state visit to London.

Until very recently, the role of the US and the UK as the biggest arms dealers in the world fatally compromised well-meaning intentions, if not to prevent foreign conflicts, at least not to make them worse. The Blair government, primed by the *Scott Report* into the arms-to-Iraq scandal, came to power in 1997 with an election pledge not to 'issue export licences for the sale of arms to regimes that might use them for internal repression or international aggression, nor where they might intensify or prolong existing armed conflicts or where they might be used to abuse human rights', a description that might have been written (and probably was) with Indonesia's strife-torn empire in mind. On taking office, Labour ministers suddenly discovered that they could not revoke existing contracts, and by the end of 1997 no fewer than forty licences were in existence, permitting the export of a wide range of military equipment to Soeharto's regime. Only six requests for licences were refused between 2 May and 31 December 1997, even though the dictator, who was soon to fall from power, continued ruthlessly to crush opposition in Indonesia itself and in occupied territories like East Timor. The self-interested policy of Indonesia's neighbour, Australia, was determined not by the prospect of arms sales but by its ambition to get its hands on East Timor's abundant offshore resources; in 1989 the Australian government signed the notorious Timor Gap Treaty, dividing up East Timor's oil and gas fields between itself and the island's Indonesian colonizers, in spite of evidence that the Indonesian Army was systematically raping and prostituting the female relatives of the leaders of the resistance movement. In January 2000, only months after East Timor had finally been liberated, I met a young woman whose older sister had been forced into concubinage with a series of Indonesian Army officers, handed from one to another every few months. She gave birth to four children by different Indonesian fathers in this period, living evidence of a policy of calculated sexual humiliation and enforced racial mixing that is also horribly familiar from the wars in former Yugoslavia.

Srebrenica, Sarajevo, Omarska, Manjaca, Trnopolje: a massacre, a siege, three concentration camps. Once again, in our own time, the mostly unfamiliar names of foreign towns and cities have taken on a dreadful significance. The scale of the atrocities is smaller: humanitarian agencies say that between 3,000 and 5,000 detainees were held at Omarska, a camp for Bosnian Muslim detainees set up by Serb nationalists near the town of Prijador in north-west Bosnia, as part of their programme of ethnic cleansing, while the Bosnian government believes it was nearer 11,000. Prisoners were starved, stabbed, shot and even castrated; they recalled stiflingly hot nights punctuated by the sounds of shots, screaming and then silence. Dusko Tadic, a Serb traffic policeman and paramilitary, was later convicted on eleven counts of crimes against humanity by an international tribunal sitting at The Hague, and the evidence against him supplies a ghastly insight into operations at the camps. At Omarska, Tadic specialized in inventing gruesome forms of torture, including forcing an inmate to chew off another prisoner's testicles and setting off a fire extinguisher in the mouth of another detainee; at Trnopolje, he carried out similar atrocities, as well as rape. Some of the Serbs who carried out these outrages had once been neighbours of the prisoners they tortured and murdered, and the emaciated appearance of a detainee at Trnopolje, Fikret Alic, shocked the world when the camp was filmed by ITN and photographed by the *Guardian*. What happened at Omarska was not comparable to Auschwitz, declared the Jewish camp survivor Elie Wiesel, but it 'was sufficiently serious to shake the world's conscience and to justify international intervention and international solidarity'. The Bosnian government estimates that nearly 150,000 people were held in 57 camps established by the Serbs in the first four months of the Bosnian war in 1992.

So what went wrong? What happened to the good intentions expressed, for the most part sincerely, in the aftermath of the Second World War? On a smaller scale, what took place in Yugoslavia in the first half of the nineties had most of the ingredients – aggressive forms of nationalism, racial hatred, concentration camps, crimes against civilians – that inspired the architects of the post-war settlement to put in place structures, principally the UN in 1945 and the Universal Declaration of Human Rights in 1948, to ensure that recent horrors would not be repeated. The short answer is the Cold War, a grim stand-off in which the superpowers for the most part respected each other's spheres of influence but squabbled, at least once going as far as the brink of nuclear war, over client states in the Caribbean and South-East Asia. The US protested, but did not intervene, when the USSR brutally suppressed the uprising in Hungary in 1956 and the reform movement led by Alexander Dubček in Czechoslovakia in 1968; the Russians appeared to back down over the Cuban missile crisis in 1962, although they had in fact made a secret deal in which the Americans promised, in return, to remove some of their own missiles from Turkey. The missile crisis demonstrated how fragile the post-war settlement had become, even if the actual wars that took place were surrogate conflicts, chiefly in Korea and Vietnam, or civil wars in which the superpowers supported one side against another; the CIA sought to maintain American influence in Africa by backing Holden Roberto in Angola, for instance, while the KGB bankrolled the murderous Mengistu Haile Mariam in Ethiopia. The advantage of this arm's-length aggression, from the superpowers' entirely self-interested point of view, was that indigenous populations bore the brunt of casualties and destruction of infrastructure, a lesson the Americans learned from their disastrous involvement in South-East Asia; it was the Soviet Union's failure to grasp it that led to their catastrophic invasion of Afghanistan, deservedly known as Russia's Vietnam and one of the chief causes, along with the Chernobyl disaster, of the disintegration of the Soviet Union. This metamorphosis in the nature of war is vividly expressed in an extraordinary statistic: at the beginning of the twentieth century, the ratio of military to civilian casualties was 8 to 1; by the final decade the figures had reversed. It is civilians – the elderly, the sick, women and children – who now bear the brunt of destruction in the course of a war. They are also, as we have seen in the US, the UK, Spain and Israel, the preferred target of terrorists.

For decades, these messy and sporadic conflicts around the globe obscured what had been set in place in the 1940s, and the subsequent body of law enshrined in international treaties and declarations that confirmed it. In that sense, the arrest in London of General Pinochet in 1998 was sensational not because it was unprecedented or a venture into unknown legal territory, but because someone had finally summoned up the will to do it – to use existing international law against a former head of state who had made sure to grant himself immunity against prosecution in his own country. It came at a moment when events elsewhere – the Balkan crisis and genocide in Rwanda in 1994, when the international community stood by and allowed the massacre of more than 800,000 Tutsis – had already created a crisis of conscience; also in 1998 President Clinton visited Rwanda and belatedly apologized for his failure to intervene during the three months of slaughter four years earlier. (One of the more useful functions of Clinton's final years in office was his unprecedented decision to make these apologies; Guatemala received one in 1999, when Clinton admitted American involvement in the slaughter of 200,000 people during the country's protracted civil war. Sadly, it did not prevent him from endorsing Plan Colombia, a programme of mostly military aid to that country, in a doomed attempt to halt the cocaine trade. As Clinton left office, the US was supplying money, helicopters and military advisers to an army implicated in massive human rights abuses during another, just as deadly, civil war.)

It was the failure to intervene in Rwanda – along with the massacre at Srebrenica in 1995, when 7,300 Muslim men were slaughtered by General Mladic's army as Dutch UN peacekeepers watched helplessly – that determined Western reaction to the Kosovo crisis in the spring of 1999. Confronted once again with the prospect of massacres in former Yugoslavia, this time in the form of Serbian aggression against the majority Albanian population in the Yugoslav province, the international community, including Russia, tried to negotiate a settlement at Rambouillet, a chateau thirty miles from Paris. The pressure on both sides, Serbs and Kosovars, to sign an agreement was backed up by a threat of NATO air strikes against Yugoslavia, an outcome that was spelled out to the country's President, Slobodan Milosevic, by the US Special Envoy, Richard Holbrooke. When Milosevic remained obdurate, the plans for a bombing campaign swung into action, the first air strikes taking place on the evening of 24 March. Arguments still rage about the NATO action, which was opposed by Russia and followed by atrocities on the ground – although involving far fewer fatalities, it later transpired, than was claimed at the time – and a refugee crisis on a much larger scale than anything that had taken place before the bombing commenced. What can be said with certainty is that the campaign demonstrates both a new determination on the part of Western governments, particularly the UK and the US, to intervene on humanitarian grounds in parts of the world where their national interests are not directly involved, and a major flaw in the method they have chosen to do it. The same flaw has undermined UN peacekeeping operations in different parts of the globe, and is not difficult to identify; it is the neo-colonial assumption that the lives of troops from interventionist nations are hugely more valuable than those of the civilians they are supposed to protect. As we saw in the 1991 Gulf War, the conflict in Kosovo, and Afghanistan in October 2001, strategy is currently determined by this single consideration above all others, resulting in hi-tech air wars, using frighteningly inaccurate bombs and missiles, that do nothing to protect civilian lives on the ground; on the contrary, their effect is still being felt in Kosovo at the beginning of the new century, as the Albanian majority take their revenge, often on entirely innocent Serb families, for the burning and looting of Albanian villages during the bombing campaign.

In the early days of the 78-day conflict, the hysterical nature of the American attitude to casualties was revealed when two of its personnel were taken prisoner by Milosevic's forces. Although they were unharmed, President Clinton issued wild threats and their fate dominated military briefings and press coverage for the next few days. The genesis of this disproportionate response, at a time when Yugoslav soldiers and civilians were dying every night, can be traced back, if not directly to Vietnam, to the disaster in Somalia in 1993. On that occasion, American troops unwisely set off in hot pursuit of Mohammed Aideed, a local warlord whose men had killed several

Pakistani peacekeepers; Aideed responded by shooting down two American helicopters, killing 18 soldiers and wounding 75 others. He proceeded to display some of the mutilated American corpses in front of TV cameras, prompting a furious reaction at the White House and in the US at large. Although any casualties are a tragic result of war, the subsequent American insistence on arm's-length intervention has undoubtedly protected its own military personnel at huge cost to civilians in other countries, including Yugoslavia – where the NATO bombing of a TV station in Belgrade may have been a war crime – and of course Iraq.

An unofficial doctrine appears to be in force that says that only Americans can kill Americans; as I pointed out in Chapter 4, 32,000 people die each year in shooting incidents in the US, a figure comparable with the casualties in a medium-sized war, while the number of Americans who die in overseas conflicts, in honourable causes, is negligible. One of the risks of this strategy is that it has allowed humanitarian intervention to be characterized, by talented propagandists like Milosevic – himself indicted for war crimes by the Hague Tribunal – as a new form of Western imperialism. It is, in effect, an evasion of moral responsibility, whose consequences are now sufficiently well known to risk placing the entire future of intervention in jeopardy. It is also the reason why so many people felt uneasy about the bombing of Afghanistan, even if civilian casualties were exaggerated by the Taliban. The West may one day have to accept that the so-called 'collateral damage' – loss of civilian life and destruction of infrastructure – caused by its preference for air strikes is too high, and return to more effective methods of warfare, principally on the ground, which will inevitably involve injury and loss of life among its own troops. There is no doubt that this would involve a change in the aims and objects of national armed forces, one that should be made clear so that recruits know in advance that they may be required to fight not just for their own country but to save the lives of civilians in distant territories. (Nor is it the case that the expansion of the military's role to include peacekeeping and delivering humanitarian relief has been universally welcomed; in Britain, it has been derided as 'Oxfam with guns' and attracted the accusation that humanitarian intervention is a distraction from the army's proper role, which is, presumably, killing people.) Much the same dilemma faces the UN, whose unarmed peacekeeping forces have in the past proved ineffective in too many locations, forcing the organization to consider a more forceful presence. Mary Kaldor, Director of the Global Civil Society Programme at the London School of Economics, has advocated a tough alternative, which she calls 'cosmopolitan law-enforcement'; what she is suggesting is that peacekeeping is an outmoded concept in locations where civil society has broken down, and that UN troops should play a more active role in the restoration of order and civil institutions. This does not mean the kind of reckless pursuit that American forces indulged in with farcical consequences in Somalia; it does mean, *inter alia*, that troops wearing the UN blue helmet would no longer face an official reprimand if they returned fire, as the British contingent of the United Nations Protection Force in Bosnia (UNPROFOR) did in 1993 when they came under attack from Serbs as they escorted a relief convoy from Kladanj to Tuzla. It certainly involves, in Kaldor's formulation, 'risking the lives of peacekeepers in order to save the lives of victims', bringing to an end an era in which the Western democracies, even when acting on behalf of the international community, tried to assume the role of world policeman at little cost, other than financial, to themselves – attracting, en route, the accusation that unequal conflicts like the Gulf War were a convenient showcase for American arms manufacturers. There are indications that both the UN and the British government, though not the Americans, are already moving in this direction; Tony Blair's decision in the late 1990s to instruct British troops in Bosnia to search for and arrest indicted war criminals demonstrated a willingness to give British forces an active part in punishing wrongdoers and preventing future conflict. The government's decision in 2000 to send troops to Sierra Leone, ostensibly to ensure the safe evacuation of European Union passport holders but in actuality to bolster the fragile government of President

Kabbah, is further evidence that it is willing to take risks in the course of its new humanitarian mission. It also appeared to be readier than the Americans, in the autumn of 2001, to commit ground troops to the conflict in Afghanistan.

Yet the problems associated with humanitarian intervention should not be allowed to obscure the motives behind it, or its successes. The NATO campaign in Kosovo was followed, less than eighteen months later, by the fall of Milosevic, who was driven from office after losing a general election. Even the Russians, faced with a display of people power on the streets of Belgrade, reluctantly withdrew their support for their erstwhile ally, making way for a new government led by Vojislav Kostunica. Although Milosevic insisted he would remain active in Yugoslav politics, there was widespread rejoicing that his own people had rejected a man who was regarded by the international community as the prime mover in three Balkan wars.

It is clear that, in the 1990s, governments as well as individuals began to think seriously about their responsibility to prevent ethnic conflicts, massacres and torture throughout the world, not just in their own backyard but in the Balkans, Africa and Asia. In effect, there was a belated attempt to implement the precedents created in 1946, however imperfectly, by the Nuremberg Tribunal, which tried the surviving Nazi leadership as Europe began to recover from the ravages of the Second World War. The change was as much moral as legal, a return to the idealism that flowered briefly in the immediate post-war period and was snuffed out, as far as governments were concerned, during the superpower confrontation and nuclear arms race. Indeed, the international tribunals set up to hear the cases of individuals charged with war crimes, for Yugoslavia at The Hague in 1993 and for Rwanda at Arusha in Tanzania in 1994, were a direct legacy of Nuremberg; Dusko Tadic, the Serb torturer I mentioned earlier in this chapter, was the first defendant to be convicted by an international tribunal for forty-one years, a small-time thug following in the footsteps of Nazi leaders like Hermann Goering and Karl Dönitz. In one respect at least, the Hague Tribunal has already gone further than the judges at Nuremberg, establishing that rape, which has tended in the past to be regarded as a regrettable side-effect of war, constitutes both a war crime and a crime against humanity. Charges have been brought against Serb police who ran a rape camp at Foca, and a Croatian paramilitary leader who failed to prevent a subordinate from raping a female prisoner who was under interrogation. The rape convictions of three Bosnian Serbs at The Hague in February 2001 were rightly hailed as a legal landmark.

The Nuremberg Tribunal already seems, to generations born long after its hearings, like ancient history. Yet its significance for a lengthy list of late-twentieth-century tyrants, who never dreamed its provisions would apply to them, cannot be overestimated. Nuremberg was the first time that defendants had been charged not just with war crimes but the novel offence of crimes against humanity, which included acts committed by a government against its own citizens regardless of whether war had been declared. From the beginning, it was clear that it was easier to make the case for intervention – unavoidable, in fact, after the Holocaust – than to apply it even-handedly, as events in 1946 quickly proved. The trials and convictions of 22 alleged Nazi war criminals (3 were acquitted) were open to the charge, repeated to this day, that what was being handed out was simply victors' justice. This claim was confirmed by the extraordinary and entirely political decision that the Tokyo Tribunal, set up to try offences committed in the Far East, should not prosecute the Emperor of Japan, Hirohito, whose regime was responsible both for war crimes and crimes against humanity; the Allies had certainly intended to try Hitler, who escaped justice by committing suicide in the Berlin bunker, and the decision not to indict Hirohito seems to have been taken by the Americans, 'by the good grace of General Douglas MacArthur', according to one authority. There were no judges from neutral countries at the Nuremberg Tribunal and, at the end of the trials, their near-universal enthusiasm for the death penalty sat uneasily with the notion of a court set up to assert and protect human rights; 12 of the defendants were hanged and, in a gruesome symbolic act, their bodies cremated in the ovens at Dachau. No one was called to account for the hundreds of thousands of civilian deaths caused by the atomic bombs dropped by American warplanes on the Japanese cities of Hiroshima and Nagasaki, or the firestorm inflicted in 1945 by Allied bombers on non-combatants in Dresden; the Russians, whose purges at home went politely unmentioned until the Cold War changed attitudes to our Second World War ally, cynically blamed the Germans for their own massacre of Polish officers in the Katyn Forest. As the American Supreme Court Judge Robert Jackson frankly remarked to President Truman, the Allies had 'done or are doing some of the very things we are prosecuting Germans for'.

Yet, in spite of its imperfections, the Nuremberg Charter that empowered the Tribunal in 1945 established important legal precedents. One was Article 7, which struck down the defence – which General Pinochet's lawyers would unsuccessfully attempt to resurrect in 1998 – that heads of state were immune from prosecution. It stated that the 'official position of defendants, whether as Heads of State or responsible officials in Government Departments, shall not be considered as freeing them from responsibility or mitigating punishment'. This was a succinct summary of a principle expounded at greater length in the trial judgment, explaining why the principle of sovereign immunity could not be upheld:

Crimes against international law are committed by men, not by abstract entities, and only by punishing individuals who commit such crimes can the provisions of international law be enforced ... It was submitted that ... where the act in question is an act of State, those who carry it out are not personally responsible, but are protected by the doctrine of the sovereignty of the State. In the opinion of the Tribunal, [this contention] must be rejected ... The principle of international law, which under some circumstances, protects the representative of a state, cannot be applied to acts which are condemned as criminal by international law. The authors of these acts cannot shelter themselves behind their official position in order to be freed from punishment in appropriate proceedings.

This was, in essence, the view the House of Lords came to in the Pinochet case just over half a century later. Its meaning has always been clear: Admiral Dönitz, who had been head of state of Germany from 1 to 9 May 1945, after Hitler's suicide, was convicted of 'waging aggressive war', partly because he gave orders in that capacity to the Wehrmacht to continue the war in the East; he was sentenced to ten years' imprisonment, although he was acquitted on charges relating to his conduct of submarine warfare. The Nuremberg Charter also established another important principle, universal jurisdiction over crimes against humanity, which authorized the judges to hear charges regardless of where the alleged offence had been committed. Such crimes are, in law, analogous to piracy, which any state may punish; this doctrine was stated as early as 1927, when a judge of the International Court of Justice, in a case between France and Turkey, declared that 'the right and duty to ensure public order does not belong to any particular country; any country, in the interest of all, can exercise jurisdiction and punish'. But Nuremberg applied it specifically to crimes against humanity, and it entered international law when both the Charter and the judgments were recognized by the UN General Assembly in 1946; universal jurisdiction has since been confirmed in a series of treaties and conventions, including the United Nations Convention Against Torture in 1986, which obliges states that have ratified it to prosecute alleged torturers who enter their territory. The signatories include Britain, which is therefore required, under Article 7, to extradite anyone found in its jurisdiction who is alleged to have committed torture or to 'submit the case to its competent authorities for the purpose of prosecution'. Indeed, this legal principle, known as *aut dedere aut judicare* – that all states must either extradite or try anyone accused of crimes against humanity – is now widely accepted as an obligation even on governments that have not signed up to the convention.

In 1998, when Pinochet's hubris led him to book an agreeable shopping and medical trip to London, the legal apparatus to seize him had long been in place. What had changed was the moral climate, as an increasing number of lawyers, judges and human rights activists around the world began to look for ways to implement existing laws that outlaw torture and crimes against humanity. Once again, as we saw with protests against globalization in Chapter 8, the impetus came from below, not from governments; Pinochet had visited London several times before, under both Conservative and Labour administrations, without mishap. Even those politicians who had shown themselves ready to intervene in former Yugoslavia, and supported the setting-up of the Hague and Arusha tribunals, had little stomach, it seemed, for pursuing former or serving heads of state other than the West's current demon figures, Saddam Hussein and Milosevic. (At the beginning of the Kosovo conflict, some British newspapers declared, without apparent irony, that Milosevic was worse than Saddam, who was in turn worse than Hitler.) That was why the news of Pinochet's arrest reverberated around the world, making an impact far beyond Spain, Chile and the UK, the three countries that were directly involved in the extradition process. Dozens of serving and former heads of state saw Pinochet's fate as a warning, even if they had previously felt safe in their presidential palaces or sumptuous retirement homes. Several abruptly reconsidered their travel plans, realizing that not just judges but organizations like Human Rights Watch, Amnesty International and the Redress Trust were drawing up indictments that might be put into action, as happened to Pinochet in Britain, in an apparently neutral third country. In 2001, one of those affected was the Israeli prime minister, Ariel Sharon, who was said to have been advised by the security service that a number of countries were unsafe for him to visit. Sharon has been accused of complicity in the massacres carried out by Lebanese militiamen at two refugee camps, Sabra and Shatila, in Beirut in 1982. The list includes Belgium, where twenty-three survivors of the killings filed complaints against Sharon, using a controversial law which allows Belgian courts to prosecute foreigners for human rights violations committed in other countries. Similar complaints have been filed in Brussels against Saddam Hussein, Fidel Castro, the former Iranian president Hashemi Rafsanjani and the Rwandan president, Paul Kagame.

The narrowest escape took place in Vienna in the summer of 1999, when Saddam Hussein's number two, Izzat Ibrahim al-Douri, fled the country only hours after a Green MP presented the Austrian Ministry of Justice with evidence that he had committed genocide at Halabjah, where thousands of Kurds were bombed and gassed in 1988. Al-Douri, who had originally planned to spend a month at the plush Doeblinger Clinic in Vienna, had enjoyed only a week's R & R when he was tipped off that the MP, Peter Pilz, was asking the Austrian Ministry of Justice to arrest him; without waiting to find out the government's response to the request, al-Douri jumped on to the next flight to Amman – there were, of course, no direct flights to the pariah state of Iraq – and scurried across the border to Baghdad. 'I am ashamed of the Austrian government,' his accuser, Peter Pilz, declared theatrically. 'The country is becoming a paradise for mass murderers.'

Al-Douri is not the only mass murderer with a taste for expensive foreign clinics. In Jakarta, ex-President Soeharto had often travelled abroad for treatment, a habit that also came to a sudden end in the summer of 1999. Planning a trip to Europe, Soeharto applied to the German Embassy for an assurance that he would not face arrest if he arrived in the country and booked into his usual clinic; word came back that if Portugal were to seek his arrest and extradition for genocide in its former colony of East Timor, the German government would have no choice but to comply with the legal process. A corruption investigation was later launched against Soeharto in Jakarta, where he was alleged to have embezzled so much money that his wealth outstripped that of the Indonesian state, and the former dictator placed under house arrest when his lawyers pleaded he was too ill to appear in court; they would go to him, said state prosecutors, if Soeharto insisted he was unable to come to them. On 3 August 2000 the former dictator was formally charged with corruption, with the government's lawyers alleging he had transferred $570m from seven charitable trusts to his family. The charges were the opening shot in a battle to discover the whereabouts of a sum of money estimated at somewhere between $15bn and $40bn, stolen from the state treasury during Soeharto's long presidency. In Spain the indefatigable Judge Garzón followed up his arrest warrant for General Pinochet with a similar request through Interpol to Argentina; Garzón indicted the former leader of the junta, Leopoldo Galtieri, and 47 other military commanders whom he accused of genocide and torture, most of them now living in retirement in Buenos Aires and other Argentine cities. The writ named 600 Spanish victims of the junta, including a sixteen-year-old girl, Ana Cristina Corral, who was allegedly kidnapped, tortured and executed by an Argentine general, Antonio Domingo Bussi, in a clandestine detention camp. Garzón demanded, under the *aut dedere aut judicare* principle, that the Argentine government hand the men over to stand trial in Spain or begin prosecutions itself.

Some former dictators and generals, no longer safe in their home countries, have been lucky enough to find protectors elsewhere. Perhaps the most notorious case was that of Colonel Mengistu, whose seventeen-year-rule in Ethiopia coincided with the slaughter of 200,000 people; Mengistu, whom the Ethiopian government wished to try for crimes against humanity, was given sanctuary in Zimbabwe by Robert Mugabe, whose own security forces were granted an amnesty for massacres in Matabeleland in the 1980s. In 1999 Mengistu apparently felt confident enough to visit South Africa, ignoring international calls for his arrest. While General Radislav Krstic, who commanded Serb troops at Srebrenica, was put on trial at The Hague in July 2000, accused of genocide, his superior Ratko Mladic remained at large, living in a suburb of Belgrade, shielded by Milosevic until his fall from power in September 2000. Milosevic himself was handed over to The Hague, where he faced a long list of charges, a few months later. Another President, Idi Amin of Uganda, was exiled to Mecca by the Saudi authorities after they discovered that their not-very-welcome guest, then living in Jeddah, had been involved in a plot to ship arms to northern Uganda. It is something of a mystery why the British government, which has an extradition treaty with Saudi Arabia, has not yet asked the Saudis to hand over Amin, whose 75,000 victims included British citizens.

Justice came closest to being done in Senegal, where Hissène Habré, the former dictator of Chad, was indicted in February 2000 on charges of torture. Habré, who is known as an African Pinochet, is accused of responsibility for 40,000 murders during his eight-year dictatorship in Chad; he had the bad luck to take refuge in a country where Judge Demba Kandji, widely regarded as an African equivalent of Spain's Judge Garzón, was prepared to press charges. Former dictators often complain, somewhat disingenuously, that they have not been convicted of the crimes attributed to them, at the same time doing their very best to avoid appearing in court, so Habré's forthcoming trial was seen as an important precedent by human rights activists around the world. Then, in July that year, Judge Demba was abruptly removed from his post by a body presided over by Senegal's President, Abdoulaye Wade, and his place on the Chambre d'Accusation given to another judge. The following day, the court ruled (wrongly) that Senegal had no jurisdiction over crimes committed in Chad and dismissed all the charges against Habré. 'This is a dark day for Chad and for Africa,' said Delphine Djiraibe, President of the Chadian Association for the Promotion and Defence of Human Rights. 'But facts are stubborn things and the evidence of Habré's crimes is finally being presented to the courts and to the world. Hissène Habré has not seen the last of his victims.'

What we are seeing, in the first years of the twenty-first century, are the early manoeuvres in a struggle not just to bring mass murderers to justice but to ensure that their eventual fate is a deterrent to others. International criminal tribunals have been mooted for Sierra Leone, Iraq and Cambodia, and valuable lessons have been learned from the protracted Pinochet saga and the experience of the Hague and Arusha tribunals. But the urgent need for a permanent tribunal was demonstrated by the events of 11 September, which raised the question of what should happen to Osama bin Laden, chief suspect in the bombing of the twin towers and the Pentagon. Supporters of the idea of an International Criminal Court, first mooted at a conference in Rome in 1998, argued that the terrorist attacks proved the need for an impartial tribunal where someone accused of crimes on this scale could get a fair trial. They also pointed out that it was the US, which had suffered this terrible assault on its citizens, which had done most to delay the establishment of the ICC. In 1998, 120 countries had voted in favour of its statute, while seventy-three nations had also taken the next step in the protracted process, signing the Rome treaty, in the following six months. (The signatories included not just members of the EU but Chile, Argentina, Senegal, Sierra Leone and Zimbabwe.) But the American government had remained objurately opposed, insisting that it would never agree to its own citizens appearing before such a tribunal – not such a remote possibility, given that the history of the US in the last half century has included the My Lai massacre in Vietnam and attempts to assassinate foreign leaders like Fidel Castro. When President Clinton did a U-turn on his final day in office, signing the Rome treaty only hours before his presidency ended, it was little more than a PR stunt, carried out in the knowledge that his successor in the White House would be even more hostile to the court. Sure enough, one of the first actions of the new President was to instruct his lawyers to try and find a legal means of unsigning the treaty as speedily as possible.

This was, of course, before the suicide-hijackings, which invigorated the debate about how best to enforce international justice. President Bush's assertion that he wanted bin Laden 'dead or alive' alarmed many observers, who saw it as a return to the Wild West way of doing things, as well as displaying scant regard for the rule of law. By a curious accident of timing, the British government actually ratified the ICC, becoming the forty-second country to do so, only three days before it joined the Americans in bombing Afghanistan, where bin Laden was said to be hiding. This is not as contradictory as it seems, for it was never intended that the ICC's jurisdiction would be retrospective; with another eighteen ratifications needed before the court could be set up, it was always clear that bin Laden, like Pinochet and Idi Amin, was beyond its remit. But the British endorsement, however quietly done, was a further demonstration of the gradual conversion of the world's democratic nations to an enforceable model of international justice. After decades of prompting by courageous individuals – reporters, lawyers, judges and human rights activists – governments are moving closer to achieving the ambitious goals set out at Nuremberg in 1946. The culture of impunity enjoyed by powerful people for centuries is slowly being replaced by a new world order, in which the actions of dictators and terrorists are interpreted as an assault on humanity as a whole rather than on individuals or single states. Even if the US chooses to remain outside that process, it represents a revolution in the way we think about power, and a new confidence in our ability to challenge its most flagrant abuses.

11 September 2001

Empire not only manages a territory and a population but also creates the very world it inhabits . . . [A]lthough the practice of Empire is continually bathed in blood, the concept of Empire is always dedicated to peace – a perpetual and universal peace outside of history

– MICHAEL HARDT AND ANTONIO NEGRI

Perhaps the most surprising thing about the terrorist attacks on the East Coast of the US on 11 September 2001, is how many people were *not* surprised by them. This may seem a paradoxical observation to make about events that struck most observers as completely unprecedented, and sent most of the world into a state of numbed shock. Yet the exclamations of horror were accompanied by another discourse, carried on mostly in private, in which people expressed the feeling that there was a grim inevitability about what had happened. It was not that anyone had foreseen an attack on so breathtaking a scale, or with so many civilian casualties. But something that came as news to many Americans – that their country is distrusted by millions of people, and disliked by more than a handful of Islamic fundamentalists – had been known for a very long time beyond its shores. While only a fanatical minority expressed any sympathy at all with the terrorists, there was a sense that America's mystifying disengagement from the world, symbolized by the fact that the majority of its citizens do not possess passports and the tearing up of international treaties, has allowed American governments to pursue ruthless policies which have created untold misery in every corner of the globe. This perception means that the suicide-bombings raised complex moral and practical issues, one of them being the fear that invoking America's right to self-defence, as President George W. Bush immediately did, presaged the kind of military response which, along with covert operations and campaigns to destabilize foreign economies, had made the US a target for terrorists in the first place. While dazed Americans asked 'Why do they hate us so much?' the rest of the world waited to learn the answer to an equally important question: what has American learned from this terrible episode? It was a question that might decide the future security of the entire world and as days turned into weeks, and Bush appeared not to have authorized an immediate bombing campaign in Asia or the Middle East, there was a widespread sense of relief and even optimism. Lawyers and human rights activists argued that the assault on the US should be dealt with as a crime, by the international community acting through the UN, and asked for proof of Osama bin Laden's direct involvement in the attacks. They argued that he and other leaders of the al-Qaida terrorist organization should be tried in a court of law, either in the US or at an international tribunal like those in operation at The Hague and Arusha. The American government was reluctant to produce conclusive evidence linking bin Laden to the suicide-bombers – it was not until an amateur videotape was discovered in Afghanistan in December, in which he suggested that some of the hijackers did not know they were on suicide missions, that doubts were finally laid to rest – but for just under four weeks, in the autumn of 2001, it looked as though the American government was displaying both unexpected restraint and an unwonted respect for international law. There is no doubt that in this interval it enjoyed the moral high ground to an unprecedented degree and disarmed even some of its most persistent critics.

On 7 October, the optimists were proved wrong. As members of the President's inner circle revealed much later, George Tenet, the director of the CIA, presented Bush with a plan to wipe out al-Qaida bases in Afghanistan as early as 12 September, the day after the attacks. The reluctance of the War Cabinet to offer evidence against bin Laden is explained by a single circumstance, Tenet's obsession with the al-Qaida leader, which meant that his guilt was assumed from the start. That Bush accepted Tenet's plan, after a day's deliberation, may be a reflection of his complete inexperience in the area of foreign policy – questioned by a reporter during his Presidential campaign, he was unable to name the man who was to become a key ally in the 'war against terrorism', General Pervez Musharraf of Pakistan – and of his predisposition to listen to an organization his father had once headed. It also demonstrates a perplexing faith in an intelligence service that, in spite of its director's obsession with al-Qaida, had completely failed to pick up even a hint of the devastating attacks that bin Laden had masterminded. 'These are very sophisticated guys,' Bush said later, justifying his decision. 'They understand [Afghanistan]. They know what they're doing.' Tenet's plan relied on high-level bombing by the USAF while operatives from the agency and special forces assisted local opposition groups – the Afghan warlords who had once fought the Russians and were now not-very-reliable enemies of the Taliban – on the ground. Although everyone in the War Cabinet seems to have agreed they were about to embark on a new kind of war, they were wrong in almost every respect. What *Time* magazine characterized as 'a war fought by others, with the US role both obvious and covert, a combination of brute force, financial muscle and behind-the-scenes finesse' will be familiar to anyone who has studied the long history of American intervention abroad in the period that followed the Second World War. The US has always employed foreign proxies, as its search for a general to lead a military coup in Chile in the early 1970s demonstrates; nor is there anything new about its use of economic pressure, covert or otherwise; nor about employing the CIA to support opposition forces, no matter how dreadful their human rights record (and some mujahidin commanders in Afghanistan had been accused of as many atrocities as the Taliban). The use of high-level bombing emerged as the favoured US military tactic in 1991, when it was used successfully in the Gulf War, and gained even greater support after the débâcle in Somalia, when American public opinion became increasingly hysterical about the prospect of casualties. That the Bush administration was uncomfortable about its dependence on air superiority is evident from its private rhetoric, which reveals that the President's closest associates had convinced themselves that on this occasion they were prepared to countenance American casualties. Donald Rumsfeld, Bush's Defence Secretary, admitted that the US had come to be perceived as 'risk-averse', a perception it intended to dispel in Afghanistan, while Stephen Hadley, Condoleezza Rice's deputy at the National Security Council, made the explicit assertion that 'America is getting serious, because it is going to put its people at risk'. This was, as events in Asia were quickly to prove, a self-deluding myth; the first American casualty in combat, leaving aside accidents and the death of a CIA interrogator killed during an uprising by captured Taliban soldiers at Mazar-i-Sharif in November, was not reported until 4 January 2002, almost three months into the campaign. By then, thousands of Afghan civilians had been killed and many more injured in the bombing. Those casualties, and the way an existing refugee crisis in Afghanistan had been exacerbated by the war, were largely responsible for the American government losing the moral advantage it had enjoyed after the suicide-bombings.

The changed mood was vividly demonstrated on Christmas Day 2001, when an Anglican cleric – someone at the heart of the British establishment, soon to be discussed as a possible replacement for the retiring Archbishop of Canterbury – observed in a sermon that the suicide-bombings were a 'judgement' on the West. Michael Scott-Joynt, Bishop of Winchester, was talking specifically about the failure of wealthy countries to help impoverished nations. But it was clear that the muted criticism that was the order of the day in the wake of 11 September, when any direct censure of the US was regarded as heartless, was rising in volume. This is not to say that the initial expressions of horror and compassion were anything other than genuine. But the fact that they coexisted with a much less sympathetic *political* critique had been obscured by an understandable reluctance to add to the burdens of the bereaved. The gradual emergence of that critique is not to suggest that anyone who perished in the suicide-bombings deserved the ghastly fate visited upon them; on the contrary, stories of individual heroism – the New York fire fighter struggling *up* the stairs of the north tower of the World Trade Centre as survivors made their way down; the couple who jumped to their deaths, hand in hand, from the burning building; the passenger who called his wife from a hijacked plane to say that he was going to fight back – offered glimpses of the human spirit at its best. No one could deny that for those directly touched by it – widows and widowers, children who lost a parent, emergency workers whose colleagues perished – life would never be the same again. Nor did anyone question the devastating impact of their loss as the smouldering ruins of Ground Zero, as the southern tip of Manhattan swiftly came to be called, became a symbol of their bereavement. The use of the military term – Ground Zero is the point where an atomic bomb is detonated – expressed the feeling of millions of Americans that what had happened was the equivalent of the pre-emptive nuclear strike they had feared throughout the Cold War.

But is possible to acknowledge all these things without subscribing to the theory that the pre-eminent nation in the modern world had suffered a completely inexplicable attack by terrorists motivated by hatred of its superior values. The crux of the argument over 11 September is whether that day is to be understood historically or as a freak event, standing outside history. Bush's public rhetoric revealed a nostalgia for a time of simple loyalties and equally simple solutions; it also, unsurprisingly for an administration whose primary interests were commercial rather than political, favoured ahistorical readings of the atrocity. (For his critics at home and abroad, Bush's arrival in the White House in January 2001 marked a take-over of American government by the oil industry.) That this kind of lawless talk did not play well outside the US was quickly apparent, especially as it came from a President whose legitimacy had been in question before and after his inauguration. Within days of the attacks, there was a pressing need to place them in a context that displayed a more sophisticated grasp of history and politics, and the former British defence secretary Michael Portillo was one of the first to supply it. Writing in *The Times* on 13 September, in a column whose intent seemed to be to maximize America's sense of outrage and mobilize support elsewhere in the world, Portillo compared the attacks on the World Trade Centre to the atomic bomb dropped on Hiroshima in 1945 and America's military losses in the Vietnam War:

The US lost 55,000 servicemen during the Vietnam War. The number killed in the atomic explosion at Hiroshima was 78,000. The death toll from the destruction of the World Trade Centre is in the same league as major acts of war that have scarred nations for generations.

In pure numbers, it is not. A death toll of 2,992 in New York, the city's own official figure, is closer to the number of people executed and murdered in Chile after the American-inspired coup led by General Pinochet in 1973; by an eerie coincidence, the suicide-bombings happened on the same day of the same month, marking the twenty-eighth anniversary of the overthrow of the Allende government. It would be fairer to compare the casualties in New York to the massacres at Halabjah in 1988 (between 6,000 and 8,000 Iraqi Kurds), Srebrenica in 1995 (7,300 Bosnian Muslims) and Mazar-i-Sharif in 1998 (between 5,000 and 8,000 of the Hezara minority murdered by the Taliban). Like the attack on the twin towers, all three were deliberately targeted on civilian populations; Halabjah was an air attack, involving chemical weapons, while the remaining two were carried out by soldiers on the ground, who singled out and slaughtered male civilians over a period of hours.

Portillo was writing at a moment when the figures were inflated by the difficulties facing rescuers, double reporting of casualties and the fact that many people reported missing by anxious relatives and friends later turned out to be safe. (He wildly overestimated the number of victims in New York while using as a comparison one of the lower figures for people killed by the atomic bomb dropped *by* the Americans on Hiroshima; the city authorities estimated total casualties at 200,000. Nor did Portillo mention the number of *Vietnamese* who died in that catastrophic war in South-East Asia.) Besides the deaths in New York, a total of 224 people died on the hijacked plane that crashed in Pennsylvania, a fourth aircraft that flew into the Pentagon, and in the damaged wing of that building. This means that the official death toll in all four terrorist incidents is 3,216, just over half the number feared dead in the immediate aftermath, when the New York authorities estimated the number of fatalities in the city alone as 6,275. But as the *New York Times* memorialized the victims in hundreds of heart-wrenching obituaries, revealing among other things the ethnic diversity of the city, a clearer picture of the sequence of events at the World Trade Centre was beginning to emerge. And the paper's research quickly seemed to suggest that many more people had escaped from the twin towers than was initially realized.

The first attack happened at 8.46 a.m. East Coat time, the second 16 minutes later at 9.02, a gap which was to make the difference between life and death for many office workers. Thanks to the strict evacuation procedures in force after the 1993 terrorist attack on the twin towers, when a bomb exploded in an underground car park, around ninety-nine per cent of workers on the floors below the points of impact found their way out or were led to safety. The number of casualties was reduced by the timing of the assaults, which happened before many people got to work; it has been estimated that there were between 5,000 and 7,000 people in each tower, rather than the 50,000 who might have been expected to be in the buildings later in the day. (This may be the source of the preposterous anti-Semitic rumour that 4,000 Jewish workers had been warned in advance and did not report for work that day.) Most of those who died were in the north tower, the site of the first impact, where everyone on or above the ninety-second floor perished; everyone on the ninety-first floor survived, while twenty people on the eighty-third died. In the south tower, about two-thirds of the office workers had been taken to safety before the second plane crashed into floors seventy-eight to eighty-four of the building; four people who worked on higher floors had an amazing escape, stumbling down a smoke-filled staircase to ground level. There was angry criticism of eighty-three lift mechanics who ran from the complex after the first impact, leaving most of the ninety-nine lifts – the fastest means of escape – unattended. One in seven of the victims were fire, police or security personnel, creating a wave of appreciation, in a country where private enterprise has iconic status, of the sacrifices made by public service workers.

It might be thought that the death toll on 11 September was grim enough, without manipulating it to serve political ends. Yet there is no doubt that this is what happened. The wild exaggeration of Portillo's article was scaled down as doubts about the initial casualty figures began to emerge. Yet senior members of the Bush administration, the Major of New York and pundits continued to cite the higher figures long after their inaccuracy had been widely acknowledged. In mid November, the host of a popular New York talk show was still referring to 6,000 victims. Towards the end of the same month, the official New York death toll had been revised down to 3,899 and three news organizations – the *New York Times*, Associated Press and *USA Today* – were suggesting it was no higher than 2,950. Yet Colin Powell, President Bush's Secretary of State and by no means a hawk within the administration, was still using a figure of 5,000. To this day, it is not uncommon to hear or read references to five or six thousand casualties in New York alone, a claim often made in a context where someone is being chided for failing to support the war in Afghanistan or for asking why the suicide-bombings have received so much attention compared with, say, civilian casualties in Chechnya.

There were few more blatant examples of a politician using the victims for political ends than Tony Blair's mawkish speech at the end of October, when he reminded the wavering British public why the 'war against terrorism' was necessary. Faced with rapidly falling support for the conflict in opinion polls and anxiety among backbench Labour MPs, the prime minister explicitly asked his listeners to identify with the dead. 'Never forget those answer-phone messages,' the prime minister urged, 'never forget how we felt imagining how mothers told children they were about to die.' The speech backfired, too obviously an attempt to reinstate the dominant discourse of the period immediately after 11 September: that while massacres and catastrophes had been regrettably common in the final decade of the twentieth century, the terrorist attacks on the East Coast were qualitatively different. By now, it was beginning to be possible to analyse the reasons why this had seemed to be the case only seven weeks before, and the answers were not comforting for politicians. First there was the choice of target. Unlike most of Europe, where a whole string of terrorist organisations – the IRA, ETA, the Red Brigades, the Baader-Meinhof Gang, the November 17 organization in Greece – have been operating for years, the US has been relatively immune from such attacks on its own territory; two exceptions, the 1993 explosion at the World Trade Centre and the 1995 Oklahoma City bombing, were seen very much as aberrations. The fact that terrorists had dared to strike simultaneously at New York City and Washington, the country's financial, cultural and political capitals, was genuinely astonishing. So was the novel method, which turned what is perhaps the pre-eminent symbol of Western freedom and affluence, the jet plane, into a weapon of mass destruction. The victims – English-speaking, with mostly familiar names – were easy for Americans and Europeans to identify with and long lists of the dead were published in newspapers in several countries. (No one in Western Europe or the US published definitive lists of civilian victims in Bosnia, Iraq or Afghanistan; it did not even happen after two previous terrorist outrages planned and executed by al-Qaida, at the American embassies in Nairobi and Dar es Salaam in 1998, which killed 224 people, most of them Africans.)

Above all there was the fact that the second hi-jacked plane was captured on film as it approached and crashed into the south tower of the World Trade Centre, as was the subsequent collapse of both towers and nearby buildings. Seldom have such spectacular events been filmed and transmitted instantly; wars these days are either subject to news management, which for the most part keeps violent death off camera – the slaughter of retreating Iraqi troops in the Gulf War being a very good example – or ignored. How would we have reacted to the massacres in Rwanda in 1994 if we had been forced to watch individual Tutsis being hacked to death nightly on our TV screens? On 11 September, viewers saw people falling to their deaths from burning buildings and terrified New Yorkers running to escape flying debris. So powerful were these images that they eclipsed the other terrorist attacks that day and the devastation at the crash sites in Pennsylvania and the Pentagon has been very nearly forgotten; reviews of the year, printed in newspapers at the end of December 2001, focused exclusively on the World Trade Centre. In any other circumstances, an assault on the headquarters of the American military, Rumsfeld's own headquarters in the heart of Washington, would have received wall-to-wall coverage. Yet it is the wreckage of 'those glittering towers', in Margaret Drabble's words, that continues to obsess both the public and the world's media.

There can be little doubt that the conjunction of symbolic meaning – there could scarcely be a more dramatic example of hubris than the twin towers – and the availability of events in New York to the media were crucial in shaping reactions to 11 September. Anyone who had missed the first reports of the terrorist attacks was able to catch up later in the day, as rolling news programmes endlessly repeated the footage. One British TV channel even added music to the images, a decision made in the heat of the moment which its executives later publicly regretted. Yet the effect of this exposure to real events – as opposed to 'reality TV', a title reserved in Britain for gladiatorial game shows – was not what might have been predicted. Most people in Europe and the US correctly thought they had never seen anything like it, but they had been exposed to a pretty unrelenting cinematic diet of *simulacra* of catastrophe. A culture addicted to recreational violence was suddenly confronted with the genuine article and the parallels with standard Hollywood disaster scenarios, from *Towering Inferno* and *Independence Day* to the *Die Hard* movies, were utterly disconcerting; repeated viewing, as though someone kept playing back the same video time after time, actually increased the watchers' sense of *un*reality. It also raised irresistible expectations of a different ending, Steve McQueen or Bruce Willis leading a ragged band of survivors from the World Trade Centre, which were continually frustrated. Viewers were trapped in a cycle of repetition without resolution, multiplying the sense of helplessness which is a natural reaction to disasters on this scale; the experience was not unlike consuming pornography, in the sense that people were exposing themselves to the same horribly stimulating sights many times over, renewing the original state of shock and keeping their emotions at the highest possible pitch. Viewers were thus encouraged to make a vicarious identification with the victims, a response that had not been invited in other instances of mass murder: the hundreds of thousands of dead in Rwanda remained an undifferentiated – and, as Africans, racially 'other' – multitude. On this occasion, by contrast, people's natural reactions were unnaturally extended by the coverage, creating an atmosphere in which American retaliation was both assumed and easier to justify.

Of all the immediate reactions, the *Mirror*'s front page headline on 12 September was perhaps the most egregious: 'War on the World', the words superimposed on a photograph of a fireball engulfing the twin towers. As if this elision was not disturbing enough, the paper's back page produced another in a quote from Bush: 'Freedom itself was attacked by a faceless coward. Freedom will be defended.' The following day, *The Times* printed a photograph of wreckage at the World Trade Centre which looked eerily familiar; at a moment when all eyes were on New York, it took a while to register that the jagged steel spars called to mind pictures of Grozny, the Chechen capital systematically destroyed by the Russians in a brutal civil war. But the paper's headline was unthinkable in terms of that conflict, which President Putin has been allowed to prosecute unmolested by the rest of the world: 'Good will prevail over evil.' On Friday, the *International Herald Tribune* rallied its readers: 'Bush Vows to "Lead World to Victory".' The claim was patently absurd, given that a world united behind the US would have no one to go to war with, other than extra-terrestrials. But the media coverage did serve a useful purpose, highlighting the narcissistic fantasy which explains why the US is disliked so much beyond its shores.

It was still being reproduced in January 2002, when *Time* magazine made Rudy Giuliani its person of the year; Giuliani, the magazine declared, was not just major of New York but 'mayor of the world'. While Giuliani undoubtedly inspired and comforted New Yorkers in the weeks after the attack on the World Trade Centre, his relevance in the slums of Guatemala City, a Palestinian refugee camp or even a run-down council estate in South London is not immediately obvious. Nor did the notion of the US as a beacon of liberty find a sympathetic audience in those countries around the world where direct American intervention, or its support for despotic regimes, has had disastrous consequences. The list is too long to print in full, but it includes Nicaragua, El Salvador, Guatemala, Columbia, Chile, Vietnam, Cambodia, Indonesia, East Timor, Iran, Iraq, Pakistan, Palestine/Israel and of course Afghanistan, where the US supported anyone who was prepared to oppose the Russian occupation, even welcoming the Taliban when they seized power in 1996. For critics of American foreign policy, inside the country as well as abroad, the freedom and prosperity enjoyed by the middle classes have been achieved at a very high cost right round the world. Indeed it is hard to think of an occasion when a nation's illusions about itself have been so dramatically exposed or when a single class – white, affluent, insular – has been so successful in repressing alternative forms of discourse. In an earlier chapter of this book, I quoted figures demonstrating that millions of Americans – black, Hispanic, poor whites – are excluded from the affluent lifestyle that Middle America expects as its due; their experience is more like that of the poor in developing countries, with whom some of them identify, and many of them were unconvinced by Bush's rhetoric about going to war to save the world. But their voices were largely excluded from the mainstream, while other dissenting constituencies – academics, intellectuals, liberal columnists, even a handful of Republican critics of the administration – faced derision and accusations of anti-American behaviour. The irrepressible satirist Michael Moore posted a series of bitingly sarcastic commentaries on his website, one of them a parody of an old John Lennon song entitled 'All We Are Saying Is Give War A Chance'. But the writer Susan Sontag was pilloried for suggesting – reasonably enough, given the degree of deranged courage the act requires – that the suicide-bombers should not be described as cowards. The attack on Sontag was predictable in an atmosphere in which many Americans were festooning their homes, offices and websites with the Stars and Stripes, a response whose less benign analogue was an upsurge of racism. The chief targets were what have become known as 'hyphenated' Americans, people with Arab, Asian or North African backgrounds, who were regarded with immediate suspicion if they spoke foreign languages among themselves or were seen reading foreign newspapers. This xenophobia appeared to have the government's imprimatur when more than a thousand Arabs and Arab-Americans were arrested and held without trial, even though the FBI conceded that only a handful, perhaps ten or fifteen, were seriously suspected of having links with al-Qaida; there were reports that some of the suspects had been badly beaten by other prison inmates. That many Arabs are secular and some Muslims native-born New Yorkers or Londoners was largely ignored; an American-born convert to Islam, the scholar Hamza Yusuf, was visiting the White House at the President's request when the FBI turned up unannounced at his home in California. In the *Guardian*, George Monbiot listed a series of incidents that illustrated the state of suspicion and intolerance created by the attacks: a fifteen-year-old girl suspended from high school in West Virginia for trying to found an anarchy club and for wearing a T-shirt bearing the slogan 'Against Bush, Against Bin Laden'; a nineteen-year-old student in North Carolina who was accused by FBI agents of being in possession of 'anti-American material', namely a poster campaigning against Bush's support for the death penalty; an anti-war campaigner, Nancy Oden, surrounded by armed soldiers at a civilian airport in Maine and forbidden to fly on the grounds that she was a 'security risk'. On a visit to London from New York in December 2001, Edward Said, Professor of English and Comparative Literature at Columbia University, told me that people with an Arab or Asian background – he is an American citizen but was born in Palestine – felt under threat. 'Most of my Indian or Pakistani friends, Iranians, North Africans, we all feel singled out,' he said. In this hysterical atmosphere, there was widespread astonishment when the man arrested on suspicion of trying to blow up a flight from Paris to Miami, three days before Christmas, turned out to be an Englishman, Richard Reid from South London.

'We have shown the world that we cannot be defined as cowards and weaklings. We do not hide in the corner when the going gets tough. Each and every one of us has proved that we are great by showing our patriotism,' declared Adam Balz of Wisconsin in a letter to *Time* magazine. With the dominant public mood composed of sentimentality, patriotism and paranoia, the Bush administration rushed through a series of executive orders that constituted one of the most sustained assaults ever mounted on civil liberties in the US. The President signed orders that reduced client-attorney privilege for defendants suspected of terrorist offences, and made outside scrutiny of government more difficult by restricting access to presidential papers from previous administrations, an action that was challenged in court by a group of American historians. Perhaps the most egregious of these measures was the setting up of closed military tribunals to try foreign terrorist suspects, a practice condemned by American governments when similar courts were set up in a long list of repressive countries: Burma, China, Colombia, Egypt, Kyrgyzstan, Malaysia, Nigeria, Peru, Russia, Sudan and Turkey. The tribunals have the power to sentence defendants to death – suspects will have what the Attorney General, John Ashcroft, euphemistically described as 'death eligibility' – but the decision of the judges will have to be unanimous, a concession designed to allay anxiety in Europe about possible executions. ('The lack of due process is particularly egregious in death penalty cases,' the American government declared presciently in a recent report on the use of closed tribunals in China.) In another indicator of his increasing reliance on the CIA, the President also relaxed the ban on assassinations of foreign leaders, imposed twenty-five years before. Some of America's allies, notably Britain, Canada and Russia, seized the opportunity to rush through Draconian anti-terrorist legislation of their own, leading to the accusation that authoritarian ministers were dusting down measures that would have been unacceptable in any other circumstances. The British Home Secretary, David Blunkett, candidly admitted that the country had become a target for groups like al-Qaida because of its support for the bombing of Afghanistan, casting further doubt on the stated reason – that Britain was as much at risk as the US – for joining the 'war against terrorism'. The irony that politicians were busily destroying the freedom of their citizens in order to save it was not lost on opponents of the bills and executive orders that streamed from European governments and the White House.

There were even calls, from unnamed FBI officials, for torture to be permitted in order to force prisoners suspected of terrorist offences to talk. 'FBI and Justice Department investigators are increasingly frustrated by the silence of jailed suspected associates of Osama bin Laden's al-Qaida network, and some are beginning to say that traditional civil liberties may have to be cast aside if they are to extract information about the Sept. 11 attacks and terrorist plans,' the *Washington Post* reported at the end of October. The agents interrogating four suspects held at New York's Metropolitan Correctional Centre were frustrated by their silence, the paper reported, and had begun to discuss the possibility of using sodium pentothal, the so-called 'truth drug'. They were also arguing for the use of 'pressure tactics, such as those employed occasionally by Israeli interrogators, to extract information'. Some of these shocking proposals found support in the mainstream media. The Fox News Channel allowed advocates of torture to put their case on TV, while a *Newsweek* columnist, Jonathan Alter, mused that 'in this autumn of anger, even a liberal can find his thoughts turning to . . . torture'. Alter said he was not necessarily advocating the use of 'cattle prods or rubber hoses', just 'something to jump-start the stalled investigation of the greatest crime in American history'.

In this atmosphere, it is hardly surprising that some of the attitudes expressed by members of the American public towards the war in Afghanistan were frankly callous. By 6 December, two months into the conflict, a crucial milestone was passed: American opponents of the bombing claimed that civilian deaths now stood at 3,767, more than the death toll in all four suicide-hijackings in the US. Professor Marc W. Herold of the University of New Hampshire published a detailed breakdown of civilian casualties, listing seven dates when they had been particularly heavy. 'The critical element remains the very low value put upon Afghan civilian lives by US military planners and the political elite,' he wrote. On the penultimate day of December 2001, another episode of civilian carnage was added to the roll call, this time in a village in eastern Afghanistan called Qalaye Niazi. The Americans sent a B-52 and two B-1 bombers to attack the village, apparently after being told by local warlords that it contained an al-Qaida compound. The intelligence was wrong, possibly even malicious – this was one of the several occasions when American bombers appeared to have been used to settle old scores – and Western reporters who made their way to the area found the pitiful remains of women and children lying in the streets: clumps of hair, pools of blood, exercise books. Local people said more than 100 civilians had been killed in the raid, a figure difficult to confirm when so many of the victims had been blown apart, but the UN later said it had reliable information that more than fifty civilians had died, including twenty-five children. The American military first of all denied any 'collateral damage', its preferred euphemism for civilian casualties, then blamed any injuries on al-Qaida and the Taliban. A few days later Donald Anderson, influential chair of the House of Commons Foreign Affairs Committee, counselled caution about the continued bombing campaign: 'If we value Afghan lives as much as American, we will have to be extremely careful,' he observed. Beside the direct effects of the bombing, there was also evidence of major violations of human rights on the ground by some of America's allies in the war. The most notorious incident, at the Qala-i-Jhangi fortress controlled by the notorious warlord Abdul Rashid Dostum, leader of the mainly Uzbek Junbish militia, near Mazar-i-Sharif in November, resulted in hundreds of deaths after a revolt by Taliban prisoners.

Even so, any attempt to suggest moral equivalence between the deaths of Afghan civilians and the victims of 11 September prompted outrage in some quarters of the US. This may have been because American readers and viewers were to some extent protected from facing the consequences of the war by their own media. 'It seems perverse to focus too much on the casualties or hardship in Afghanistan,' wrote Walter Isaacson, chair of CNN, in a memo to staff. 'You want to make sure that when [viewers] see civilian suffering there, it's in the context of a terrorist attack that caused enormous suffering in the US.' Isaacson ordered journalists to make sure that images of suffering Afghans were accompanied by a commentary reminding viewers that the American bombing was in retaliation for the fact that the Taliban harboured terrorists. The European press, on the other hand, was brutally frank about what was happening in the war. Towards the end of October, Richard Lloyd Parry of the *Independent* visited a hospital in the Pakistani border town of Quetta, where Afghan refugees were being treated for wounds sustained in air attacks. His front-page report, under the headline 'Families blown apart, infants dying', was accompanied by a photograph of an Afghan woman and her baby, both visibly suffering from shrapnel wounds; Lloyd Parry reported that other children from the same family had died in an American bombing raid. The very next day, the paper printed a letter from Mark Diederichsen, writing from Las Vegas, in which he roundly condemned Lloyd Parry's 'disgusting' article:

Don't you realise that over 5,000 [*sic*] innocent, unsuspecting civilians in the US were pulverised, their bodies smashed into millions of unidentifiable parts, many completely disintegrated into ashes? How on earth can you compare that to a couple of dead and a handful of people in a hospital with cuts on their faces?

Another correspondent, Carey Smith, accused the journalist of being 'detached from reality'. Writing from Bush's home state of Texas, Smith insisted:

We all know war is hell – look at New York. Want to see innocent civilian death? Again, try New York. Is it possible to fight a war and not hit civilians? Never been done in history. I for one am fresh out of sympathy for Afghanistan.

Smith went on to claim that 'the Afghan people ultimately are responsible for the poor choices they have collectively made, and collectively, must face the consequences'. Of course these opinions were not shared by compassionate Americans, who were as worried as onlookers in Europe, the Middle East and Asia about their government's conduct of the war. But callous expressions of disregard for the suffering of Afghan civilians played no small part in creating a widespread perception abroad that the 'war against terrorism' was actually a cover for the kind of unilateral action the US government had undertaken, with the support or at least indifference of its population, on many previous occasions in the past. Indeed for a world that was supposed to have changed out of all recognition on 11 September, things were beginning to look, at least where the behaviour of the one remaining superpower was concerned, very much like business as usual.

Nor did the Bush administration appear unduly concerned by its failure to achieve one of its major objectives, the capture of bin Laden and Mullah Omar, the Taliban leader. On the contrary, a Pentagon spokesman confirmed early in January 2002, with baffling casualness, that the government had more or less given up hope of finding the two men. American-led forces in Afghanistan were going to stop 'chasing the shadows', remarked Read Admiral John Stufflebeem, and concentrate on looking for remaining pockets of Taliban and al-Qaida fighters. That the Americans were prepared to abandon the search for their favourite demon figures with such ease makes sense in only one circumstance, that the publicly stated war aims were part of a much more ambitious plan: to destroy al-Qaida training camps in Afghanistan and remove their protectors, but also to confirm the capacity of the American government to intervene militarily in a volatile part of the world with impunity. In all these aims the administration could claim success; there had been no further terrorists attacks on the US mainland, apart from a spate of anthrax scares that appeared to have nothing to do with al-Qaida, and America's closest allies had demonstrated their reluctance to criticize an administration with which many of them were not politically in sympathy. The long-term outlook might reasonably be described as ominous, for the US had not only failed to face up to the causes of the worst ever terrorist attack on the American mainland but been reinforced in its belief in the efficacy – and the moral rightness – of unilateral military retaliation. This marked an abrogation of responsibility on the part of Bush's European counterparts, especially Tony Blair, who was in a better position than almost any other world leader to impress upon an inexperienced President that terrorism cannot be defeated by military means alone. British prime ministers had learned this in Northern Ireland over a thirty-year period in which internment, brutal treatment of terrorist suspects and the full force of the British army had failed to stop a *de facto* civil war. It was only a willingness to negotiate and address the *political* causes of terrorism that finally brought about an uneasy ceasefire, brokered by Blair and his then Secretary of State for Northern Ireland, Mo Mowlam, in 1998.

Yet the conflict in Afghanistan had not even drawn to a close when leading members of the Bush administration began preparing the American public for the next phase in the 'war against terrorism'. There was a repetition of what had by now become ritual warnings to Iraq, a sore point for the Bush family ever since the President's father failed to finish off Saddam Hussein at the end of the Gulf War, and mutterings about terrorist bases in Somalia and Sudan.

The bellicose noises from Washington finally prompted public expressions of disquiet in Europe, where the British Foreign Office reiterated its view that there was no evidence that Iraq had been involved in the 11 September attacks; the arbitrary nature of this search for new enemies was revealed in the President's State of the Union address at the end of January 2002, when he identified an 'axis of evil' that consisted, bizarrely, of Iraq, Iran and North Korea. But an article published in *Time* magazine in the first week of 2002, which included on-the-record interviews with leading members of the Bush administration, seemed to offer a carefully orchestrated insight into its future plans. As well as confirming the extent to which the war in Afghanistan was being run by the CIA, it included the chilling warning given to the President by George Tenet only twenty-four hours after the attacks: 'We have a sixty-country problem.' The remark goes some way to explaining assertions from leading members of the administration that the 'war against terrorism' might last years, perhaps even decades. What the CIA director appeared to be suggesting was a variation on Trotsky's formula of 'permanent revolution', a state of permanent war whose object is, of course, lasting peace.

In one sense, Tenet's apocalyptic announcement is an indicator of the embattled atmosphere that pervaded the White House Situation Room on 12 September. It also demonstrates that if the American public was only just discovering the extent of the hostility towards their country, the CIA was all too well aware of it. But what is striking about the deliberations of the War Cabinet that day is the absence of any degree of reflection or self-questioning. Even the curious fact that Tenet turned up to the meeting accompanied by two CIA agents who had been covert operatives in Afghanistan during the 1980s does not seem to have prompted a discussion of the agency's less than glorious history in that country. '[The CIA] had owned whole parts of Afghanistan then,' *Time* magazine reported laconically. 'And they had come to the White House to tell the President that they could own Afghanistan again.'

It was what Bush wanted to hear. What was not on the agenda was an examination of his own and previous administrations' toleration of, if not actual encouragement of, Isamic fundamentalism in Afghanistan and elsewhere. There is considerable irony in this instance of collective denial, for one of the explanations offered for the events of 11 September is a 'clash of civilizations': Islam versus the West, and civilized post-Enlightenment values versus religious fanaticism. The right-wing Prime Minister of Italy, Silvio Berlusconi, seized on the phrase and used it in public, while Samuel Hunting-don's book of the same title leapt onto the *New York Times* bestseller list in the wake of the terrorist attacks. That a rather more complex analysis might be required was suggested by the presence on the same list of half a dozen books designed for the credulous, from collections of prayers to a mawkish volume in which a 'psychic TV host' claimed to recount his conversations with the recently deceased. The combination of simple-minded patriotism and born-again Christianity displayed by these texts, along with the President's tremulous repetition of 'God bless America' at the end of each address to the nation, was a reminder that the US remains one of the most religious nations in the world – Bush, Ashcroft and other members of the administration are evangelical Christians – and that Christianity is often invoked in that country as an authority for dubious moral enterprises. While Tony Blair's religiosity is mocked with encouraging frequency in the British press, the same is not true of Bush in the American media, and the US is an uncomfortable environment for convinced secularists. Agnostics and atheists, including Edward Said, detected not a clash of civilizations but a contest between two forms of fundamentalism, Christian and Islamic, in the response to the current crisis. If the religious fanatics who crashed into the World Trade Centre were convinced that they had the approval of Allah, it was clear that a disturbing number of American citizens believed that their government's retaliation had been embarked upon with the Lord's approval.

It was also apparent that that government's hostility to the Tali-ban, who became public enemy number one along with bin Laden on 11 September, was a very recent phenomenon. When the Taliban seized Kabul on 26 September 1996, they were widely regarded as a stabilizing force after years of civil war in Afghanistan. One of their first acts was to break into the UN compound where the former President Najibullah had taken refuge with his brother, castrate both men, tie them to the back of a jeep and drag them in the dust until they were dead, then string their bodies from a lamp post. The State Department in Washington responded a few hours later by announcing that the US intended to establish diplomatic relations with the new regime. Although the Taliban did not exactly go out of their way to conceal the grim theology they espoused, declaring their intention to impose Islamic law on Afghanistan, the Clinton administration said there was nothing objectionable about this project. The stage was set for a five-year experiment in which human rights abuses became an everyday occurrence, with women and gay men singled out for especially barbaric treatment. Many of the abuses – the way women were denied education and medical treatment, the public executions in sports stadiums – were documented in annual reports from the State Department, as well as being the subject of endless denunciations by Amnesty International and other NGOs. Nor was there any doubt in Washington that the regime, far from being an indigenous entity, was bankrolled chiefly by two sources: the Pakistan intelligence service, whose creation it was, and bin Laden's terrorist organization. A little-noticed report on terrorism published by the Congressional Research Service only two days after 11 September confirmed once again that Pakistan 'is providing the Taliban with material, fuel, funding, technical assistance and military advisors', all of which had been known for years. Yet far from putting political and economic pressure on Pakistan to stop supporting the Taliban and terrorist groups within its own borders – the report also described how the military dictatorship headed by General Musharraf 'has tolerated terrorists living and moving freely within its territory' – the American government had decided it could live with this bunch of zealots; the administration warmed to the Taliban in 2000 after Mullah Omar banned poppy growing, the source of much of the heroin that was finding its way to Europe and the US, and gave them financial assistance as recently as the spring of 2001. Even in Europe, official condemnation of the regime was muted, which is why Tony Blair's conversion to the cause of Afghan women at the Labour party conference in October 2001, quickly followed by feminist declarations on their behalf by Cherie Blair and Laura Bush, was received with some cynicism.

There is no doubt that US governments, which had in the past intervened all over the world to overthrow democratically elected leaders – from Prime Minister Mossadegh in Iran to President Arbenz in Guatemala – were prepared to tolerate gross human rights abuses by the Taliban in Afghanistan. Ignoring protests from Afghan refugees, women's groups and NGOs, they turned on the regime only when Mullah Omar's alliance with al-Qaida took the lives of more than 3,000 American citizens. Even then, American anger remained highly selective and some of the regimes it initially tried to enlist as allies – notably Iran, repeatedly named in Congressional reports as the chief state sponsor of terrorist bombings – were and are as unpleasant as the Taliban. But the most vivid illustration of the US's complicity with Islamic fundamentalists, undermining the moral authority of the 'war against terrorism' from the outset, is its close relationship with Saudi Arabia.

While initial attempts to explain the motives of the 11 September suicide-bombings focused on the plight of the Palestinians, it is a striking fact that most of the nineteen hijackers were Saudi citizens. Saudi Arabia is an authoritarian state that was until very recently prepared to tolerate and export Islamic fundamentalism, as long as its adherents trained and carried out their holy war abroad. The King's official title is Custodian of the Two Holy Mosques of Mecca and Medina, and the Saudis were happy to finance the mujahidin in their fight to expel the Soviet army – who represented atheistic communism – from Afghanistan. But the fervent Islamic warriors have proved increasingly difficult to control. On four occasions in the last six years, Saudi citizens who trained in terror camps in Afghanistan, Chechnya, Kosovo or Bosnia have been among the terrorists who bombed American targets in Kenya, Tanzania, Yemen and – more worryingly for the ruling family – Saudi Arabia itself.

There is no doubt that America's refusal to force Israel to comply with UN resolutions and withdraw from the occupied territories is a potent source of rage in Arab countries. But it is vital to understand that championing the perfectly genuine cause of the Palestinians also allows undemocratic rulers – including King Fahd of Saudi Arabia and Bashar al-Assad of Syria, who lectured Tony Blair about Israel during a flying visit to Damascus – to divert popular anger away from their own dreadful human rights record at home. In a recent essay, Barnaby Mason, diplomatic correspondent for the BBC World Service, addressed the apparent paradox that the hostility of so many Arabs towards their own autocratic governments has been turned against the 'freedom-loving West'. The reason, he wrote, is that Western countries, and the United States in particular, are 'the chief supporters of those governments'. Young Arab men, often, but not always, encouraged by religious leaders, despise the double standards of Western democracies that boast about freedom at home yet support vile regimes in the Middle East. And nowhere is this more the case than Saudi Arabia. The kingdom is an absolute monarchy, a theocracy that regularly appears on lists of the top four countries in the world for carrying out executions, many of them in public. Amnesty International has repeatedly accused the Saudi authorities of serious human rights violations, including the use of torture; flogging is a common punishment in the kingdom and Amnesty noted an 'alarming increase' in amputations in the year 2000, including seven cases of cross-amputation (removal of the right hand and left foot). Yet Bush and Blair have been careful not to extend their strictures of the Taliban to the Saudi regime, and their wives have remained silent about the kingdom's disgraceful treatment of women.

Girls and boys are strictly segregated, and the Saudi authorities allow the madrassas or religious schools to begin teaching the puritanical Wahhabi form of Islam to boys as young as eight or nine. The Wahhabis espouse a literal interpretation of the Koran which encourages hostility to almost every aspect of the modern world, especially secular values and equal rights for women; it is the same joyless ideology that inspired the Taliban, with results we have all become familiar with. Yet when these young Saudi boys become men, they are denied virtually all forms of engagement in public life – political parties and trade unions are banned – while contact with women is strictly controlled. At the same time, the Saudi authorities buy arms from the very Western countries whose values their youth has been taught to hate; in 1997 British arms manufacturers, with government approval, sold weapons worth £1,576m to the Saudi authorities, including 56 combat aircraft. But it is the monarchy's cosy relationship with the American government, to the extent of allowing large numbers of American troops to be stationed at bases in Saudi Arabia, that has increasingly become the target of home-grown terrorists. In this volatile situation, where the survival of the corrupt House of Saud is far from guaranteed, the authorities were relieved to see the dangerous energies of their young men channelled into conflicts elsewhere; according to Saudi intelligence, no less than 25,000 Saudi men have received military training abroad since 1979. Saudi-born Osama bin Laden and his lieutenants are perfect representatives of this deadly exodus, and his rhetoric embodies the toxic combination of religious zeal and anti-American sentiment that inspires so many of his admirers. 'After Belief,' bin Laden wrote in 1996, 'there is no more important duty than pushing the American enemy out of the holy land.'

While al-Qaida itself may have only a few thousand members, it is believed to have provided funding and training for many other terrorist groups around the world. A BBC foreign affairs reporter, Gordon Corera, estimated that up to 30,000 trainees have passed through its camps; as well as the Taliban, al-Qaida is said to have links with terrorists in Egypt, Algeria, Uzbekistan, Chechnya and other flashpoints, including the disputed territory of Kashmir, where India and Pakistan came close to a nuclear exchange in the first weeks of 2002. A former American ambassador to Riyadh told the *New York Times* that it was, in retrospect, a huge blunder on the part of the Saudis and their American allies that this was ever allowed to happen. 'Alarm bells should have rung,' said Wyche Fowler Jnr.

'Someone should have said, wait a minute, we can't have people marching off to choose their own *jihad*, without examining the foreign and security repercussions.'

This analysis has almost certainly been made many times within the Bush administration since 11 September, but it does not go nearly far enough. Islamic terrorism is a response to a deeply corrupt and unjust political system throughout the Middle East, where a single circumstance – the possession of the huge reserves on which the oil-hungry US depends – has shaped American foreign policy. It has often been observed that there are no Arab democracies in the sense that the West understands the word, a situation that American governments (and, in varying degrees, European leaders) have been prepared to live with in return for strong Arab states: not just the House of Saud but, until he over-reached himself in 1990, the murderous dictatorship of Saddam Hussein. The suicide-bombings have at long last exposed the contradiction at the heart of this policy, which is that ruthless self-interest – support for friendly dictators, theocrats and mass murderers – cannot in the end protect American citizens from its consequences. not just the rage of the starving and dispossessed, but the twisted passion that takes root in countries where natural forms of expression, principally engagement in the political process, are denied. The chilling prospects for the future were neatly summarised in an article by Steven Simon and Daniel Benjamin in *Survival*, the journal of the International Institute for Strategic Studies. In January 2002 they warned:

There is little reason to believe that ruling elites will offer a route to political self-expression that does not go through the mosque and madrassa. An integral part of this religious orientation will be resentment, even hatred of western societies. The globalisation juggernaut of cultural intrusion into these traditional societies will certainly fuel this hatred and make religious terrorism even more likely.

Against this background, the Bush administration's declaration of an open-ended 'war against terrorism' is reckless, irrelevant and self-defeating. No country, no matter how wealthy or militarized, has the ability to bomb its way out of the crisis that faces the world at the beginning of the twenty-first century. The US can destroy terrorist training camps, but new ones will spring up in their place and every mistaken map coordinate, every accidental air strike on innocent civilians, creates new recruits. The *political* lesson of 11 September is all too clearly embodied in Foucault's maxim that power creates resistance, and resistance new forms of power: B-52s and cruise missiles on the one hand, suicidal fanatics and box-cutters on the other.

Nor can one country, acting more or less unilaterally, solve the problem of international terrorism. The events of 11 September were a crime against humanity and require a response from the international community, working through the UN, to capture and punish the people who planned and financed them. A *pax Americana* whose object is to safeguard peace, prosperity and freedom only within its own borders is no longer viable. The American government, and even more importantly the American people, have to re-engage with the rest of the world and recognize that cooperation, not domination, is the only safe strategy. Meanwhile the moral imperative for the rest of us – to support democracy, justice and forms of society where religion is a matter of private conscience rather than state policy – has never been more overwhelming.

Notes

Introduction

(p. xi) *I am inclined to agree with Nietzsche . . . Die fröhliche Wissenschaft* (1882), III, 130.

(p. xvi) *'One of the problems of a free society . . .'* Quoted in Seymour Hersh, *The Dark Side of Camelot* (HarperCollins, 1998), p. 208n.

(p. xxiii) *particularly Amnesty International and . . .* Both human rights organizations can be contacted via their websites, which also provide details of how to join each organization: www.amnesty.org and www.humanrightswatch.org

PART ONE: *Sins of the Fathers*

1. One of Us: Augusto Pinochet Ugarte

(p. 3) *'It is firm and continuing policy . . .'* Quotations from official American sources in this chapter come from documents released under the Freedom of Information Act in the course of the Clinton administration's Chile Declassification Project. Thousands of these documents can be accessed at the Freedom of Information Act electronic reading room, whose web address is http://foia.state.gov. For an invaluable commentary on some of the most important documents, I recommend the National Security Archive at George Washington University in Washington DC. Its website can be accessed at www.gwu.edu/-nsarchiv.

(p. 3) *'The pain of those . . .'* AP (wire service), 15 September 1999.

(p. 6) *the Chilean government concluded . . .* Figures from *Chile: Transition at the Crossroads. Human Rights Violations under Pinochet Remain the Crux*, published by Amnesty International, March 1996, p. 17.

(p. 6) *When Baltasar Garzón . . .* Quotations and figures in this chapter are English translations from Judge Garzón's indictment, dated 30 April 1999.

(p. 6) *Dawson Island . . .* For a full account of what happened to surviving members of the elected government, see Samuel Chavkin, *Storm Over Chile: The Junta Under Siege* (Lawrence Hill Books, revised edition 1989), Chapter 3.

(p. 7) *Even Pinochet's offer . . .* Pinochet profile, *New Yorker*, 19 October 1998, p. 50.

(p. 7) *The wartime pontiff . . .* The history of Pacelli's relations with the Nazis is described in detail in John Cornwell, *Hitler's Pope: The Secret History of Pius XII* (Viking, 1999).

(p. 7) *One of his first actions . . .* Cornwell, p. 208.

(p. 7) *Pius consistently refused . . .* Cornwell, Chapter 14.

(p. 7) *At the conclusion . . .* Cornwell, p. 223.

(p. 7–8) *links with 'the very right-wing . . .'* Cornwell, p. 280.

(p. 8) *According to documents . . .* Reported in the *Guardian*, 3 July 2000, p. 13.

(p. 9) *The Vatican's letter . . .* *Daily Telegraph*, 20 February 1999, pp. 1, 2.

(p. 9) *Yet the Pope's . . .* *Guardian*, 19 February 1999, p. 7.

(p. 10) *'The Pope visited . . .'* *Daily Telegraph*, 20 February 1999, p. 2.

(p. 10) *The former British Prime Minister . . .* *Independent*, 27 March 1999, p. 7.

(p. 11) *In March 1971 . . .* Chavkin, p. 60.

(p. 11) *In congressional elections . . .* Chavkin, p. 72.

(p. 12) *At the extradition hearing . . .* *Daily Telegraph*, 28 September 1999, p. 11.

(p. 12) *A member of . . .* *Guardian*, 29 September 1999, p. 9.

(p. 12) *Yet the General's . . .* Garzón incorporated Contreras's evidence at his own trial in his indictment of Pinochet.

(p. 13) *Ernest Barcella . . .* Also included in the Garzón indictment.

(p. 13) *'Quite frankly . . .'* Chavkin, p. 89.

(p. 14) *Twenty years later . . .* *Chile: Transition at the Crossroads*, p. 16.

(p. 15) *a man named 'Papi' . . .* Quoted in Geoffrey Robertson, *Crimes Against Humanity: The Struggle for Global Justice* (Allen Lane, 1999), p. 364.

(p. 15) *Even pregnant women . . .* Details from *The Pinochet Case: The Chilean Government is Making a Mockery of Its Duties to Its Citizens and International Law*, Amnesty International, 27 January 1999.

(p. 16) *Yet Pinochet whined . . .* *Sunday Telegraph*, 18 July 1999, p. 2.

(p. 16) *a dramatic report . . .* *Daily Telegraph*, 30 September 1999, p. 12.

(p. 16) *From the beginning* . . .   Hansard, 6 July 1999.

(p. 20) *Kissinger is said* . . .   Chavkin, p. 47.

(p. 21) *In 1976 at a time* . . .   *Independent*, 1 July 1999, p. 2.

(p. 23) *including a neuro-radiologist* . . .   In a letter to the *Guardian*, published on 18 February 2000, Ivan Moseley, a consultant neuro-radiologist, stated that 'many normally-functioning people of General Pinochet's age have scans which show marked changes, and the reverse is also true'.

2. One of the Boys: William Jefferson Clinton

(p. 24) *'[The] President only wanted* . . .' From 'Why My Friend Bill Had to Lie', *Guardian*, 30 January 1999.

(p. 24) *'[Clinton] has offended* . . .' *Independent on Sunday*, 14 February 1999.

(p. 25) *an attempt 'to reclaim* . . .' Henry Porter, introduction to the *Starr Report* (Orion Books, 1998).

(p. 25) *'with his head held high* . . .' *Guardian*, 30 January 1999.

(p. 26) *'unusually sordid and* . . .' *Independent on Sunday*, 14 February 1999.

(p. 27) *a sympathetic biographer* . . .   Gail Sheehy, *Hillary's Choice* (Simon & Schuster, 1999).

(p. 28) *'The President said* . . .' *Starr Report*, Narrative section XIV, D2. The full text is available on the internet at www.icreport.access.gpo.gov/report

(p. 29) *This is how he explained* . . .   *Starr Report*, Narrative XIV, D4.

(p. 29) *'Earlier in his marriage* . . .' *Starr Report*, Narrative VII, B.

(p. 29) *Hillary Clinton appeared* . . .   First issue of *Talk* magazine, summer 1999.

(p. 30) *After surviving* . . .   Sheehy, pp. 247–8.

(p. 31) *'attacking Gennifer Flowers'* George Stephanopoulos, *All Too Human: A Political Education* (Hutchinson, 1999), p. 439.

(p. 31) *He also recorded* . . .   Stephanopoulos, p. 68.

(p. 31–2) *Clinton dismissed her allegation* . . .   *Starr Report*, Narrative VIII, C.

(p. 32) *that Clinton raped her* . . .   *The Times*, 25 February 1999, p. 19.

(p. 32) *Clinton's behaviour* . . .   Sheehy, p. 372.

(p. 32) *'Does it count* . . .' Erica Jong, *What Do Women Want?* (Bloomsbury, 1999), p. 151.

(p. 33) *'In the evaluation of* . . .' *Starr Report*, Narrative I, B2.

(p. 33) *'The charges . . .'* Starr Report, Narrative XIV, D3.

(pp. 33–4) *The following day . . .* Starr Report, Narrative XIV, D3.

(p. 34) *On 26 January . . .* Starr Report, Narrative XIV, D4.

(p. 34) *the conviction rate . . .* Observer, 30 July 2000.

(p. 34) *'How could he have . . .'* Stephanopoulos, p. 68.

(p. 34) *a hurried, incomplete blowjob . . .* Starr Report, Grounds, note 81.

(p. 36) *Stephanopoulos even recalled . . .* Stephanopoulos, p. 189.

(p. 37) *The stage for the drama . . .* This account of Clinton's relationship with Lewinsky is drawn from the *Starr Report*, Narrative II–XII.

(p. 40) *Gore Vidal . . .* Quoted in Christopher Hitchens, *No One Left to Lie to* (Verso, 1999), p. 84.

(p. 41) *'The effect . . .'* Sigmund Freud, 'The Taboo of Virginity', *On Sexuality*, Pelican Freud Library, vol. 7 (Penguin, 1977), p. 271.

3. Not One of Us: Saddam Hussein al-Takriti

(p. 43) *In July 1981 . . .* Ministerial visits to Iraq are listed in *Arming Saddam: The Supply of British Military Equipment to Iraq 1979–1990*, published by CAAT (Campaign Against the Arms Trade, 11 Goodwin Street, London N4 3HQ).

(p. 44) *The* Guardian *had no hesitation . . .* 17 July 1981.

(p. 44) *Britain's trade with Iraq . . .* Report of the Inquiry into the Export of Defence Equipment and Dual-use Goods to Iraq and Related Prosecutions (*Scott Report*), Sir Richard Scott, 1996, vol. 1, p. 155.

(p. 45) *Saddam Hussein has mythologized . . .* See the judicious account of his early career in Adel Darwish and Gregory Alexander, *Unholy Babylon: The Secret History of Saddam's War* (Victor Gollancz, 1991), Chapter 7.

(p. 46) *a diplomat at the US Embassy . . .* Declassified American documents quoted in this chapter come from the State Department's electronic reading room cited in Chapter 1, http://foia.state.gov.

(p. 47) *According to the historian . . .* Peter Mansfield, *The Arabs* (Allen Lane, 1976; revised Penguin edition, 1992), p. 262.

(p. 49) *'Persian-pukes prepare to die'* A fuller version of this song appears in my book *Misogynies* (revised Vintage edition, 1996).

(p. 50) *The declaration of war . . .* Scott Report, vol. 1, p. 152.

(p. 50) *In 1979 just under . . .* Arming Saddam, p. 2.

(p. 50) *In the days of the Shah . . .* Scott Report, vol. 1, p. 152.

(p. 51) *UK exports to Iran . . .* Scott Report, vol. 1, p. 156.

(p. 51) 'From the start . . .' John Hughes-Wilson, *Military Intelligence Blunders* (Constable Robinson, 1995), p. 313.

(p. 51) *At a meeting . . . Scott Report*, vol. 1, p. 154.

(p. 52) *British companies sold . . . Scott Report*, vol. 1, p. 156.

(p. 52) *I discovered that . . .* Joan Smith and Anita Bennett, 'Secret Talks Begin on £1bn Contract for Britain in Iraq', *Sunday Times*, 4 July 1981, p. 1.

(p. 52) *Amnesty International issued . . .* Cases cited appear in *Iraq: 'Disappearances': Unresolved Cases since the Early 1980s*, Amnesty International, October 1997.

(p. 53) 'the perfect Orwellian . . .' Darwish and Alexander, p. 213.

(p. 54) *Export Credits Guarantee Department . . . Arming Saddam*, p. 4.

(p. 54) *In any case after representations . . . Scott Report*, vol. 1, pp. 155–6.

(p. 54) *ministers were aware . . . Scott Report*, vol. 1, p. 156.

(p. 54) *Ministry of Defence, Mr Sandars . . . Scott Report*, vol. 1, p. 156.

(p. 55) 'The United Kingdom has been . . .' *Arming Saddam*, p. 3.

(p. 55) *Iraq's economy . . .* Hughes-Wilson, p. 316.

(p. 56) 'to help British companies . . .' *Arming Saddam*, p. 4.

(p. 56) *the Kurdish town of Halabja . . . Massacre by Gas*, published by Minority Rights Group (379 Brixton Road, London SW9 7DE), 1989.

(p. 58) *The purpose of the visit . . . Arming Saddam*, p. 4.

(p. 59) *Lord Trefgarne, a junior trade minister . . . Arming Saddam*, p. 5.

(p. 59) 'We did not just . . .' The Times, n.d.

(p. 59) 'gung-ho for defence sales' *Scott Report*, vol. 1, p. 436.

(p. 60) 'found himself exposed . . .' *Scott Report*, vol. 1, p. 433.

(p. 60) 'would give a green light . . .' *Scott Report*, vol. 1, p. 434.

(p. 60) 'the guidelines are penalizing . . .' *Scott Report*, vol. 1, p. 456.

(p. 61) *It reported that Iraq . . . Scott Report*, vol. 1, p. 448.

(p. 61) 'Iraq's position . . .' *Scott Report*, vol. 1, p. 443.

(p. 61) 'the nature of the Iraqi regime . . .' *Scott Report*, vol. 1, p. 455.

(p. 62) *when the change . . . Scott Report*, vol. 1, p. 458.

PART TWO: The Policing of Private Life

4. Fooling the People

(p. 67) 'Parnell's amours . . .' Quoted in Ronald Hyam, *Empire and Sexuality: The British Experience* (Manchester University Press, 1990), p. 32.

(p. 67) *'You know, I get . . .'* Quoted in Seymour Hersh, *The Dark Side of Camelot* (HarperCollins, 1998), p. 389.

(p. 68) *'I was taken . . .'* *Daily Telegraph*, 20 November 1999, p. 8.

(p. 73) *Each year 32,000 Americans . . .* *Guardian*, 15 May 2000, p. 15.

(p. 73) *656 people have been . . .* *The USA's Hour of Shame*, Amnesty International, 10 August 2000.

(p. 73) *a select group of countries . . .* *Facts and Figures on the Death Penalty*, Amnesty International, 3 August 2000. China executed at least 1,077 people in 1999, and Iran 165, while hundreds are believed to have been killed in Iraq, where accurate figures are difficult to obtain.

(p. 74) *Al Gore admitted only . . .* *International Herald Tribune*, 14 July 2000, p. 7.

(p. 75) *Yet in May that year . . .* *Guardian*, 29 May 2000.

(p. 75) *Gore's Republican opponent . . .* *The USA's Hour of Shame*, 10 August 2000.

(p. 75) *'but the devil on . . .'* George Stephanopoulos, *All Too Human: A Political Education* (Hutchinson, 1999), p. 63.

(p. 75) *'We're not inflicting pain . . .'* Stephanopoulos, p. 214.

(p. 76) *The Islamic regime in Saudi Arabia . . .* *Daily Telegraph*, 15 August 2000, p. 12.

(p. 76) *1 in every 20 . . .* *US: Stark Disparities In Drug Incarceration*, Human Rights Watch, 8 June 2000.

(p. 79) *'sublime indifference'* Hyam, p. 32.

(p. 79) *the distinguished soldier . . .* There is a full account of the disgrace and death of Macdonald in Hyam, Chapter 2.

(p. 80) *'the rich, if caught . . .'* Colin Spencer, *Homosexuality: A History* (Fourth Estate, 1995), p. 324.

(p. 81) *The nineteenth-century statesman Lord Palmerston . . .* Hyam, p. 28.

(p. 81) *'almost unique among . . .'* Hyam, p. 28.

(p. 81) *Lord Rosebery's sexual orientation . . .* Hyam, p. 26.

(p. 83) *'keep bureau fully . . .'* Hersh, p. 391.

5. The Body Enclosed

(p. 86) *'The chastity of women . . .'* Quoted in Roy Porter, *English Society in the Eighteenth Century* (Penguin, 1982), p. 39.

(p. 86) *'A woman who has . . .'* Mary Wollstonecraft, *A Vindication of the*

Rights of Woman (1792; Everyman edition, published by J. M. Dent, 1929), p. 79.

(p. 86) *there were 64 Enclosure Acts . . .* Porter, p. 226.

(p. 87) *'The poor man . . .'* Porter, p. 228.

(p. 87) *'An amazing number . . .'* Porter, p. 228.

(p. 88) *'From the respect . . .'* Wollstonecraft, p. 154.

(p. 89) *'It has long since . . .'* Wollstonecraft, p. 144.

(p. 89) *'people in my way . . .'* Quoted in Porter, p. 41.

(p. 91) *'Whilst [women] are . . .'* Wollstonecraft, pp. 154–5.

(p. 92) *'One of the most terrible . . .'* Lawrence Stone, *Road to Divorce: A History of the Making and Breaking of Marriage in England 1530–1987* (OUP, 1990), p. 168.

(p. 92) *'I cannot avoid feeling . . .'* Wollstonecraft, p. 79.

(p. 93) *'the cult of the family . . .'* Porter, p. 44.

(p. 94) *'Losing thus every . . .'* Wollstonecraft, p. 79.

(p. 94) *'Of all the regulations . . .'* Quoted in Claire Tomalin, *The Life and Death of Mary Wollstonecraft* (Weidenfeld, 1977), p. 145.

(p. 95) *'If Clare [sic] thinks . . .'* Quoted in Leslie Marchand, *Byron: A Portrait* (The Cresset Library, 1987), p. 332.

(p. 96) *'All other injuries . . .'* Stone, p. 231.

(p. 97) *a form of indentured labour . . .* James Walvin, 'Symbols of Moral Superiority: Slavery, Sport and the Changing World Order, 1800–1850', in J. A. Mangan and James Walvin (eds.), *Manliness and Morality: Middle-class Masculinity in Britain and America, 1800–1940* (Manchester University Press, 1987), p. 244.

(p. 98) *'In keeping with . . .'* John Tosh, *A Man's Place: Masculinity and the Middle-class Home in Victorian England* (Yale University Press, 1999), p. 55.

(p. 98) *'Oh my dear girl . . .'* Tosh, p. 55.

(p. 99) *The novelist Margaret Oliphant . . .* Republished in Bridget Bennett (ed.), *Ripples of Dissent: Women's Stories of Marriage from the 1890s* (Dent, 1998), pp. 315–32.

(p. 99) *The theme of rape . . .* Republished in Bennett, pp. 130–40.

(p. 101) *'Herself the supreme type . . .'* Quoted in Paul McHugh, *Prostitution and Victorian Social Reform* (Croom Helm, 1980), p. 17.

(p. 101) *'Round the fire . . .'* Quoted in Judith R. Walkowitz, *Prostitution and Victorian Society: Women, Class and the State* (CUP, 1980), p. 27.

(p. 101) *'masses of rottenness . . .'* Walkowitz, p. 151.

(p. 101) *'Let those who have never . . .'* Walkowitz, p. 73.

(pp. 101–2) *Rates of venereal disease . . .* Walkowitz, p. 49.

(p. 102) *'syphilis was endemic...'* Walkowitz, p. 50.

(p. 102) *'there is no comparison...'* Walkowitz, p. 71.

(p. 103) *When Florence Nightingale...* McHugh, p. 37.

(p. 103) *One articulate young woman...* McHugh, p. 155.

(p. 104) *'It is awful work...'* Walkowitz, p. 109.

(p. 104) *'comfortable concentration camp'* Betty Friedan, *The Feminine Mystique* (1963; Laurel Books edition, 1984), p. 282.

6. Back to the Future

(p. 107) *'We will not stand back...'* *Guardian*, 31 May 2000, p. 6.

(p. 109) *'Such degenerates...'* Quoted in Richard Plant, *The Pink Triangle* (Mainstream Publishing, 1987), p. 32.

(p. 109) *'an innate indication of...'* Sigmund Freud, *On Sexuality*, Pelican Freud Library, vol. 7 (Penguin, 1977), pp. 48–9.

(p. 111) *a precedent in 1811...* Bonnie S. Anderson and Judith P. Zinsser, *A History of Their Own: Women in Europe from Prehistory to the Present*, vol. 2 (Penguin, 1990), p. 221.

(p. 111) *Very few women were lesbians...* Quoted in Richard Davenport-Hines, *Sex, Death and Punishment: Attitudes to Sex and Sexuality in Britain since the Renaissance* (Fontana, 1991), p. 139.

(p. 112) *'By the 1920s...'* Anderson and Zinsser, pp. 221–2.

(p. 113) *'one of the high priests...'* Quoted in Colin Spencer, *Homosexuality: A History* (Fourth Estate, 1995), p. 286.

(p. 114) *'If Oscar Wilde...'* Davenport-Hines, pp. 133–4.

(p. 114) *'the same kind of vice...'* Spencer, p. 287.

(p. 114) *'He looks well...'* Spencer, p. 288.

(p. 115) *'lay hold of a certain...'* Davenport-Hines, p. 142.

(p. 115) *in 1911 a London magistrate...* Spencer, p. 324.

(p. 115) *'conditions of bonding...'* Juliet Mitchell, *Mad Men and Medusas: Reclaiming Hysteria and the Effects of Sibling Rivalry on the Human Condition* (Allen Lane, 2000), p. 28.

(p. 115) *between 1920 and 1924...* Davenport-Hines, p. 147.

(p. 115) *between 1945 and 1955...* Spencer, p. 360.

(p. 117) *American soldiers who were...* Spencer, p. 349.

(p. 117) *'I want to see men...'* Plant, p. 67.

(pp. 117–18) *the remarks of Himmler...* Plant, p. 102.

(p. 118) *Lord Chief Justice Goddard...* Davenport-Hines, p. 315.

(p. 118) *A Somerset man* . . . Davenport-Hines, p. 308.

(p. 119) *In the* Sunday Express . . . *Daily Telegraph*, 23 May 2000, p. 29.

(p. 120) *The suggestion that the defendants* . . . Davenport-Hines, p. 303.

(p. 121) Time *magazine attacked* . . . Quoted in Sheridan Morley, *Dirk Bogarde: Rank Outsider* (Bloomsbury, 1996), p. 96.

PART THREE: *The Peasants' Revolt*

7. Sex and Drugs and . . . Children

(p. 129) *'The "double" sexual morality* . . .' Freud, ' "Civilized" Sexual Morality and Modern Nervous Illness', published in Elisabeth Young-Bruehl, *Freud on Women* (The Hogarth Press, 1990), p. 174.

(p. 129) *'If we are to escape* . . .' Germaine Greer, *The Female Eunuch* (1970; Paladin edition, 1971), p. 116.

(p. 132) *'Women supposedly have* . . .' Natalie Angier, *Woman: An Intimate Geography* (Virago, 1991), pp. 334–5.

(p. 134) *Couples who married* . . . Lawrence Stone, *Uncertain Unions and Broken Lives: Intimate and Revealing Accounts of Marriage and Divorce in England* (OUP, 1995), p. 36.

(p. 135) *'My awareness of* . . .' Sheila Rowbotham, *Promise of a Dream: A Memoir of the Sixties* (Allen Lane, 2000), p. 115.

(p. 136) *'Women do have sexual* . . .' Greer, p. 115.

(p. 137) *'Lifelong marriage or* . . .' *Independent on Sunday*, 28 May 2000, p. 10.

(p. 138) *'She was surrounded* . . .', Andrew Morton, *Diana: Her True Story* (Michael O'Mara Books, 1993), p. 45.

(pp. 138–9) *'We had both found* . . .' Rowbotham, p. 78.

(p. 140) *'As a rule* . . .' Sigmund Freud, *On Sexuality*, Pelican Freud Library, vol. 7 (Penguin, 1977), p. 382.

(p. 140) *' "Civilized" Sexual Morality* . . .' Young-Bruehl, pp. 173–4.

(p. 143) *'a separation of our attitudes* . . .' *Nova*, July 2000.

(p. 144) *'putting muscle back* . . .' Melanie Phillips, *The Sex-Change Society: Feminized Britain and the Neutered Male* (Social Market Foundation, 1999), p. 344.

(p. 144) *one in four British women* . . . *Evening Standard*, 30 June 1999, p. 4.

(p. 144) *The statistics suggest* . . . Obtained by phone from the Office for National Statistics (ONS), November 1999.

(p. 145) *divorced women outnumbered* . . . *Population Trends 95*, spring 1999.

(p. 146) *Between 1971 and 1994* . . . *Social Focus on Women*, Central Statistical Office, 1995, p. 18.

(p. 146) *The differential is startling* . . . ONS, May 2000.

(pp. 146–7) *nearly two thirds* . . . *Social Focus on Women*, p. 18.

(p. 147) *poor exam performance* . . . ONS, May 2000.

(p. 147) *the three million children* . . . ONS, May 2000.

8. Globalize This!

(p. 149) *'This is no longer . . .'* Joan Smith and Andrew Gumbel, *Independent on Sunday*, 5 December 1999, p. 16.

(p. 149) *'Not since the student . . .'* Barbara Gunnell and David Timms (eds.), *After Seattle: Globalization and its Discontents*, published by Catalyst (Bury House, 33 Bury Street, London SW1Y 6AX), April 2000, p. 29.

(p. 149) *'If you want . . .'* Conversation with author, April 1997.

(p. 151) *'The WTO speaks . . .'* *Independent on Sunday*, 5 December 1999. People for Fair Trade and Network Opposed to WTO can be accessed at www.peopleforfairtrade.org. The WTO's reply to some of these charges can be found at www.wto.org.

(p. 151) *'All the WTO's . . .'* *Independent on Sunday*, 5 December 1999. The Ruckus Society website can be accessed at www.ruckus.org.

(p. 152) *1,200 groups from 85 countries* . . . *After Seattle*, p. 29.

(p. 153) *in the Saudi case* . . . *Guardian*, 11 May 2000.

(p. 153) *the World Health Association* . . . Its website and reports can be accessed at www.who.int.

(p. 153) *in 1960 the gap* . . . *After Seattle*, p. 21.

(p. 155) *Meacher welcomed a report* . . . *Guardian*, 17 June 2000.

(p. 156) *Five months later* . . . *International Herald Tribune*, 16 June 2000.

(p. 158) *Around the world* . . . *After Seattle*, p. 26.

(p. 160) *The primatologist Jane Goodall* . . . Quoted in Carole Jahme, *Beauty and the Beasts: Woman, Ape and Evolution* (Virago, 2000), p. 344.

(p. 160) *An American lawyer* . . . Steven Wise, *Rattling the Cage: Towards Legal Rights for Animals* (Profile Books, 2000), p. 237.

(p. 161) *Alan Lopez* . . . *WHO Issues New Life Expectancy Ratings*, 4 June 2000.

(p. 162) *It is worth pointing out . . .* *International Herald Tribune*, 27 June 2000, p. 1.

(p. 163) *a woman living in Africa . . .* WHO, *Pregnancy Exposes Women in Poor Countries to a 200-fold Risk of Dying vs Rich Countries*, 5 June 2000.

(p. 163) *Overall, the WHO, says . . .* WHO, *Gender, Health and Poverty*, June 2000.

(p. 164) *Tony Blair's government . . .* *Guardian*, 19 June 2000.

(p. 165) *the incomes of the richest . . .* ONS, May 2000.

(p. 165) *Nor is it an accident . . .* Figures from Unicef, June 2000.

9. Never Again: The Continuing Quest for Justice

(p. 167) *'Any man's death . . .'* John Donne, Meditation XVII.

(p. 167) *'Whereas the soldier . . .'* Mary Kaldor, *New and Old Wars: Organized Violence in a Global Era* (Polity Press, 1999), p. 131.

(p. 167) *'Man's capacity . . .'* Reinhold Niebuhr, *The Children of Light and the Children of Darkness* (1944).

(p. 168) *in a recent book . . .* Wolfgang Benz, *The Holocaust: A History* (Profile Books, 2000), p. 119.

(p. 169) *As I was writing this book . . .* *Daily Telegraph*, 27 June 2000, p. 19; *Guardian*, 27 June 2000, pp. 1–2.

(p. 171) *by the end of 1997 . . .* Strategic Export Controls, *Annual Report 1999*, Department of Trade and Industry, p. 49.

(p. 172) *Dusko Tadic . . .* Geoffrey Robertson, *Crimes Against Humanity: The Struggle for Global Justice* (Allen Lane, 1999), p. 287.

(p. 172) *What happened at . . .* Elie Wiesel, foreword to *The Tenth Circle of Hell* by Rezak Hukanovic (Little, Brown, 1997), p. vii.

(p. 173) *at the beginning of the twentieth century . . .* Kaldo~

(p. 177) *It certainly involves . . .* Kaldor ~ Pinoc~

(p. 179) *'by the good g~~ ~* Juris~ ~

(p. 180) ~ *~* The Pinoc~

(p. 180) 'Crimes again~ ~

International, p. 27.

(p 181) *Such crimes are, in law . . .* ~national, p. 11.